To Rabbi Greenstein —
I hope you enjoy
these stories as I did.

The ArtScroll Series®

Rabbi Nosson Scherman / Rabbi Meir Zlotowitz
General Editors

In the Footsteps

by
Rabbi Paysach J. Krohn
author of
The Maggid Speaks and *Around the Maggid's Table*

Published by

Mesorah Publications, ltd

of the Maggid

Inspirational Stories and Parables
about Eminent People
of Yesterday and Today

FIRST EDITION
First Impression . . . December 1992
Second Impression . . . December 1992
Third Impression . . . January 1993
Fourth Impression . . . October 1993

Published and Distributed by
MESORAH PUBLICATIONS, Ltd.
Brooklyn, New York 11232

Distributed in Israel by
MESORAH MAFITZIM / J. GROSSMAN
Rechov Harav Uziel 117
Jerusalem, Israel

Distributed in Europe by
J. LEHMANN HEBREW BOOKSELLERS
20 Cambridge Terrace
Gateshead, Tyne and Wear
England NE8 1RP

Distributed in Australia & New Zealand by
GOLD'S BOOK & GIFT CO.
36 William Street
Balaclava 3183, Vic., Australia

Distributed in South Africa by
KOLLEL BOOKSHOP
22 Muller Street
Yeoville 2198
Johannesburg, South Africa

Typography by Compuscribe at ArtScroll Studios, Ltd.

Printed in the United States of America by Noble Book Press
Bound by Sefercraft, Quality Bookbinders, Ltd. Brooklyn, N.Y.

הרב שלום מרדכי הכהן שבדרן
שערי חסד, ירושלים

ר״ח חשון תשנ״ג

לכבוד ידידי הרב פסח יוסף קראהן נ״י
בנו של ידידנו הדגול האהוב לכל,
רב פעלים מוה״ר אברהם זעליג זצ״ל.

שמעתי שאתה עומד להוציא לאור ספר משלים והנהגות
מגדולי ישראל, עיני העדה.

הנני מוסר לך ברכתי ברכות כהן הדיוט שתצליח בכל
דרכך ולהפיץ מעיינותך חוצה.

ממני הדורש בשלומך
ידידך באהבה

[חתימה]

RABBI
ISRAEL GROSSMAN
BATEI WARSAW
JERUSALEM, ISRAEL

Tel. 371056 .טל

ישראל גרוסמן
רב ור"מ ורזמ"ץ
פעיה"ק ירושלים תובב"א
מחבר ספרי שעורי מתיבתא שעורי גיטין
שעורי קדושין שעורי בכ"ק שרת הליכות ישראל
שרת משכנות ישראל שרת נצח ישראל
שרת אורח ישראל
בתי ורשא ירושלים

בעזהי"ת י' סיון תשנ"ג

קראתי בזה להרב"ק את ידידי הנכבד מו"ה בן ציון עמנה הכהן
שליט"א בן מו"ה קרין שי'

אשר ספרי מאמרו קץ ספרו שידבר על פ" נ"א
וכראתי הרעיונות של מרשה הם ספר כמסורת התג' ...

[remaining handwritten text]

בכ.פ.פ"ל
ישראל גרוסמן

ישיבה שער התורה-גרודנה

Yeshiva Shaar Hatorah-Grodno

בס"ד

אהרן זליג הלוי עפשטיין
ראש הישיבה

Rabbi Zelik Epstein
Rosh Hayeshiva

ב"ה י' אייר שנות השמטה

כבוד ידי"נ הגאון הרב ר' ... שליט"א

117-06 84th Avenue Kew Gardens, N.Y. 11418
(718) 846-1940

ביהמ"ד גבול יעבץ
ברוקלין, נוא יארק

דוד קאהן

ב"ה

בס"ד

בס"ד רח"א צפ'... אוגב צאת הברית, ואתחזק לקיים ... ימשיך לישראל, ואלאה אומרה
... לע"ט יום ...

בחרוות (סה"א)(א"צג) כיון שחושב אומר לפן זא השא אומר הין זא הכאס אומר הין זא שען ...
אומר הין זא שען ... אומר הין זא קודק ... אומר הין זא קרקף ... אומר הין זא שען אומר שען ...
אומר הין זא שבת ... אומר הין ... אומרים ... קבור ודפא אומרים ... קבור ודפא אומרים ... קבור
... שהוא אומרית אין קרית ... ואומר באשא... יום ... כל לאה אמני
הרי שעלרו ... חכמין לש של ... יבי ... ה ... ואומרים הבר ... על ... אולצים ...
... הבצרים ופ... הבכחרית הקרה ... קהר ... וספרי זרכן ...
(שאומר ... או אמרן כן צבוקים ... הראית שפרא'... ... כאה ... כאן בחרות
... , סיון, נסן פרן, הרכת צרוה , קרה אבלאה, ו...
...ך ... הש... בכל כצבסת ... "ספר הא"צ" ... ... יבים קאות וערכים כואות
... וכ... ... אידות ... ובו וית ... ישראל, הכך אתה'ק
... שבחקת ... ... רב ... אחד מהשקרים ... ... ושעור
...

וקף אין ... אשיה וארוכך ... משולחת שאשין ... ... מאוכק מלאנק ...
ואתך ... תרו'ת ... ... צ... ... ...

...

...
בוב קאהן
...

৶ Table of Contents

Part C: Deeds of Distinction 115

Part D: Torah — Teachers and Talmidim   177

Part E: Who and What We Are   249

Author's Preface

אֲבָרְכָה אֶת ה' בְּכָל עֵת תָּמִיד תְּהִלָּתוֹ בְּפִי

I am deeply grateful to the *Ribono Shel Olam* for having granted me the opportunity to complete this work and thereby present to the reading public a third book in the *Maggid* series.

Shlomo *HaMelech* wrote (*Koheles* 4:12): "וְהַחוּט הַמְשֻׁלָשׁ לֹא בִמְהֵרָה יִנָתֵק — A three-ply cord will not unravel quickly." From the moment I began to work on the first *Maggid* book, with R' Sholom Schwadron, the renowned *Maggid* of Jerusalem, and throughout the research and writing of the two that followed, I was fortunate to establish personal ties with many special people from all walks of Jewish life who were kind enough to share their stories with me. During this same period there developed within me and within the members of my family, a heartfelt affection for many of the eminent people about whom I came to write.

It is my hope and prayer that these bonds with the people of today and yesterday, developed over the past number of years, will, like the three-ply cord, remain with us as a source of strength and inspiration towards the piety, goodness and sincerity inherent in the holy nation that is *Klal Yisrael*.

❧ ❧ ❧

In 1930, R' Shimon Schwab, today the *Rav* and *Mara D'Asra* of the German *kehillah* in Washington Heights, had the opportunity to spend a Shabbos in Radin with the Chofetz Chaim. On Friday night [*Rosh Chodesh Nissan*] many people crowded into the Chofetz Chaim's tiny home to hear words of *mussar* and *chizuk* from the great Torah sage.

In his talk, the Chofetz Chaim said, "We know that the manna that fell from Heaven [as food for the Jews in the desert] had whatever taste anyone wanted it to have. All one had to do was concentrate on the food one wished the manna to taste like, and one would experience just that flavor." (See *Shemos Rabbah* 25:3.)

"However," the Chofetz Chaim asked, "what if one ate the manna without thinking of a particular taste? What flavor did it have then?"

The sainted *tzaddik* waited for someone to answer, but no one replied. He then proclaimed, in Yiddish, a poetic truism that he meant to apply both to the question at hand and to life in general. "*Az menn tracht nisht, hut es kein taam nisht.* [If one does not think, it is senseless.]" Hence, if one did not give any thought regarding the manna before eating it, it was indeed bland and tasteless.

The *Gemara* in *Yoma* (75a) notes that manna is described in the Torah (*Shemos* 16:31) as having the appearance of זֶרַע גַּד לָבָן — lit., a white coriander seed. The *Gemara* there infers, though, that the unusual word (גַּד) in the *passuk* is used to teach us that the manna was as alluring as אַגָּדָה — a narrative, a story.

In what manner are manna and a narrative similar? Perhaps it is that both the manna and a worthwhile story are capable of being different things to different people. A noteworthy story may have one message for a child, yet on a deeper level transmit a different message to an adult. One person may see man's goodness as the primary lesson in a story, whereas another may see Hashem's Divine intervention as the point of the same episode.

Manna, because of its very nature, forced one to think, and that indeed is the essence of every significant story — to be thought provoking. Otherwise, as the Chofetz Chaim said, it is senseless.

❧ ❧ ❧

A *maggid* has the uncanny ability to tell precisely the right thought-provoking story in order to convey with exactness his intended message. In 1964, by incredible acts of *hashgachah pratis* (see the Introductions to **The Maggid Speaks** and **Around the Maggid's Table,** published by ArtScroll/Mesorah), my father, Rabbi Avrohom Zelig Krohn, *z'l,* came to know and befriend the world-famous *Maggid* of Jerusalem, Rabbi Sholom Mordechai HaKohen Schwadron, as well as Rabbi Yisroel Grossman, a *dayan* in Jerusalem, who then stayed in our home for close to six months.

On that visit, and on R' Sholom's subsequent visits to America, I accompanied him on many of his travels. I came to realize that wherever he lectured and whenever he met people — be it at a Torah convention, a *kinus,* a *beis hamidrash* in a yeshivah or even in a *shul* after *davening* — he invariably had the appropriate "*maamar Chazal*" (Talmudic teaching), the precise *midrash,* or the proper *passuk* pertaining to the discussion at hand. However, more than anything else, he always had the right "*gevaldikeh maiseh*" (exceptional story).

Rav Sholom has always felt that a *maiseh* is a wonderful medium to convey a message. Ideally, it should accomplish one or more of a number of goals. It should either encourage people to a higher level of *zehirus b'mitzvos* and *midos,* assist them in gaining an appreciation and understanding of an exalted individual — be that individual from the learned or lay people of *Klal Yisrael* — or make them more acutely recognize the beneficence that the *Ribono Shel Olam* showers upon us, His beloved people. Ultimately, though, a magnificent story or parable should inspire a person to bring forth the greatness that lies within him.

It is with these same goals in mind that I present this work of stories and parables to the reading public. If the entries in this book are able to inspire, teach, or guide even in a small measure, I am humbly grateful to the *Ribono Shel Olam* for allowing me this great opportunity, for in essence that would be following **In The Footsteps of The Maggid.**

Acknowledgments

Torah learning in America and in all English-speaking countries has been changed forever by the foresight of such outstanding individuals as Rabbi Nosson Scherman, Rabbi Meir Zlotowitz, and Rabbi Sheah Brander, who founded ArtScroll/Mesorah Publications. Their meticulous dedication to enhancing the *dvar Hashem* — be it in *Torah Sheb'al Peh* or *Torah She'biksav* — has set a standard of excellence for future generations.

Rabbi Aharon Kotler (1891-1962) once said that when a person is learning Torah, it is as though Hashem is speaking to him, and conversely, when a person is *davening*, it is he who is speaking to Hashem. Imagine the *Ribono Shel Olam* choosing three individuals in a generation to be His voice to hundreds of thousands of His people. Imagine the merit in store for individuals who have not only enhanced Hashem's voice to us, but through their work (*siddur*, *machzor*, *zemiros*, etc.) have enhanced, as well, our voice to Hashem.

The Talmud (*Berachos* 7b) states: "שְׁמָא גָרִים — A name [a person bears] has an influence [on his life]." In that sense, R' *Nosson* has given, R' *Meir* has enlightened and R' *Sheah* has assisted thousands in their enhancement of Torah study and observance. May the *Ribono Shel Olam* grant all His emissaries, and these three in particular, the strength and the vitality to continue in their great work and bring all their projects to fruition.

❀ ❀ ❀

I feel honored and grateful that the following people took time to share with me some of their life experiences and relate to me stories and parables they felt would be helpful for this work: Rabbi Yisroel Belsky (Brooklyn), Rabbi Dovid Birnbaum (Brooklyn), Rabbi Yosef Buchsbaum (Jerusalem), Rabbi Shlomo Cheshin (Jerusalem), Rabbi Moshe Chodosh (Jerusalem), Rabbi David Cohen (Brooklyn), Rabbi Yaakov Eisen (Montreal), Rabbi Yitzchak Engel (Jerusalem), Rabbi Yaakov Galinsky (Bnei Brak), Rabbi Avie Gold (Brooklyn), Rabbi Tuvya Goldstein (Brooklyn), Rabbi Moshe Grossman (Brooklyn), Rabbi Yitzchak Grossman (Migdal HaEmek), Rabbi Yisroel Grossman (Jerusalem), Rabbi Chaim Halperin (London), Rabbi Avrohom Kabalkin (Jerusalem), Rabbi Kolman Krohn (Lakewood), Rabbi Zvi Kushelevsky (Jerusalem), Rabbi Yoni Levinson (Brooklyn), Rabbi David Lopian (Brooklyn), Rebbetzin Zipa Lopian (Gateshead), Rabbi Shlomo Lorincz (Jerusalem), Rabbi Shlomo Leib Mund (Montreal), Dr. Avigdor Newman (Brooklyn), Rabbi Yisroel Reisman (Brooklyn), Rabbi Mayer Roberg (London), Rabbi Moshe Rosenfeld (London), Rabbi David Sanders (Brooklyn), Rabbi Yosef Scheinberger (Jerusalem), Rabbi Mordechai Shapiro (Miami Beach), Rabbi Tzvi Shenker (Bnei Brak), Rabbi Avraham Shmulevitz (Jerusalem), Rabbi Moshe Mordechai Shulsinger (Bnei Brak), Rabbi Meir Shuster (Jerusalem), Rabbi David Soloveitchik (Jerusalem), Rabbi Peretz Steinberg (Kew Gardens Hills), Rabbi Yisroel "Bruddy" Stern (London), Rabbi Shlomo Teitelbaum (Kew Gardens), Rabbi David Trenk (Adelphia), Rabbi Eliyahu Valt (São Paulo, Brazil), Rabbi Simcha Wasserman, z'l (Jerusalem), Rabbi Mendel Weinbach (Jerusalem), Rabbi Pinchas Winer (Jerusalem) and Rabbi Nisson Wolpin (Brooklyn). Each of these people took a personal interest in this project, and the work has been enhanced because of it. I hope this effort lives up to their expectations.

These individuals were generous enough to lend me tapes, *sefarim* or publications from their personal libraries: Rabbi Avram Bogopulsky (Binghamton), Rabbi Avrohom Dolinger (Bnei Brak), Rabbi Shoul Dolinger (Ashdod), Rabbi Dovid Kleinkaufman (Kew Gardens), Mr. Benny Lachman (Far Rockaway), Mr. Avrohom Monczyk (Far Rockaway), Mr. Avie Pfeiffer (Lawrence), my *mechutan* Mr. Freddy Pfeiffer (Montreal) and Rabbi Tzvi Schactel (Monsey).

Over the last few years, Rabbi Sholom Ber Eber (Brooklyn), the Homburger family (London), Mr. Michael Rothschild (Brooklyn), Rabbi Eli Teitelbaum (Brooklyn) and Rabbi Yaakov Salomon (Brooklyn) have become close friends who have afforded me opportunities and perceptive advice for which I will always be grateful.

❁   ❁   ❁

Every person should have either a *Rav, Rebbe* or *Rosh Yeshivah* to whom he turns for leadership, guidance and instruction. (See *Pirkei Avos* 1:17.) I have been blessed to have the world-renowned *talmid chacham,* Rabbi David Cohen of Brooklyn, as a *Rebbi* and *moreh derech* for more than twenty special years. He has shared my joy and felt my pain. He has been a strength, a guide and an inspiration. His vibrant personal interest in my endeavors has been a source of motivation. May he and his family experience only Hashem's blessings and goodness.

❁   ❁   ❁

My mother, Mrs. Hindy Krohn, an accomplished writer and author (*The Way It Was* — ArtScroll/Mesorah) in her own right, served as the initial editor and advisor throughout this entire work. As mentioned earlier, it was her open home that allowed Rabbi Sholom Schwadron and Rabbi Yisroel Grossman to become integral parts of our family. The series of *Maggid* books is a by-product of the *hachnasas orchim* of both her and my late father, Rabbi Avrohom Zelig *z"l.*

Mrs. Nina Indig, in her meticulous way, has a method of editing a manuscript which enhances, yet simultaneously manages to retain, the author's original intent. She is masterful at what she does, and I am fortunate to have had her apply her expertise to this work.

I have a special sense of *hakaras hatov* to my son-in-law and daughter, Rabbi Shlomo Dovid and Chaviva Pfeiffer, who read and commented on each of the stories, shared their insights with me, and worked on the index of topics. My son Eliezer and nephew Avrohom Zelig Abraham compiled the index of Biblical and Talmudic sources which appears in the back of this book. I appreciate Yehuda Landy's photography for the cover, Nichie Fendrich, for her diligence in "seeing the book through," Bassie Gutman, for typsetting and pagination, Mrs. Faygie Weinbaum and Mrs. Ethel Gottlieb, for proofreading, Mrs. Chavie Friedman, Mindy Kohn, and Mrs. Esti Dicker for their meticulous corrections, Yehuda Gordon for his "special delivery" service, Eliyahu Babekov for his travel assistance, and the entire ArtScroll staff, each in his or her own field of expertise: Avrohom Biderman, Efraim Perlowitz, Yossi Timinsky, Shimmy Goldblatt, Said Cohen, Yuri Gutkin, Eli Kroen, Avraham Kay, Rabbi Yosef Gesser, Yitzchok Saftlas, Sheila Tannenbaum, Lea Freier, Chaya Gitty Zaidman, Mrs. Esther Feierstein, Raizy Brander, Mrs. Devorah Morgenstern and Mrs. Estie Schreiber.

❧ ❧ ❧

A writer without a reader is like a sunset on a foggy day. Obscured in a mist of clouds, a sunset can be seen only by those willing to rise above the haze. With a plethora of English-written Judaica available today, an author needs a certain *siyata d'shmaya* to have his work read. The Zohar writes: 'הַכֹּל תָּלוּי בְּמַזָּל אֲפִילוּ סֵפֶר תּוֹרָה שֶׁבַּהֵיכָל — Everything depends on good fortune, even the Torah scroll in the Ark.' I therefore thank you for choosing this work and taking the time to read this *sefer*/book. Since the publication of the first *Maggid* book, the *Ribono Shel Olam* has granted me the very special opportunity of meeting many wonderful people in many different places. I never imagined that I would have the *zechus* to share these stories and parables with people of all ages. I realize now the thirst in *Klal Yisrael* for an inspirational story or an encouraging parable. Your words, comments and stories are all deeply appreciated. In reality, you were the inspiration for this work.

❧ ❧ ❧

Time is one of man's most precious possessions. What we do with our time identifies us and defines us. However, because of the many daily demands on our time, we each must set priorities to determine what gets done and what gets delayed. How fortunate is the man whose wife is able to shoulder the burden of these daily demands so that her husband can pursue a goal they both feel has the potential to serve a segment of *Klal Yisrael*.

The researching, selecting, writing and rewriting, editing and re-editing of these stories and parables has taken thousands of hours. The time had to come from somewhere. My wife, Miriam, provided the atmosphere and the encouragement to reassure me that the project of bringing to the fore yet another *Maggid* book, containing the ideas and accounts of the deeds of *tzaddikim* and *tzidkaniyos* of yesterday and today, was indeed worthwhile — even at the expense of so much time. May it be the will of the *Ribono Shel Olam* that my wife and I merit to see our children and their children grow in Torah, *yiras Shamayim* and *midos* in the footsteps of the people who have come to be our "acquaintances" by virtue of this work.

Paysach J. Krohn   פסח יוסף קראהן
November 7, 1992   י"ב חשון תשנ"ג
Kew Gardens, New York   מוצש"ק פרשת "התהלך לפני והיה תמים"

Part A:

With Others in Mind

⊷§ Of Straps and Scraps

R abbi Hillel Rosen* and his wife were waiting on line to use the phone. They were in a catering hall in Monsey to attend the wedding of the daughter of a close friend, but their minds were elsewhere. Rabbi Rosen, who had come from Brookline, Massachusetts (a suburb of Boston) earlier in the day for this wedding had been given the honor of reciting one of the *berachos* (blessings) under the *chuppah*. He was still in a state of shock at what had happened to him since arriving in New York.

The original plan had been so simple. He was to come to Queens, the area where the family of the *kallah* lived. From there he would be taken to my home where he would stay the night, drive with us to the wedding, returning to our home afterwards, and then leave for Brookline the next day. But he never made it to Queens, and it was a wonder that he even got to the wedding at all.

Now at the phone booth he was thinking about his children at home. He and his wife were hoping that their children's day hadn't been as "eventful" as theirs. He hoped that they had gone to school, come home, had supper and were now doing their homework.

However, when he finally got to use the phone and to call his daughter, the first thing she asked him excitedly was, "Did you lose your *tallis* and *tefillin?*"

"What?" exclaimed R' Hillel. "How could you know about that?"

And then, over long-distance telephone wires, father and daughter exchanged stories.

❀   ❀   ❀

---

* Name has been changed.

Early that afternoon, Rabbi Rosen and his wife had made their way into Manhattan and were walking near the diamond district on 47th Street. As they were talking, they were suddenly interrupted by a frantic woman who babbled at them in broken English with a heavy Spanish accent. She asked them for directions to a particular street, conveying to him that she was lost and confused. Rabbi Rosen tried to calm her down and slowly began to describe the direction in which she should walk in order to reach her destination. But the woman seemed to have difficulty understanding, and persisted with her questions.

Rabbi Rosen, who was carrying his attaché case, put it down for a moment and began to motion with both hands as he spoke to the woman. Suddenly, comprehension showed on her face and she pointed towards her left. Nodding, he looked in the same direction, but when he turned around again, the women was gone. He looked down and realized that his attaché case, containing his *tallis*, *tefillin*, *sefarim* and telephone book was gone as well. About half a block away he saw a man and a woman running. R' Hillel began to give chase but his wife, frightened, called him back. The fact that they were in New York City made her fear that perhaps the robbers might have guns!

It had all happened so quickly. R' Hillel was stunned! He now realized that it was all a setup. The woman was there as a decoy to divert his attention from what he was carrying, and her cohort was there to grab the attaché case which, they probably assumed, contained diamonds. After all, the thieves must have reasoned, Rabbi Rosen looked Jewish, he was in the diamond district, and he was carrying a case. Therefore, twisted logic dictated, what else could he be holding but diamonds?

"Now what?" he said to his wife in utter frustration. How would they get to Queens? Where were they supposed to stay overnight? How would they get to the wedding? Should they call the police? How could they identify anyone? They could, of course, have called the *kallah's* family for assistance, but they refused to disturb the atmosphere of *simchah* in that home.

The Rosens spent the rest of the day filling out forms at a nearby police station, and then made their way to the Port Authority Bus

Terminal where they boarded a bus to Rockland County. Bitter, bewildered and bereft of their belongings, they made their way to the wedding, not telling anyone what had transpired.

❧ ❧ ❧

Yechiel Ratzabi, a deeply pious Jew from Israel, had just come to America the day before. This was his first trip to the States and, as he walked along the streets of Manhattan, he was overwhelmed by the huge buildings and the frantic bustle of the city caused by a confusing maze of buses, cars, trucks and taxis. The constant wave of humanity that seemed to blur through the streets and avenues moved at a pace he had never witnessed before. He paused for a moment and looked around with awe.

And then he saw the most startling thing! A disheveled, dirty-looking man, obviously inebriated, was standing in front of a city garbage can leafing through a book that looked like a *mishnayos!* Yechiel had heard strange things about the "Big Apple," but this was "the pits" and rotten to the core! He stood off to one side and waited to see what the man would do with the *sefer*. After a few moments the man shrugged and tossed the *sefer* into the garbage bin, where it lay with crushed soda cans, torn candy wrappers and yesterday's papers.

Yechiel rushed to the bin, took out the *sefer*, brushed it off and kissed it. He looked back into the bin and then, as he says in Hebrew, *"Ra'iti retzuot yotzot m'ashpah,* (I saw straps emerging from scraps)." He thought they looked like the straps of *tefillin*, so he began to tug at them. Sure enough, at the other end of the straps was the *bayis* (the black square casing which contains the four *parshios*) of the *tefillin shel rosh* (for the head). He searched some more and found *tefillin shel yad* (for the arm) as well, plus one more *sefer*. He kissed each of the *tefillin* and the new-found *sefer*, and wrapped them all in a plastic bag which he had with him.

It was getting dark and Yechiel rushed to meet his friend Shlomo Raful* at a subway station two blocks away, as planned. As he and Shlomo descended into the subway station, Shlomo asked him what

---

* Name has been changed.

he was carrying in the bag. "You'll never believe this," said Yechiel with a smile.

As Yechiel began to tell his story, Shlomo started to laugh. "Don't you realize what happened?" Shlomo exclaimed. "Someone probably robbed a Jew of what he was carrying, ran away, searched through the material, kept what he wanted and threw out the rest, and you happened to find it!"

"What?" cried Yechiel. "You mean there could be other things back in that garbage bin that belong to this Jew who is missing his *tefillin?*"

"That's possible," came the reply, "but there is nothing we can do about that now."

"Who says?" snapped Yechiel. "There is a *mitzvah* of *hashavas aveidah* (returning a lost object). I am going back right now to see what else is there."

"But that is foolish," Shlomo insisted. "You are here only one day, you don't know the subway system or how to get around. You'll get lost. Remember, you're in New York, not Bnei Brak."

Yechiel was undaunted. He smiled and said simply, "לְפוּם צַעֲרָא אַגְרָא (Reward is in proportion to exertion [*Pirkei Avos* 5:26]). I'm getting off at the next station."

Shlomo saw that it was hopeless to try and convince Yechiel not to go back, so he got off at the next station as well, determined that Yechiel would not have to face this adventure alone.

They retraced Yechiel's steps and, about an hour later, came back to that same garbage bin. Night had spread its cloth over the New York skyline, and on this dimly lit corner of Broadway and 46th Street, two dedicated Jews searched through refuse and rubbish trying to do a *mitzvah*. They sorted and separated what they thought might be of value from the obvious garbage, and found a toothbrush, a small *siddur*, a frequent-flyer card and a *tefillin* bag. In the *tefillin* bag, they saw Rabbi Rosen had had the foresight to insert his business card. They compared the business card to the frequent-flyer card and decided that the names matched, and so the two of them, Yechiel and Shlomo, did a dance for joy on Broadway.

Now it would be simple. They were going back to Brooklyn, for that was where the card said Rabbi Rosen lived — in Brookline. To

Shlomo and Yechiel, who had very little experience with the English language, Brookline was Brooklyn just spelled differently by different companies. After all, they were pronounced the same, weren't they?

When they finally descended the steps of the elevated train station in the Boro Park section of Brooklyn, they began to inquire about Dartmouth Street. No one seemed to know where it was, and many insisted there was no such address in Brooklyn. Finally, someone with knowledge of English and geography read the business card and realized that Yechiel and Shlomo were 200 miles away from where they thought they were. They were given an instant lesson in phonetics. When they realized their error, they decided to call the number on the business card. It was the Rosens' daughter who got the call from a stranger informing her that perhaps her father had lost his *tefillin*.

❦   ❦   ❦

"But where are these people now?" R' Hillel asked his daughter. "How can I contact them?"

The daughter dutifully dictated a number where Yechiel could be reached. R' Hillel called Yechiel and they arranged to meet the next afternoon in Manhattan.

He returned to his table at the wedding *seudah*, a burden lifted from his shoulders. Now, for the first time, he began to tell me his story. I offered to drive from the wedding in Monsey to Brooklyn so that he would not miss even one morning without his own *tefillin* but R' Hillel would not hear of it. "I don't know much about New York," he said, "but I know that you don't pass through Brooklyn on the way from Monsey to your home in Queens. I won't allow you to go out of your way for me."

I realized that the next morning I had a *bris* to perform in Boro Park. Incredibly, the *bris* was to take place only one block away from where Yechiel was staying! Another call was made and it was arranged that we would meet Yechiel early in the morning, before *davening*, so that Rabbi Rosen could *daven* with his own *tefillin*.

R' Hillel and I eventually invited Yechiel to our respective homes in our communities and helped Yechiel raise money for the project which had brought him from Israel. Yechiel was able to help children from disadvantaged homes cover their tuitions in *yeshivos* with funds that were raised for him by his two new friends.

❈ ❈ ❈

Yechiel Ratzabi found more than *tefillin* that afternoon in New York City. He found a way into people's hearts because of his ultimate sincerity and piety.

❧ A Step Cast in Greatness

Rabbi Isser Zalman Meltzer's (1870-1953) love for his fellow Jew was legendary. Every *rav*, every layman, Yeshiva *bachur* (student) and even every child with whom he came in contact walked away feeling extravagantly wonderful about themselves. In his conversations with people he sought to build their self-esteem and this was particularly so when he spoke to *bachurim* in learning. Additionally, his concern for others always took precedence over his own welfare.

In this remarkable story told by Rabbi Shlomo Lorincz, a former Knesset representative for Agudath Israel, we come to appreciate R' Isser Zalman's priorities.

During the 1940s, the Israelis and Arabs were constantly battling each other in a war of nerves and attrition. Arabs shot bombs and hurled grenades throughout Jerusalem. Almost no section of the Holy City was spared, and thousands of people sought protection in underground shelters scattered throughout the area.

R' Isser Zalman, however, refused to go to a shelter. Regardless of the intensity of the bombing, he would always tell his wife, Rebbetzin Baila Hinda, that his learning of Torah was the best protection.

One afternoon the grenades and bombs were falling with a ferocity never witnessed before. The *Rebbetzin* was terrified and she pleaded with her husband to take refuge in the underground shelter nearby. This time she would not tolerate his refusal. Reluctantly, R' Isser Zalman closed his *gemara* and agreed to go with her to the local shelter.

As he made his way down the many stairs from his house into the courtyard, a grenade fell nearby and exploded. Shrapnel tore painfully into R' Isser Zalman's leg. (He had to wear a cast for over a year to ensure that it healed properly.) His wife began to scream for help, but R' Isser Zalman stopped her at once.

"You cannot summon help now," he insisted, his great anguish apparent as he spoke. "It is a life-threatening danger for anyone to be outside now. It would be wrong to have people come here to help me now if at the same time they would be endangering their own lives. I will have to wait here until there is a lull in the bombing, and then we can call for help."

And that is exactly what he did. In excruciating pain and suffering he tolerated his agony so that he would not jeopardize, even for a moment, the safety of another Jew.

⪧ Connections

A number of years ago, Mr. Label Acker* of Brooklyn received a letter from his granddaughter in Israel. The letter was so touching and memorable that Mr. Acker has saved it to this day, proudly sharing its contents with numerous people.

A well-known *mechanech*, Rabbi Moshe Grossman of Brooklyn, who teaches at Yeshiva Darchei Torah in Far Rockaway, has retold this episode numerous times to his *talmidim*. I am grateful that he shared it with me as well, for I believe there are outstanding lessons to be gleaned from this story.

Mrs. Henya Lerman,* the granddaughter of Mr. Acker, was working for a company in Ramat Gan, Israel, which was owned by an Orthodox Jew, Mr. Heshy Fleisher. Financial times in

---

* All names in this story have been changed.

Eretz Yisrael were difficult, jobs were at a premium and Mrs. Lerman knew that she was fortunate to have a good job.

Mrs. Lerman, however, was concerned about her future with the company. In three months she would be giving birth to her first child. When she was ready to return to work, would her position still be waiting?

The job was critical for Mrs. Lerman because, unfortunately, her husband had been out of work for the past six months and her brother, who was living with them, also was unemployed. Hence, at the moment, she was the sole support of the family.

One afternoon, the owner of the company, Mr. Fleisher, was having lunch with a group of his employees. It was an informal gathering, and the casual conversation drifted from one topic to the next.

At one point, Mrs. Lerman voiced her fear of losing her job in the near future. She explained her predicament at home, as others at the table discussed their own financial concerns as well.

Mr. Fleisher, unwilling to commit himself, gracefully sidestepped the issue and people began to talk about their past histories and families. When Mrs. Lerman mentioned that she came from the East Flatbush section of Brooklyn, Mr. Fleisher turned suddenly and said, "When did your family live there?" Mrs. Lerman ventured a guess as to the exact years that her grandparents lived there, but that was not enough for Mr. Fleisher. He wanted to know her father's name, her mother's maiden name, her grandfather's name, her grandfather's occupation, where he *davened*, whether he was still alive ... Mrs. Lerman was taken aback by the torrent of questions.

Suddenly Mr. Fleisher left the room. When he came back, his eyes were red and it was obvious that he had been crying. After he composed himself, he told the following story.

❈　❈　❈

Many years ago, he said, there were two electricians who lived in the same neighborhood in East Flatbush. One was a member of the electrical union and was quite successful. The other, a non-union man, scraped together a meager living by searching throughout the city for miscellaneous small jobs. The two men *davened* in the same *shul* and were somewhat friendly, occasionally walking home together. However, their families did not know each other well.

One day the non-union electrician had a massive heart attack and within days he passed away. The other electrician came to be *menachem avel* (console the mourners). He couldn't help but notice the impoverished manner in which the mourners lived. While talking with the widow, he asked her if she had enough food for herself and the children. The widow claimed that she did, but when the electrician went into the kitchen and looked inside the refrigerator, he found it almost empty.

That afternoon he bought enough food to fill the refrigerator and some of the kitchen cabinets. Every day of the *shivah* (seven days of mourning), he replenished and added to the supply of food. The widow tried to dissuade him from what he was doing, but with all the people coming in and out of the house throughout the *shivah*, she really could not stop him.

Almost two months after her husband had passed away, the widow called the electrician. She told him that her basement was filled with wires, cables, drills, switches, screwdrivers, hammers, outlets and other electrical materials for which she had no use. "For a hundred dollars I'll sell you all the electrical material in the basement," she offered.

The next evening the electrician came to her house and began to work in the basement. For three weeks he spent his evenings sorting, organizing, separating and arranging all the various electrical paraphernalia that had accumulated over the years.

Once he had the material organized he called all the electricians and carpenters he knew and informed them that on a particular Sunday afternoon there was going to be a sale on electrical material and that it would be worth their while to attend.

The sale brought in more than three thousand dollars, all of which was given to the widow and her family.

When Mr. Fleisher finished telling this story to his spellbound audience, he turned to Mrs. Lerman and said, "The union electrician was your grandfather, and I was one of the *yesomim* (orphans). It was my father who had passed away, and it was my mother and brothers and sisters, as well as I, who benefited from your grandfather's *tzidkus* (righteousness).

"Mrs. Lerman," he continued, "you will always have a job in my company. Tomorrow morning, if your husband and brother come to my office, I will have jobs for them as well."

🦋　🦋　🦋

"Thank you, Zaide," Mrs. Lerman had written her grandfather. "I am so proud to be your granddaughter."

> Shlomo *HaMelech* wrote (*Koheles* 11:1): "שַׁלַּח לַחְמְךָ עַל פְּנֵי הַמָּיִם כִּי בְרֹב הַיָּמִים תִּמְצָאֶנּוּ — Send your bread upon the waters, for after many days you will find it." The good that is done today reaps rewards tomorrow. It is only a matter of time until that tomorrow comes.

⋙ *Favorable Reaction*

It was known by all the *talmidim* (students) of the Mirrer Yeshivah in Jerusalem that their *Rosh Yeshivah*, Rabbi Chaim Shmulevitz (1902-1978), made it a point to participate in all of their *simchos* (festive occasions). Whether it was the wedding of a *talmid*, or the *bris* or *bar mitzvah* of a *talmid's* child, R' Chaim would be among the first to arrive. And though he might have to wait until the festivities began, he never seemed impatient or in a hurry to leave.

That R' Chaim would extend such courtesy to his regular *talmidim* was understandable. However, he did this even for the *bnei Torah* (Torah scholars) of other *yeshivos* who attended his weekly *shiur* which was open to the general public.

R' Chaim's son, R' Avraham, recalls that when R' Chaim was asked why he would go out of his way for the once-a-week *talmidim*, he answered matter-of-factly, "I owe it to them as a matter of *hakaras hatov* (gratitude). They come to listen to my *shiur*, and I appreciate that!"

Customarily, it is the student who feels a debt of gratitude towards the *rebbi*/teacher, but here, to the contrary, R' Chaim (admitting what most others would not) acknowledged his pleasure in people coming to listen to him!

This credo of *hakaras hatov* was ingrained in R' Chaim's life because to him it was an ethical trait basic to the Torah way of living.

He once pointed out that when Hashem told Moshe *Rabbeinu* (*Bamidbar* 31:2) to avenge the Jewish nation against the Midianites, Moshe didn't go himself but, instead, sent Pinchas, along with a thousand warriors from each of the tribes, to carry out the mission (ibid. 31:6). The *Daas Zekeinim* (ibid.) and *Midrash Tanchuma* (*Matos*, Chap. 3) explain that Moshe himself did not wage war against the Midianites because he felt a sense of gratitude towards them, for it was in their country that he found a safe haven when he was forced to escape from Pharaoh in Egypt (see *Shemos* 2:15). Moshe lived by the concept that "בֵּירָא דְשָׁתִית מִינֵיהּ לֹא תִשְׁדֵי בֵּיהּ עַפְרָא — One should not throw earth into a well from which he drank water." (See also *Bava Kamma* 92b.)

Yet, asked R' Chaim, if Hashem himself told Moshe to wage war against Midian, no logic in the world should have superseded that command. How could Moshe have sent others instead?

R' Chaim explained that in reality the imperative of *hakaras hatov* is so strong that Moshe understood that it was impossible for Hashem to have meant that Moshe himself should be involved in the war against Midian. Rather, what Hashem intended when issuing His command was that Moshe should make sure that the task was accomplished. And that he did.

In light of this explanation, the following story, told by Rabbi Avraham Shmulevitz is illuminating.

Rabbi Meir Kleiman (1915-1988), a *talmid* of the Novorodok Yeshivah in Poland, was a man saturated with the study of *mussar* (ethical behavior). In his quiet, unassuming manner he personified through his speech and actions all that he absorbed from his *rebbeim* in Novorodok.

After he came to Jerusalem, he published and reprinted forty-one mussar sefarim so that they would be available to the public. Additionally, he was involved with the Bais HaMussar (House of Ethical Study) in the Chaya Soroh shul in the Meah Shearim section of Jerusalem, where such Torah luminaries as Rabbi Elya Lopian (1872-1970), Rabbi Chaim Shmulevitz and (yibadel l'chaim) Rabbi Sholom Schwadron would come to deliver inspirational and provocative shmuessen (mussar lectures). People from all over Jerusalem would flock to listen to these personalities.

Following every shmuess, R' Meir would lead the assembled in an emotional and heart-rending recitation of various chapters of Tehillim.

In the last year of Rabbi Chaim Shmulevitz's life, R' Meir's daughter had a son. R' Meir made his way to R' Chaim's home, wishing to inform him about the upcoming bris. (One does not actually invite people to a bris, but merely informs them about the occasion. This is because if one is actually invited he is not permitted to refuse such an invitation. See Pesachim 113b and ArtScroll Bris Milah p. 100).

R' Meir was met at the door by R' Chaim's wife, who asked him about the nature of his visit. "I've come to tell the Rosh Yeshivah about the upcoming bris of my grandson, which will take place tomorrow morning," he said.

"Please don't go in to see my husband," pleaded the Rebbetzin, who was always trying to protect and conserve his strength. "He is very weak and it will be a strain for him to go to the bris. If you do talk to him," continued the Rebbetzin, "he will feel obligated to come."

"I understand," he replied. "I wouldn't want to impose on the Rosh Yeshivah. I hope he feels better." With that, R' Meir left.

The next morning when R' Meir arrived at the shul where the bris was to take place, R' Chaim was already there! Unable to believe his eyes, he was both overjoyed and overwhelmed, for by now he understood the effort R' Chaim had to make in order to attend.

How was it that R' Chaim came to be there?

It seems that the day before, when Rabbi Kleiman was speaking to the Rebbetzin, R' Chaim actually heard his voice in the front room of his home. After he left, R' Chaim asked his wife why he had come. She explained that he had come to notify the *Rosh Yeshivah* about the upcoming *bris* of his grandson, but that she had encouraged him not to impose on R' Chaim because of the strain it would entail for him to attend.

However, R' Chaim said to his wife, "I must attend that *bris!* I feel such a sense of *hakaras hatov* to him. He says the *Tehillim* (at the *mussar* gatherings) so beautifully and I am always moved by it. It is only proper that I should attend his *simchah.*"

And that he did, with great effort and great exuberance.

◆§ Shattered!

The Talmud (*Berachos* 7b) teaches that there is even more value in being of service to a Talmudic scholar than there is in listening to his discourses: גְּדוֹלָה שִׁמּוּשָׁהּ שֶׁל תּוֹרָה יוֹתֵר מִלִּמּוּדָהּ. This is because when one is of service to a Torah scholar he has the opportunity to closely observe the scholar's behavior and conduct, which becomes embedded in his heart more deeply than any lecture (See *Maharatz Chiyus, Berachos* 7b).

The Talmud (ibid.) deduces this lesson from the manner in which the prophet Elisha's relationship with his mentor, the prophet Elijah, is described. Elisha is introduced (*Melachim II*, 3:11) as the one who poured water (as his attendant) over the hands of Elijah. No mention is made regarding Elisha having studied under Elijah.

Interestingly enough, the following story, told by Rabbi Yisroel Belsky, a *Rosh Yeshivah* in Yeshiva Torah Vodaath in Brooklyn, also deals with a *talmid* serving a *rebbe* by pouring water over his hands. Although the sensitivity we witness in this episode is remarkable, it almost went unnoticed. It was only in retrospect that an awareness was gained of what really happened.

In 1954, a young *bachur* still in his teens left "the *Mesivta*" (Torah Vodaath in Williamsburg) where he had been studying, to go to learn in one of the most prominent *yeshivos* in America, Bais Medrash Elyon in Monsey, New York. The *Rosh Yeshivah* there at the time was one of the *gedolei hador* (Torah giants of the generation), Rabbi Reuvain Grozovsky (1896-1958), son-in-law of the world-renowned Kamenitzer *Rosh Yeshivah*, Rabbi Baruch Ber Leibowitz (1870-1941). When the *bachur* came to the *yeshivah*, R' Reuvain was already quite ill. He had suffered a stroke which left the right side of his body paralyzed.

The students of Bais Medrash Elyon were given certain assignments on a rotation basis. (Naturally, newcomers were initiated almost immediately.) The assignments included traveling to a nearby farm and watching the cows being milked so as to assure that the milk for the *yeshivah* community would be considered *chalav Yisrael*; putting away the *sefarim* which had been used by the *bachurim* in the *beis hamidrash* (study hall) throughout the day; and assisting the ailing *Rosh Yeshivah* by sleeping in his room at night and being available to tend to his needs. These needs included washing R' Reuvain's left (and only mobile) hand with *"negel vasser"* when he awoke, holding a *siddur* for him so that he could recite the *Birchos HaShachar* (morning blessings), to which the *bachur* would respond with *"Amen"* as R' Reuvain finished each *berachah*, and putting the *Rosh Yeshivah's* *tefillin* on his arm and head.

Although R' Reuvain had a dedicated male nurse who attended him throughout the day, the *bachurim* did these chores every morning before the gentleman arrived. Assisting R' Reuvain was not an easy task, for his stroke had caused his speech to be slurred, making it hard to understand his requests. In addition, his left hand would sometimes jerk spontaneously and uncontrollably, making it difficult to put on his *tefillin*.

On the morning that this particular *bachur* was to help R' Reuvain, the young man was noticeably nervous. This would be the first time that he would be so close to this world-renowned *Rosh Yeshivah*. He had been forewarned that his tasks might not be easy, but he was hoping for the best. What happened was the worst.

As soon as he heard R' Reuvain stir, the *bachur*, following the instructions of those who had done it before, filled a cup of water, which he held in one hand, and carried a large basin in the other hand to catch the water after it was poured over R' Reuvain's hand.

He approached the bed with great trepidation. R' Reuvain, lying on his back, extended his left hand so that the *bachur*, whom he had never seen before, could pour the water over it. But as the young *bachur* began to pour the water, an uncontrollable spasm caused R' Reuvain to suddenly pull his hand back, and the water sloshed straight from the cup into the basin. The *bachur* felt foolish and somewhat helpless, but knew he would have to try again.

He took a step closer to the bed as R' Reuvain once again extended his thin, wavering hand. The *bachur* tipped the cup and began to pour, but in his haste and nervousness and in his eagerness to wash the hand before it could jerk back, he accidentally spilled water onto the bed, where it splashed all over the sheet and onto R' Reuvain's clothes. The young boy felt more ashamed and humiliated than he had ever felt before. He wished he could be anywhere but where he was! However, he still had his chores to complete, and only then could he head back to the *beis hamidrash* to catch the morning *minyan*.

He tried once again, determined this time not to spill water anyplace but on the *Rosh Yeshivah's* hands. He finally managed to accomplish his task as he poured the water three times. He wiped R' Reuvain's hand, and then got a *siddur* from which R' Reuvain read the *berachos* out loud. As R' Reuvain peered into the *siddur*, the young *bachur* could not take his eyes off the drenched sheet. He answered *"Amen"* dutifully and then, still embarrassed, proceeded to put on the *Rosh Yeshivah's tefillin*.

He had just turned to leave so that he could get to the *minyan* on time, when he heard the *Rosh Yeshivah* call him.

"What is your name?" R' Reuvain inquired.

"Yisroel Belsky," the *bachur* answered.

R' Reuvain asked him to sit down and engaged him in some small talk. The *Rosh Yeshivah* inquired about his family, his former *yeshivah* and his current *chavrusas* (study partners). Slowly, the *bachur* began to relax as R' Reuvain thanked him for being of assistance. After a few minutes R' Reuvain bid the young man good day and wished him *hatzlachah* (success) in his stay at Bais Medrash Elyon.

The *bachur* left the home of R' Reuvain in a relaxed frame of mind. He had undergone an awful, awkward morning, but the soothing voice of the *Rosh Yeshivah* had calmed him.

A few days later the *bachur* told some of his friends what had transpired between him and R' Reuvain. The *bachurim* in the *beis hamidrash* were shocked! Not one of them could recall R' Reuvain ever talking with his *tefillin* on! The *bachurim* began to ask one another, and to inquire of the other *Roshei Yeshivah* as well, whether anyone had ever heard R' Reuvain talk once he had his *tefillin* on.

It soon became clear (this was later confirmed by family members) that as long as anyone could remember, R' Reuvain had never intentionally uttered a word (aside from those of *tefillah* [prayer] and Torah) while wearing his *tefillin* (see *Orach Chaim* 28:1 and *Mishnah Berurah O.C.* 44 note 3). And yet, for the sake of a *bachur* whom he did not know, who had become uncomfortable and humiliated in his presence, R' Reuvain felt compelled to be lenient about a precept he had adhered to so fiercely, and speak freely while wearing his *tefillin*. His priority at that moment was to calm a young *bachur* so that his day of learning and sense of self-value would not be destroyed.

Now, decades later, Rabbi Yisroel Belsky, who himself has nurtured thousands of *talmidim*, remembers that incident as the shining example of a *rebbi's* sensitivity to a *talmid* (student).

To experience that event was to experience an eloquence of caring unsurpassed by any lecture. Indeed גְּדוֹלָה שִׁמּוּשָׁה שֶׁל תּוֹרָה יוֹתֵר מִלְּמוּדָה.

⋗§ *Shabbos Guests*

Moshe Rabbeinu admonished the Jewish nation and warned them that they would be punished severely if they did not serve Hashem with joy and happiness (see *Devarim* 28:47).

Rabbeinu Bachya (ibid.) teaches that aside from the reward awaiting those who perform *mitzvos* properly, there is a separate reward for the joy with which those *mitzvos* are accomplished (see *Rambam, Hilchos Lulav* 8:15). It would seem that this is especially true with regard to the observance of the *mitzvah* of Shabbos, for as we sing in one of the *zemiros* (songs) of Friday night, "יוֹם זֶה לְיִשְׂרָאֵל אוֹרָה וְשִׂמְחָה — This [Shabbos] day for Israel is one of light and gladness."

Iturei Torah (*Devarim* ibid.) recounts a story that illustrates this beautifully.

R' Simchah Bunim of P'shis'che (1767-1826), a *talmid* of the Chozeh [R' Yaakov Yitzchak] of Lublin (1745-1815), was a beloved *Chassidic Rebbe* whose disciples always clamored to be in his presence. If they could not manage to be with their *Rebbe* during the week, they made it a point to be with him for Shabbos.

One particular disciple, a very bitter and critical individual, once traveled to be with R' Simchah Bunim for Shabbos but arrived after Shabbos was over. When asked where he had been, he explained that he had actually been delayed and detained on the way so often that ultimately he had to spend Shabbos elsewhere.

The *Rebbe* listened to this unpopular man's story and told him the following: "Shabbos is actually a very kind and gracious host and it treats its guests with dignity. For example, when *Rosh Chodesh* comes on Shabbos, Shabbos is kind enough to give up both the regular reading of the *Maftir* and the *Mussaf* prayers to its guest, *Rosh Chodesh*. When *Yom Tov* comes with all its joy and splendor, Shabbos not only steps aside for the reading of the *Maftir* and the recitation of *Mussaf*, it also gives way for the reading of the Torah itself.

"When *Yom Kippur* comes and brings with it the wonderful portent of pardon and forgiveness, Shabbos gives way not only to the *Mussaf* prayers and Torah readings, but even the Shabbos meals themselves are set aside in *Yom Kippur's* honor.

"However, when melancholy *Tishah B'Av* with its unwelcome sadness and depression tries to come on Shabbos, a different attitude prevails. The Shabbos says, 'No, you wait and come after Shabbos!'

"Perhaps your not making it here this Shabbos," concluded the *Rebbe* to this disgruntled disciple, "is a message from Above. Unhappiness, and those who bring it, are not welcome until the joy of Shabbos is over. Change your ways and Shabbos will welcome you as well."

◆§ In the Fast Lane

When I once had the opportunity to speak on the topic of "*Midos* and *Derech Eretz* — Refining Our Character," it occurred to me to call Rabbi Avraham Kamenetzky of Brooklyn, the son of HaGaon Rabbi Yaakov Kamenetzky (1891-1986). R' Yaakov's concern for the dignity of others was legendary, and I thought that his son might have just the story that would typify both R' Yaakov's unique insight and kindness.

What he told me was classic.

R' Avraham was once driving with his father, R' Yaakov, on Coney Island Avenue in Brooklyn. Coney Island Avenue is a wide street and one of the major thoroughfares in Flatbush. They stopped at a red light, alongside a bus which was also waiting for the light to change.

As the light turned green, R' Avraham noticed that there was only one lane of traffic open ahead. Instinctively, he prepared to move quickly in order to be the first to get into the lane of moving traffic. However, R' Yaakov turned to his son and said, "You can't go yet. You have to let the bus go first."

"Why is that?" asked the surprised R' Avraham.

"*Kavod hatzibur* (communal respect)," came the reply. "There are more people on the bus than there are in this car. They deserve respect and preference!"

Who besides R' Yaakov would even think of that?

⋖§ The Right Place

In the mid-1800s Rabbi Yosef Yisrael Reichner and his wife, Faigele, lived with their eleven children in the town of Pressburg, Hungary. Eight of the children were boys, and each of them attended the local *yeshivah* elementary school and then entered the *yeshivah* for teenagers called Yesodei HaTorah. At Yesodei HaTorah they were privileged to be taught by an exceptional *rebbi* (teacher), an older gentleman by the name of Rabbi Lazer HaKohen Katz.

R' Lazer was an extremely pious man who was beloved by all members of the Pressburg Jewish community. People referred to him as the *Tzaddik* of Pressburg, and before every *Yom Tov* parents throughout the city would send their children to him for a blessing. R' Lazer lived alone in a small apartment on a block that was known as the *Z'idovska Ulitza* (Jewish Street) because of all its Jewish shops and businesses.

As the Reichner boys matured, they became imbued with a love of Torah and *mitzvos*, largely due to their association with R' Lazer. His *yiras Shamayim* (fear of Hashem), *chavivus hamitzvos* (love of *mitzvos*) and *hasmadah* (diligence in Torah study) were all worthy of emulation, and the boys in his class not only admired him but endeavored to be like him.

The years went by, and eventually R' Lazer became weak and frail and could no longer teach the young boys. He simply did not have the strength. Reluctantly, he retired from teaching and spent most of his day alone in his apartment. In Pressburg, though, there existed an organization called Toras Chessed, which gave a small stipend to older people who learned Torah in the *zechus* (merit) of *niftarim* (people who had passed away). That meager pension was to be R' Lazer's only income.

However, Mrs. Faigele Reichner did not forget what R' Lazer had accomplished with her eight sons. Therefore, every day she would send him a package of food for lunch, which contained enough for supper as well. Additionally, before every *Yom Tov* she would place money in the package so that R' Lazer could purchase something new for the upcoming holiday. This went on for more than two decades!

Shortly after Pressburg became part of Czechoslovakia in 1925, R' Lazer passed away, and a few years after that both Mrs. Reichner and her husband, R' Yisrael, also passed away.

❦ ❦ ❦

A generation went by. It was the night after *Yom Kippur* in 1944, and Nazi soldiers were furiously raiding and searching every Jewish house in Pressburg, looking for Jews to deport to concentration camps. Although the Nazis realized that the end of the war was near, their malicious hatred pushed them to try and eliminate every Jew they possibly could. Thus all Jews that were found, regardless of the passports they carried, were dragged outside their homes to be carted off to meet their bitter fate.

One afternoon two young Nazi soldiers came to the home of Ashi Reichner (one of the eight sons of Mrs. Reichner). In response to their furious pounding, Ashi opened the door and the Nazis burst in.

"How many Jews are in this house?" barked the soldier in charge.

"Only my wife is here with me," responded Ashi in a level voice.

"Find her and come with us!" ordered the Nazi.

"You should be ashamed of yourselves," said Ashi with dignity, "disturbing elderly people in their homes. What good could an old man like me be in a labor camp?"

"Out!" yelled the soldier. "Follow orders and move along if you know what's good for you! Both of you!" he shouted, turning from Ashi to Miriam, who was now standing in the doorway. "Downstairs!"

Outside, the Nazis suddenly disappeared. Ashi and Miriam could not figure out where they had gone. Perhaps, they reasoned, the young soldiers assumed that the terrified Jews would not move until their captors returned from their house-to-house search for more Jews. Ashi knew that they must take advantage of this unexpected chance for freedom. He immediately told his wife that he knew that somewhere in the left side of the city Jews were being sheltered in a bunker. His wife argued that there was a safer place in the right side of the city. She felt they should try and run there. Terrified, they argued frantically: In which direction should they run?

Their tension mounted as every frightening second passed. Their very lives might depend on the decision they were about to make! There was no time for logic, no time for thought, no time for reflection. They would have to act on instinct. Ashi knew the teaching of *Chazal* (*Niddah* 45b) that Hashem imbued women with an extra sense of insight and so he listened to his wife.

The Reichners ran as fast as they could, never looking back, towards the right side of the city and the building where Miriam had heard that Jews had found shelter.

They came to the apartment building, ran up to the second floor and knocked violently. A gentile woman answered the door, recognized them at once as Jews, and quickly ushered them in. That woman, though small in frame, was great in stature. She welcomed the terror-stricken Reichners and introduced them quickly to the other twelve people she was already shielding. Remarkably, among them were other Reichner family members: their daughter, son-in-law and grandchild who had secretly made their way there as well.

The woman in charge of the apartment became lovingly known to the people she safeguarded as "Anna Neni" (Aunt Anna). For eight months, until the Russians came and liberated Czechoslovakia, this noble woman risked her life every day as she went to the local grocer to purchase food for the people she was keeping alive. She would cover the food she bought with either wood or coal so that it would not arouse suspicion, for if the Nazis she passed in the street realized for whom she shopped, she would have been killed at once in cold blood.

In the apartment was a huge closet, behind which were two rooms in which fourteen people stayed. All who were with "Anna Neni" were saved. All who sought refuge in the bunker on the left side of the city, however, were found and killed.

☙ ☙ ☙

Incredibly, that apartment in which Ashi Reichner, his wife, daughter, son-in-law and grandchild were saved was the same apartment in which the *melamed*, Rabbi Lazer HaKohen Katz, had lived years earlier! It was in that apartment where Mrs. Faigele Reichner had kept the *Tzaddik* of Pressburg alive, that Hashem saw to it years later, to shelter her children, grandchildren and great-grandchild!

In *Shemos* (34:7) we are told, "נֹצֵר חֶסֶד לָאֲלָפִים — [Hashem] preserves deeds of kindness for thousands of generations." Rabbi Shamshon Raphael Hirsch notes that the word נֹצֵר also means "creates" or "causes to blossom." Thus the expression נֹצֵר חֶסֶד can refer to Hashem's benevolence, in which He allows an act of *chessed* performed by an individual not to remain merely an entity isolated unto itself, but rather to become a seed from which blossoms forth deliverance and happiness. At times this deliverance is granted to the same individual who performed the original act of *chessed*. However, there are times when the reward flourishes at a later date, for a descendant in a subsequent generation, as happened with the Reichners.

Our role is to plant seeds, but it is the מַצְמִיחַ יְשׁוּעוֹת, the One Who makes salvation flourish, Who in His infinite wisdom, decides on the eventual emergence of their harvests.

◦§ *Operation Bypass*

The *Gemara* (*Taanis* 25b) relates an incident that occurred when Jews were suffering from a drought. They came to R' Eliezer and asked him to pray for rain. He did, but the rains did not come. They then went to R' Akiva and pleaded with him to pray for rain. He did pray, reciting prayers that began with the phrase "אָבִינוּ מַלְכֵּנוּ — our Father, our King," and rain began to fall.

When people saw the rain they became critical of R' Eliezer, inferring from this incident that R' Akiva was the greater *tzaddik*. A *bas kol* (Heavenly voice) exclaimed, "It is not that R' Akiva is greater [in learning] than R' Eliezer; it is that R' Akiva is מַעֲבִיר עַל מִדּוֹתָיו — one who ignores the ill that others have done to him." (See *Rashi, Rosh Hashanah* 17a.) It was this noble trait, so worthy of emulation, that caused Hashem to listen to R' Akiva's prayer. When a person is willing to look away from evil that may have been done to him, Hashem, in turn, is willing to look away and disregard evil (i.e. sins) that this person may have done to Him. This person's sins, therefore, do not impede his prayers and therefore they are answered.

The following episode is an incredible manifestation of one who is מַעֲבִיר עַל מִדּוֹתָיו. It is said that Rabbi Aharon Kotler (1891-1962), the *Rosh Yeshivah* and founder of Beth Medrash Govoha in Lakewood, New Jersey, was moved to tears when he first heard this story.

R abbi Baruch Ber Leibowitz (1870-1941), the *Rosh Yeshivah* of the Kamenitzer Yeshivah in Poland, was a deeply sensitive man who rejoiced in the happiness of fellow Jews and felt their anguish when they suffered.

Rabbi Berel Wein, in his informative series of biographical tapes, relates that R' Baruch Ber was once asked why he avoided reading newspapers. One might think, suggests Rabbi Wein, that R' Baruch Ber would have explained his not reading a newspaper in light of the *issur* (prohibition) of *bitul Torah* (squandering time which could be used for learning Torah), or because of the numerous "non-kosher" articles and pictures usually found in a newspaper, which are better left unread and unseen.

However, R' Baruch Ber did not give any of those reasons. Rather, he explained that newspapers report so much tragedy, adversity and heartbreak that physically he could not bear to read about them. His empathy for other people was so intense that he literally suffered when he heard about the agony of another individual in distress.

Against this background one can well imagine the torment Rabbi Baruch Ber had to deal with in this episode of contrasting emotions.

❧ ❧ ❧

R' Baruch Ber had a daughter who was having a difficult time finding a *shidduch* (suitable partner in marriage). As time went on and the "right person" did not seem to be forthcoming, she became somewhat frustrated and despondent. Her father, who felt everyone else's pain in their moments of difficulty, felt his daughter's pain most acutely. One day, though, it finally happened. A young man from the Kamenitzer Yeshivah was suggested as a partner in marriage for R' Baruch Ber's daughter and eventually they became engaged. The joy in R' Baruch Ber's home was boundless. As was the custom of the time, the parents of the *kallah* gave the *chassan* a hat, a suit and a pocket watch as engagement gifts.

It was not unusual in Kamenitz for a *chassan* not to see his *kallah* from the time of their engagement until the wedding. Therefore, R' Baruch Ber suggested to the *chassan* that he find a *yeshivah* in another town where he would be able to learn without any distractions. The *chassan* readily agreed, and traveled to another *yeshivah* to continue his studies.

A few months later, a package from the *chassan* came in the mail, addressed to R' Baruch Ber. In it was the hat, the suit and the pocket watch that had been given to him months earlier. There was very little explanation in the letter that accompanied the returned gifts besides a few words from the *chassan* saying that the engagement was off.

R' Baruch Ber was crushed. There had been no warning that this was about to happen, and he realized that the pain his daughter would suffer from the news would be devastating. He had no choice but to tell his daughter the terrible news.

❈ ❈ ❈

Some time later, R' Baruch Ber received a letter from this same young man. In it, he explained that he had applied to become a *rav* in a small community, and during his interview with the town's Search Committee he had mentioned having once studied in the Kamenitzer Yeshivah.

The townsfolk were favorably impressed with him; however, before reaching a final decision about his candidacy, they asked for a letter of recommendation from his *Rosh Yeshivah*, R' Baruch Ber.

The young man knew how much anguish he had caused his former *Rosh Yeshivah* and couldn't muster the courage to approach him personally. Instead, he decided to take a chance and wrote a letter to R' Boruch Ber requesting a letter of recommendation.

Upon receiving this letter, R' Baruch Ber again relived the pain and embarrassment the young man had caused him. Despite everything, however, he took out a pen and paper and began to compose a message of approbation.

After he finished writing the letter, R' Baruch Ber reread it numerous times trying to see if, as he intended, a message of praise was coming across. However, the more he reviewed the letter, the less confident he felt about what he had written.

He summoned a young *bachur* named Koppel Wolpert, who did many errands for him, and asked him to bring three particular boys from the *beis hamidrash.* (R' Koppel eventually moved to Baltimore and became chairman of the board of Yeshivah Ner Yisroel. See *Around the Maggid's Table*, p. 79.)

The *bachurim* (one of whom was Rabbi Shlomo Heiman [1893-1944], eventually the *Rosh Yeshivah* of Yeshiva Torah Vodaath in Brooklyn) who were summoned were under the impression that they were being called by R' Baruch Ber for the ritual of *hataras nedarim*, to [rabbinically] absolve a vow that the *Rosh Yeshivah* might have made regarding a certain *seder* in learning. He had summoned them numerous times in the past for that very reason. However, now they were surprised as R' Baruch Ber asked them to sit down because he wanted to discuss a serious matter with them.

R' Baruch Ber began by saying, "You all remember the young man and the incident that occurred between him and my family some years ago. This same man has now requested that I write him a letter of recommendation to facilitate his being accepted as a *rav.* The pain in my heart is still great, and I am afraid that my own personal anguish may be discernible between the lines of what I have written. I ask that each of you read my letter carefully. When you have done so, please tell me honestly whether the recommendation is truly strong, or if it wavers in any way. If the words sound hesitant I will rewrite the letter because I do want to give him the highest approbation."

The three *bachurim* read the letter carefully and assured their *Rosh Yeshivah* that the letter was perfect and convincing the way it was.

Only then, overlooking the sorrow in his heart, did R' Baruch Ber mail the laudable letter in his hand.

✑ A Dance for the Ages

This following story is one of the most remarkable I have ever heard. It was told to me by one of the central characters in the episode, my uncle, Rabbi Yehuda Ackerman, a Stoliner *chassid* now living in the city of Bnei Brak, Israel. The love and concern for a fellow Jew portrayed here are so genuinely touching that the story inspires all who hear it.

A number of years ago a wealthy individual came to Israel with his family for a few weeks' vacation. He was staying in the famous Central Hotel on Rechov Pines in Jerusalem, and that is where he had most of his meals.

One Friday night, after the *seudas Shabbos*, the gentleman was strolling back and forth outside the hotel when he noticed two young *chassidic* boys rushing somewhere. "Where are you boys off to?" he asked, as they sped by.

"We're on our way to the Stoliner *Rebbe's tish.*" (The word "tish," literally translated as "table," is a term used for a gathering of *chassidim* around their *Rebbe's* table.) The gentleman thought that it might be interesting to observe a *tish* and so he asked, as he hurried to catch up with them, "Do you mind if I come along?"

"No, of course not. But you must walk quickly," they added, "because it is starting soon."

The three of them rushed down Rechov Pines, made a right turn on Rechov Malchei Yisrael, and headed into the tiny streets of Meah Shearim toward the Stoliner *shul.*

The *shul* was packed with hundreds of people who had already gathered to sing and bask in the *Rebbe's* presence. The gentleman now detached himself from the two boys, shouldered his way through the crowd, found some room for himself in the back of the synagogue and stood there unobtrusively observing the scene.

My uncle, a fervent Stoliner *chassid* for decades, had come that week to Jerusalem to be with his *Rebbe*. He, too, was at the *tish* and was sitting close to the front. As he looked around the synagogue he searched for faces that were not among the "regulars." It was then that he noticed the wealthy man in the back.

My uncle, aside from being a devout *chassid* of the *Rebbe*, is the founder and fundraiser of the Stoliner Yeshivah in Bnei Brak. Before Shabbos the *Rebbe* had told him that he must not leave Jerusalem before raising twenty-five thousand dollars for the benefit of the *yeshivah*, because the *melamdim* (teachers) were owed a great deal of back pay. Therefore, when my uncle saw the wealthy gentleman, he figured that he might be a good man to talk to.

Throughout the evening my uncle kept an eye on the man in the back of the *shul*. When he realized that the *tish* was about to end, he made his way towards him.

My uncle, a jovial and robust individual, extended his hand and, with the broadest of smiles, said, "*Gut Shabbos, Reb Yid*. Welcome to Stolin. I believe I recognize you."

My uncle knew quite well that this man had a reputation of being a philanthropist who supported many Jewish causes. He was hoping he could get him involved with his own cause.

The man looked at my uncle and replied, "*Gut Shabbos*. I believe I recognize you too."

The two men spoke for a while and then my uncle asked, "Where are you staying, and how long will you be here in town?"

"I'm staying at the Central and I'm leaving on Tuesday," came the reply.

"May I bring some of my friends to you tomorrow night at the Central, and we will make a little *Melaveh Malkah* (festive meal held Saturday night)? We'll sing a little, dance a little, tell some stories, have some good food. It will be beautiful."

The philanthropist understood quite well what my uncle's intention was, but still he smiled and said, "Fine. Come with your friends tomorrow night."

The next evening, a little while after Shabbos ended, my uncle and three of his friends went to the Central Hotel and up to the gentleman's room. They knocked on the door and waited, pacing back and forth as they worried that perhaps the gentleman had forgotten about the *Melaveh Malkah* or that something else had come up. After a few moments, however, the gentleman came to the door and invited them in.

For more than two hours they sang, told stories and relished the ambience of the evening. Finally the gentleman turned to my uncle and said, "Ackerman, what do you want from me? I know you didn't just come here to sing and dance."

My uncle smiled sheepishly and said, "You know something? You are so right. I didn't just come to sing and dance. I came for a very important reason." He then went on to explain the financial plight of the Stoliner Yeshivah and how, because of the economic hardships in Israel, the *yeshivah* was almost totally dependent on support from friends in America. "I need your help," my uncle said seriously. "The *Rebbe* told me that I must raise twenty-five thousand dollars."

Everyone in the room was quiet. The gentleman was deep in thought, his eyes closed as he reflected on the words my uncle had just spoken. "I'll tell you what, Ackerman," he said. "I'll give you a donation now, and if you raise ten thousand dollars by tomorrow night, I will match it and give you another ten!"

My uncle and his friends could not believe their ears. It had never occurred to them that the gentleman would make such a gracious offer. They shook hands on the "deal" and a few moments later my uncle left the hotel to begin his efforts to raise the ten thousand dollars.

For much of the night and all of the next day my uncle ran from person to person, telling them that he had a golden opportunity to relieve the Stoliner Yeshivah of a good deal of its financial burden if only they would help him. He collected cash, personal checks, money orders and traveler's checks. He hardly rested for a moment, and by Sunday evening he was close to his goal.

Late Sunday night he made his way to the Central Hotel, went directly to the gentleman's room and began piling all the money he had raised on the table. They counted it, and sure enough — my uncle had met the goal! He had raised ten thousand dollars! The philanthropist promptly took out his checkbook and wrote a check to the Stoliner Yeshivah for ten thousand dollars. My uncle simply could not believe what was happening. For the first time in many years he was speechless.

As he began to thank the gentleman profusely for what he had just done, the gentleman said, "Aren't you wondering why I did this?"

"Wondering?" my uncle blurted out. "To me this is a miracle. It's like *man min hashamayim* (the food that fell miraculously from Heaven for the Jews in the desert)."

"Sit down," the gentleman said. "Let me tell you a story and then you will understand."

☙   ☙   ☙

"It was twenty-five years ago," the gentleman began, "on the afternoon of my wedding day. I was so poor that my parents could not even afford to buy me a hat to wear to my *chuppah*. I lived in Williamsburg (an Orthodox neighborhood in Brooklyn, New York) at the time, so I walked to Broadway where there was a famous Jewish hat store. I went in and told the owner, 'I'm getting married tonight, but my parents are poverty stricken and can't afford to buy me a hat. Could you please do me a favor and give me a hat? I promise you that tomorrow morning I will come in and pay you with some of the money that I hope to get tonight as wedding presents.'

"The man behind the counter looked me over and then answered, 'You look like an honest *yeshivah bachur* (student). I'll give you the hat.'

"I was so happy and grateful to him," continued the gentleman. "I walked outside and a few stores down was a liquor store, also owned by a Jewish man. I knew very well that my parents couldn't afford any liquor for the wedding, so I went in and said to the man behind the counter, 'I'm getting married tonight and my parents do not have money to buy any liquor. Would you be so kind as to give me a few bottles for the wedding? I promise that tomorrow morning I will come in and pay you from the money that I hope to get as wedding gifts.'

"Here, too, the man looked me over and said the same thing the fellow in the hat store had said. 'You look like an honest *yeshivah bachur*, I'll give you the liquor.'

"He gave me the liquor and I walked out of that store with the hat in my right hand and the liquor in my left. I felt like a million dollars. I was ecstatic. I took just a few steps outside the store and there you were, Mr. Ackerman.

> [My uncle, R' Yehuda Ackerman, was known at that time as the most extraordinary dancer at Jewish weddings. Whenever he made his way into the middle of the circle where everyone was dancing, he became the focal point of frolic around which everything centered. Everyone in the hall would stop whatever they were doing just to watch him perform for the *chassan* and *kallah*. His body movements were elegant; his balancing acts, entertaining; his radiant smile ebullient, and his body's comical coordination with the music the band was playing was incredible and legendary. Somehow he managed to become the physical embodiment of the musical notes emanating from the violin, clarinet and cordovox, which were popular at the time.]

"I saw," the gentleman said, "that Hashem was so good to me in helping me get the hat and the liquor, so I figured that I would take my chances just one more time. I walked over to you and said, 'Mr. Ackerman, I know you don't know who I am, but I am getting married tonight. Would you mind coming to dance at my wedding?'

"You said that you couldn't promise anything, but you took down my name and the name and address of the wedding hall. And that night, right in the middle of the wedding, you came running into the center of the circle where everyone was dancing and you danced so magnificently. The people loved it! You made everyone so happy and you helped make it the greatest night of my life. When it was over that evening, I swore to myself that someday I would repay you."

Now, transversing all the years in between, the gentleman concluded. "Last night, when I saw you at the Stoliner *Rebbe's tish*,

I suddenly remembered what I had said to myself back then on my wedding night. I realized that now was the time to pay you back. That's why I gave you the money."

My uncle sat there astounded. He hadn't remembered the wedding from so long ago, but he would never forget this Shabbos night in Jerusalem.

The story, however, did not end there. The next time my uncle was in the city where this generous gentleman lived, he heard that the man's son was getting married. He waited until the middle of the wedding and then, as he had done so many years earlier, he ran into the center of the circle where everyone was dancing, and he danced as he had, all those years before.

And as he did, he turned and saw the gentleman standing off on the side with a great smile across his face, and tears rolling down his cheeks. He ran over to the man and, as they embraced, the man said to my uncle, "How can I ever thank you? You've made me relive the greatest night of my life."

> The *Gemara* (*Yoma* 9b) teaches that the Second *Beis HaMikdash* was destroyed because of *sinas chinam*, uncalled-for and unreasonable hatred. Here, though, was an instance of poignant *ahavas chinam*, a talented individual dancing at the wedding of a young man whom he didn't even know and never thought he would see again only because there was love. . . love of one Jew for another with no motive or incentive other than that they were both Jewish. May we all learn from this incredible story and merit together to see the building of the Third *Beis HaMikdash*.

⋐§ Hats Off!

In June of 1990, Rabbi Yaakov Salomon of Brooklyn went to buy a lightweight summer hat. He usually purchases his hats at one of the well-known hat stores in the Boro Park section of Brooklyn, and this time was no different.

The proprietor sold him a hat the size and color he wanted, and R'

Yaakov was on his way. A few days later he remembered that because he had been in a rush that particular day, he had forgotten to have his initials embossed onto the inner tab of the hat in order to make it identifiable among all the other hats that are often on his *shul's* hat racks.

One morning a week later, he went back to where he had purchased the hat and said to the owner, "I bought this hat here last week and I forgot to have my initials put in. Would you mind doing it for me now?"

"I'll be happy to do it for you," the owner said. "But what day did you buy the hat?" he asked R' Yaakov.

"I was here last Tuesday — and that's when I purchased it," came the puzzled reply.

"Are you sure that it was Tuesday?" the owner inquired.

R' Yaakov thought for a moment and said, "Yes, I am quite sure it was Tuesday."

Smiling, the owner took out a five-dollar bill and gave it to the surprised R' Yaakov. "What is this for?" R' Yaakov asked curiously.

"Last Wednesday," the owner explained, "we received a letter from the hat manufacturer telling us that the billing department had inadvertently overcharged us and that we were entitled to some money back. I had based my price for your hat, and the other summer hats I sold until that Wednesday, on what I thought the hats were going to cost me. However, when I realized that I would be getting a refund, I wanted to reimburse any of my customers that I may have overcharged."

R' Yaakov was amazed by this honesty, and when he came home he called to tell me the story. I, in turn, was so astonished by the episode that I called Rabbi Nosson Scherman, the perceptive editor of ArtScroll/Mesorah Publications, to tell him the story.

R' Nosson listened patiently to my enthusiastic retelling of the incident. He waited a moment and then said quietly, with remarkable insight, "Isn't it a shame that this is considered such a beautiful story?"

In our exuberance we must not confuse what seems extraordinary with what actually should be ordinary.

Mrs. Tova Yasner* of Flatbush, Brooklyn comes from a very close-knit family. Her parents raised her and her siblings to share in each other's joy and feel each other's pain. There are few secrets among the brothers and sisters because among them jealousy has no place and concern has no bounds.

Pesach, 1991, was a time of special joy in their family. Mrs. Yasner had recently given birth to a son and now, just a few days before *Yom Tov*, her sister, who lived a few miles away in Boro Park, had a baby girl.

The families planned to get together in Boro Park on the Shabbos immediately following the last days of *Pesach* (Thursday and Friday) for a *kiddush* in honor of the new baby.

On Friday morning, the last day of *Yom Tov*, Mrs. Yasner's brother Shimon suddenly appeared in Flatbush. He had walked from Boro Park to tell his sister and brother-in-law, R' Aaron, that the *kiddush* for their newborn niece had been canceled.

He explained that late the night before, well after the *seudah* (festive *Yom Tov* meal), their mother, Mrs. Renkin, had suddenly fainted and been rushed to the hospital. No one in the family — least of all their father, R' Pinchas, the grandfather of the newborn infant — was in the mood for a festive *kiddush*, so the family decided to postpone it.

Mrs. Yasner was very upset and told her brother that she would walk to Boro Park to visit her mother in the hospital. "It's not necessary," said R' Shimon. "She will be fine. You'll see her after Shabbos. And besides," he added, "you have your hands full here. You just had a baby yourself, the other children in the house need you, and you're expecting guests. There is no need for you to strain yourself by walking all those miles back and forth. Better that you walk in for a *simchah*."

Both Mrs. Yasner's brother and her husband tried to talk her out of going, but to no avail. They finally gave up trying to dissuade

---

* All names have been changed by personal request.

her, and it was decided that the three of them would walk together that afternoon to be with their parents in Boro Park.

Mrs. Yasner gathered her four older children together and told them that she was going to Boro Park to visit her mother in the hospital. As she informed each of her children about the arrangements she had made for them that afternoon, she instructed them not to discuss with their friends the reason she suddenly had to go to Boro Park.

Children being what they are, they did indeed tell their friends — who eventually told their parents — that their grandmother had suddenly become ill and that their mother had gone to visit her in the hospital.

Hours later, when Mrs. Yasner returned from Boro Park and went to round up her children, the people at whose homes the children had been staying asked politely about the welfare of Mrs. Yasner's mother.

She replied briefly to each inquiry, saying that everything was fine. Then she thanked her friends on the block for watching her children.

❧   ❧   ❧

That Shabbos night, after *havdalah*, Mr. Yasner called their friends and neighbors to let them know that there would be a *levayah* (funeral) the next morning. His mother-in-law had indeed passed away — early Friday morning!

The people on the block were in shock. They had seen Mrs. Yasner numerous times on *Yom Tov* and Shabbos after she had come back from Boro Park, and not once had she mentioned anything! In an act of extraordinary strength, Mrs. Yasner, inwardly torn by the tragedy, served her guests, maintained her composure and saw to it that what remained of *Yom Tov* and Shabbos was not spoiled for her close friends by information that would undoubtedly have destroyed their enjoyment of *Yom Tov* and Shabbos.

It was for this reason that her husband and brother had not wanted her to walk to Boro Park. By Friday morning her mother had already passed away. They finally agreed to accompany her to the Renkins' home when they realized that her presence would be a comfort to her father, who was terribly shocked and saddened by the tragedy.

When I heard this story, I was struck by the startling self-control of a bereaved individual, and her extraordinary concern not to disrupt or disturb the lives of others. It was then that I remembered a story which I had heard a few months earlier, told by Rabbi Berel Wein on his informative series of biographical tapes.

The *Netziv*, Rabbi Naftali Tzvi Yehudah Berlin (1817-1893) for forty years the *Rosh Yeshivah* of the great Volozhiner Yeshivah, was known to have a deep personal regard for every *talmid* in the *yeshivah*.

A concerned father of one of the *talmidim* once came to the *Netziv* and asked that the *Rosh Yeshivah* give special attention to his son for, as the father explained, "He is my *ben yachid* (only son)."

The *Netziv* replied, "I understand how you feel. I too have a *ben yachid* in the *yeshivah* — four hundred of them!"

One day the *Netziv* was walking in the hallway of the *yeshivah* on his way to give a *shiur* (Talmudic discourse). As he was about to enter the *shiur* room he noticed someone in the hall whom he did not recognize.

The *Netziv* thought that he knew everyone who studied in the *yeshivah* and was therefore surprised that this person looked unfamiliar. "*Shalom aleichem*," the *Rosh Yeshivah* said, extending his hand. "Do you learn here?"

"No," replied the gentleman. "I only came to visit the *yeshivah*."

"Where are you from?" asked the *Netziv*.

"I am from Pinsk," came the reply.

"Pinsk?" exclaimed the *Netziv*. "I have a brother who lives in Pinsk. Do you by any chance know him?"

"It happens that I do," said the gentleman.

Communication not being then what it is today, the *Netziv*

hadn't heard about his family members in quite a while. "How is my brother?" he asked eagerly.

The gentleman hesitated before replying unconvincingly, "He is all right. He is fine."

The *Netziv* told the gentleman that he was about to give a *shiur* and could not talk to him any more just then. Would he be kind enough to wait until after the *shiur* so that he could speak to him at length?

The gentleman said that of course he would wait, that it was no problem at all.

After the *shiur*, the *Netziv* and the man from Pinsk sat down to talk. "Tell me truthfully," said the *Netziv*, "how is my brother?"

The gentleman became downcast as he said sadly, "I am sorry to be the one to tell you this. Unfortunately, your brother passed away."

The *Netziv* gasped at the news and then he said slowly, "I had a suspicion that something might be wrong when I saw how hesitantly you answered me earlier in the hallway. However, I had to give a *shiur* to the *bachurim* and I had a responsibility to give them my utmost and undivided attention. Had I inquired further and become aware that my brother had passed away, I know that I would not have been able to concentrate fully on the *shiur*. My mind would have been diverted and that would have been irresponsible. I therefore waited until after the *shiur* to find out whatever news you may have."

> Self-control, mastering one's emotions, feeling with the heart but acting with the head — these are characteristics to be treasured.

The *Yalkut Shimoni* (*Mishlei* 31) relates how, on a Shabbos, the two sons of R' Meir tragically passed away. R' Meir's wife, Bruriah, knew that if her husband were to find out about this tragedy on Shabbos it would totally disrupt his Shabbos serenity.

She chose to postpone telling him the news. After Shabbos she said to her husband, "If someone asks his friend to safeguard an article for him, may he take back the article whenever he wishes?"

"Why of course," replied R' Meir. "The one who owns the article has a right to his possessions. They are his."

Bruriah then told her great husband, R' Meir, that Hashem, Who had entrusted to them two precious articles — their sons, had recalled them during Shabbos.

> Bruriah ... the *Netziv* ... a modest and unpretentious woman in Brooklyn ... The generations are different and the situations are dissimilar. Yet one quality remains unwavering: the admirable trait among *Klal Yisrael* of containing one's grief solely for the benefit of others.

⋙ *Initial Reaction*

The *Shevet Mussar* interprets a well-known phrase written by David *HaMelech* with an ingenuity that provides us with an outlook on death that reflects upon life.

Conventionally the phrase, "כִּי לֹא בְמוֹתוֹ יִקַּח הַכֹּל" — For upon his death he will not take it all" (*Tehillim* 49:18), is understood as advice from David *HaMelech* not to be intimidated by someone who becomes rich. (See ibid. 49:17.) This is because material wealth does not give one legitimate eminence. True eminence is achieved not by money, which cannot be taken after death, to the Next World, but by the study of Torah and the performance of *mitzvos,* whose accomplishment will be rewarded in the World to Come.

The *Shevet Mussar* (see *Mikdash Me'at,* ibid.) writes that "כִּי לֹא בְמוֹתוֹ יִקַּח הַכֹּל" refers to the fact that a man does not take his reputation with him when he passes away. Every man leaves a legacy in this world. It is either one of honor or one of notoriety. The consequences of a man's deeds remain in this world, even after his death, as a living testimony to what his life was all about. It therefore behooves man to act accordingly.

In this episode, told by Rabbi Chaim Yitzchok Goldberger, now of Atlanta, Georgia, we witness one of the finals acts in the legacy of life that Rabbi Yaakov Kamenetzky left behind in this world.

During the last weeks of his life, R' Yaakov was living with his daughter and son-in-law, Rabbi and Mrs. Hirsch Diskind of Baltimore. Chaim Goldberger, learning in Baltimore's Yeshivah Ner Yisroel at the time, volunteered to stay overnight in R' Yaakov's room in the Diskind home to attend to the *Rosh Yeshivah's* needs during the night.

R' Yaakov had already suffered a stroke and was no longer talking except for an occasional response to a familiar question, and even that was barely perceptible. Yet remarkably, his *Shema* at the nightly *Maariv minyan* arranged at his house was distinctly audible. Once — just once — he responded with a sentence-long greeting to a visitor who, he realized, had come from *Eretz Yisrael* to visit him. But with almost everyone who came as part of a steady stream of well-wishers he sat silently, in apparent transcendence of the world he was shortly to leave.

One morning, as Chaim was about to return to the yeshivah, the Diskinds expressed their gratitude for his nightly efforts, and as a token of appreciation they offered Chaim a copy of R' Yaakov's newly printed *sefer* on *Chumash, Iyunim B'Mikra*. Chaim asked if they could have the *Rosh Yeshivah* sign it. With little optimism, *Rebbetzin* Diskind offered to see what she could do.

That evening, Chaim came back to spend his last night at the home of the Diskinds. In the morning, as he was preparing to leave, *Rebbetzin* Diskind asked Chaim, "Did you look on the dining room table?"

On the table was the *sefer*. Chaim opened it and on the flyleaf was the name יעקב קמנצקי in the *Rosh Yeshivah's* own aged handwriting.

Chaim was beside himself with amazement. As he stared at the signature, *Rebbetzin* Diskind said, "Do you know what my father did after you left yesterday morning? He asked me for a pen and a piece of paper. Then slowly and deliberately he practiced writing his name numerous times, to make sure that his handwriting was still sufficiently legible, before signing your *sefer*. He had great *hakaras hatov* to you for your efforts and he didn't want to ruin your *sefer* by writing illegibly!"

Within a week the great *tzaddik* passed away.

❦ ❦ ❦

R' Chaim says, "Imagine a man in his mid-nineties being so deeply concerned about a young man's request that he would exert himself to have it fulfilled. Imagine a man suffering with the debilitating effects of a stroke, caring enough to recognize the good deeds that another has performed for him. Imagine a man on his deathbed sensitive to the beauty of proper penmanship!* Yet, to R' Yaakov all these things mattered. One can only marvel at the lofty stature a person reaches after having been imbued with Torah for an entire lifetime."

> Although we can no longer be inspired by his physical presence, Rabbi Yaakov Kamenetzky left behind an extraordinary legacy for us to learn from, because, as the *Shevet Mussar* notes, man does not take it all with him. His reputation and teachings remain behind.

❧ Ignore Me Not

Rabbi Akiva Eiger (1761-1837), the great *gaon* of Posen, once traveled to Warsaw, to attend a rabbinic function. The Jews in Warsaw were aware of his coming, and thousands of them streamed to the train station to greet him.

Torah scholars and lay people alike crowded alongside and behind the great *tzaddik* as he made his way into the city to meet with other Torah luminaries. Everyone in the dense throng was trying to get a glimpse of this man of tiny frame and giant stature,

---

* R' Yerucham Levovitz, sainted Mirrer *mashgiach*, taught that one should be careful and meticulous about the neatness and beauty of handwriting in a letter, as well as the quality of the paper and ink. This is part of the dictum "וְאַנְוֵהוּ – הִתְנָאֶה לְפָנָיו בְּמִצְוֹת" (*Sukkah* 11b) to beautify the *mitzvos* — even those *mitzvos* governing *bein adam l'chaveiro* (interpersonal relationships). [See *Daas Chochmah U'mussar* vol. 3 p. 235].

considered the *gadol hador* (pre-eminent Torah scholar of the generation).

After attending to his business, Rabbi Akiva Eiger announced that he wished to visit with a cousin of his whom he hadn't seen in a while, a poor shoemaker who lived outside the city.

He made his way to the small village and naturally a crowd followed close behind. When Rabbi Akiva Eiger came to his cousin's shop, the man greeted him warmly and welcomed him graciously. The shoemaker gave him the only chair in his shop — his own.

The great *gaon* spent some time with his cousin and then began his trip back to Warsaw. En route, one of the people accompanying Rabbi Akiva Eiger approached him and said, "Excuse my asking, but why did you take the time and go to the trouble of traveling to see your cousin? Surely if he wished to see you, he could have come to greet you as did so many others. Besides, it did not befit a man of your stature to inconvenience himself to make such a trip."

He thought for a moment and then, with sparkling insight, replied as follows:

"The Torah uses a unique term when it warns a Jew about his obligation to return a lost item. It addresses the one who first spots the lost item by saying, 'לֹא תוּכַל לְהִתְעַלֵּם — You may not ignore it' (*Devarim* 22:3; see also ibid. 22:1).

"The *Gemara* in *Bava Metzia* (30a) teaches that there is a time, however, when a Talmudic scholar may ignore a lost item. In a situation where it would be humiliating for him to be seen carrying that particular item he is exempt from picking it up, even if it is lost. A *talmid chacham* need not suffer embarrassment to fulfill the *mitzvah* of returning a lost item. (This exemption is only regarding this *mitzvah*).

"Interestingly, similar wording is used by the prophet *Yeshayah* (58:7) when he exhorts *Klal Yisrael*, 'וּמִבְּשָׂרְךָ לֹא תִתְעַלָּם — And don't ignore your flesh (relatives)' (see *Rashi*).

"However, here the Talmud does not make the exception it made regarding the lost item. Although the same terminology is used in both cases: לֹא תוּכַל לְהִתְעַלֵּם, regarding a lost item, and וּמִבְּשָׂרְךָ לֹא

תִתְעַלָּם, regarding concern for a relative, it is only in regard to a lost item that the Torah allows a Talmudic scholar to look away. No one may look away from a relative — even if it is humiliating. That's why I had no hesitation in going to visit my cousin."

How often do we ignore and neglect the needs of relatives, while at the very same time attending to the welfare of others who are unrelated to us? Relatives deserve priority, even if there is no honor or glory involved in helping them.

◄§ Doctor's Orders

Chazal (Talmudic sages) tell us (*Yevamos* 62b) that the *talmidim* (students) of R' Akiva perished because they did not accord honor one to another. Rabbi Aharon Kotler (1891-1962), the *Rosh Yeshivah* and founder of Beth Medrash Govoha in Lakewood, New Jersey, points out (see *Mishnas Rav Aharon,* vol. 3, p.15) that there was a specific lesson to be learned from the fact that they died during the days between *Pesach* and *Shavuos.*

He notes that the forty-nine days of *Sefirah* (lit., counting [of the *Omer*]) between *Pesach* and *Shavuos* are ones in which people of every generation prepare themselves for *kabbalas* (reception of) *haTorah* on *Shavuos.* According honor one to another, R' Aharon writes, is not merely a social grace, it is part and parcel of Torah life (see *Pirkei Avos* 6:6). Thus, R' Akiva's *talmidim* who were deficient in honoring one another failed in their Torah way of life and, therefore, could not be the ones to transmit Torah from R' Akiva to the next generation. Their dying during this time of "preparation" signified for future generations the paramount importance of maintaining each other's dignity and respect.

The following remarkable story, retold by Rabbi Moshe Grossman of Brooklyn, is a case in point.

Many years ago there lived in Jerusalem a kind individual named Dr. Nachum Kook. Dr. Kook was a general practitioner who tended to patients with all types of ailments. His unpretentious medical office was housed in the simple home in which he lived with his family. A front parlor served as a waiting room, and an interior room was used for examinations and diagnoses.

As Dr. Kook did not have a secretary or a receptionist, those who came to his office to be examined would seat themselves in the front parlor and quietly wait to be called. When he finished with each patient, Dr. Kook would come out to the waiting room and ask who was next. The individual whose turn it was would stand up and go with the doctor.

Everyone who visited Dr. Kook knew the system. It was an honor system that all his patients respected and abided by. There was, however, one exception made to this rule and that was for Rabbi Yechezkel Sarna (1895-1969), *Rosh Yeshivah* of the Chevron Yeshivah in Jerusalem. Because of Rabbi Sarna's diabetes he had to come to the office regularly, and out of deference to his imposing Torah stature, Dr. Kook made an exception for him. Thus, whenever Rabbi Sarna came to the office he would automatically be taken in next.

It happened one time that Rabbi Sarna came to the office and was seated among other patients in the parlor waiting to be called in. As Dr. Kook peered into the room, Rabbi Sarna began to get up from his seat, about to make his way towards the examining room. Dr. Kook looked around and then said to Rabbi Sarna, "Excuse me, *Rosh Yeshivah*, but first I must see this lady." Dr. Kook then motioned to an elderly lady, who had been waiting for a while, to come in.

When Dr. Kook was finished with the elderly woman, he once again went out into the waiting room and this time beckoned to Rabbi Sarna to come in. Once inside, Rabbi Sarna immediately began to apologize for getting up "out of turn."

"I know," he explained, "that you customarily take me in as soon as I come. That is why, when you finished with the other patient, I automatically began to make my way into the office."

"This is true," replied the noble Dr. Kook. "I usually do take you in before everyone else. But today I had to make an exception. You see, the lady whose turn it was is a poor old woman who does not pay me anything for her visit. It occurred to me that if I were to take anyone in before her, she would think that the reason I was giving priority to others is that since she doesn't pay me, she therefore deserves less attention than my paying patients. That is why I specifically made it a point to take her when it was her turn, so that she shouldn't in any way feel that she was getting less care than anyone else!"

❧ Two-Minute Warning

There is a beautiful poem that is used as a song at Sephardic (Syrian) brisos.

בֶּן אָדָם לָמָה תִּדְאַג עַל הַדָּמִים.

וְלֹא תִדְאַג עַל הַיָּמִים.

כִּי הַדָּמִים אֵינָם עוֹזְרִים.

וְהַיָּמִים אֵינָם חוֹזְרִים.

רְדוֹף אַחַר הַתּוֹרָה וְהַמִּצְוֹת. אֲשֶׁר הֵם לָעַד קַיָּמִים.

Son of man, why do you fret over money,
and do not fret over days?
Money does not help,
days do not return.
Pursue Torah and mitzvos, for they endure forever.

Every moment of life is precious, and it is our obligation to make the most of the time with which we are blessed in this world. All people have to function within the same confines of a twenty-four-hour day and a seven-day week. Yet there are many who achieve notable accomplishments in life, while others do not ever seem to consummate anything of significance. The difference between these two types of people is often due to the difference in their ability to master, by self-discipline, the art of deciding on priorities in order to use time intelligently. To waste minutes, hours, days, months and years of life is to waste one of Hashem's most precious gifts to man — time.

A lesson in the value of time was taught recently in a story told by Rabbi Yaakov Salomon of Brooklyn.

In the *shul* where Rav Avraham Pam, the *Rosh Yeshivah* of Yeshiva and Mesivta Torah Vodaath, *davens*, one of the regulars, an elderly man became sick and had to be hospitalized. Rav Pam, who is a *kohen*, does not visit hospitals in order to avoid the possibility of violating the law which prohibits a *kohen* from being in the same building as a dead person.* (See *Yoreh Deah* 369-374.) Therefore, instead of visiting the elderly gentleman in the hospital, Rav Pam wrote him a letter.

In the letter, he expressed his regret that the man was ill and wished him a *refuah sheleimah* (a speedy recovery). The letter, a short one, had taken the *Rosh Yeshivah* just a few minutes to write.

The gentleman was thrilled to receive the letter. He could not believe that a simple man like himself was worthy of receiving such attention from the *Rosh Yeshivah*. He put the letter under his pillow, and whenever a friend or family member came to visit him he would pull out the letter, beam with pride, and say, "Look, I received a letter from the famous *Rosh Yeshivah*, Rav Pam."

A few months later, the elderly gentleman took a turn for the worse and unfortunately passed away. His family and friends gathered together for the funeral which, because he is a *kohen*, Rav Pam could not attend.

Numerous *rabbanim* who were at the funeral were asked to give *hespedim* (eulogies). One of the *rabbanim*, a man from out of town who was friendly with one of the gentleman's children, but had not known the gentleman himself, was also asked to eulogize the *niftar* (deceased). In his *hesped*, he said, "Many of us here probably did not appreciate how special this man really was, but it should be obvious that he was an important person because Rav Pam himself, the *Rosh Yeshivah* of Torah Vodaath, took the time to write him a letter!"

❀ ❀ ❀

---

* In Hadassah Hospital in Israel, a sign is posted at the front entrance to let *Kohanim* know when there is a corpse in the hospital's morgue.

Later that week Rav Pam was told about what had been said at the funeral, and was informed how, during his hospital stay, the sick gentleman had treasured his letter. He thought for a moment, then said, "This whole incident is frightening to me. Consider what a person can accomplish in just a few moments. It took me just two minutes to write that letter, yet in the hospital it gave the recipient such cheer and comfort. Furthermore, at the funeral it gave his family and friends consolation. Do we realize what can be accomplished in just two minutes? How often do all of us have two minutes of free time? If we don't make the most of those periods, they pass by in emptiness. What frightens me," Rav Pam continued, "is that the *Ribono Shel Olam* can take this letter and say to me, 'You did something so wonderful in such a short amount of time. What are you doing with all the other two-minute spans of free time that you have?' "

Indeed! What about a call? A postcard? A friendly hello? Are there not people we know — even relatives — who would be thrilled and touched just to know that we thought enough about them to inquire about their well-being?

The *Gemara* (*Nedarim* 39b) states: "בִּיקּוּר חוֹלִים אֵין לָהּ שִׁיעוּר" — There is no limit when it comes to visiting the sick." As Abaye explains, "אֲפִילוּ גָדוֹל אֵצֶל קָטָן" — Even a great man should visit an insignificant one." Perhaps this is so, suggests Rabbi Shlomo Teitelbaum of Kew Gardens, because of the comfort and strength that the man of smaller stature receives when he realizes that in his moment of duress an important man cares.

Just as Rav Pam cared.

⋘ *Elevated!*

In the Strettiner *beis hamidrash* in Boro Park, a charitable member donated a large number of table *shtenders* for the use of the people in the *shul*. (A table *shtender* is a small lectern, placed on a table, which holds one's *siddur* or *chumash* in an elevated position, facilitating easier reading.) The gentleman brought all these *shtenders* into the *shul* on a Friday afternoon and placed them carefully on the tables, one in front of each seat, throughout the *shul*.

That Shabbos morning, Rabbi Mordechai Eliezer Leiner came into the *shul* and walked over to his *makom kavuah* (steady place [of prayer]). He could not help but notice the brand-new table *shtenders*. At first he placed his *siddur* on the *shtender*, but after a short while he decided to remove the *shtender* from the table and place it somewhere else. He had always *davened* holding his *siddur* in his hand or resting it on the table itself, and he wasn't going to change now. He picked up the *shtender* and began to walk towards the back of the *shul*, intending to place it somewhere else, when he remembered...

Many years earlier, shortly after World War II, he first met the Bluzhover *Rebbe*, Rabbi Yisrael Spira (1889-1989), in the Lower East Side of New York. He was overwhelmed by the *tzidkus* and piety of the *Rebbe* and became a devoted disciple. When the *Rebbe* started a regular *minyan*, R' Mordechai was among the first to join. The *minyan* grew until the *Rebbe* came to have hundreds of followers.

One Friday night, the *gabbai* (attendant of the *shul*) asked R' Mordechai to be the *shliach tzibbur* (leader of the assembled) and *daven Maariv*. R' Mordechai walked up to the *amud* (lectern from which the *shliach tzibbur* prays), *siddur* in hand, ready to begin as soon as the *Rebbe* gave him the signal. There was a large *chazzan's siddur* on the *amud*, open to *Kabbalas Shabbos*, but R' Mordechai closed it and peered instead into the regular *siddur* he had brought from his seat.

The *Rebbe* called him over. "Yes, Rebbe?" asked R' Mordechai in surprise.

"Did it occur to you that someone donated that *chazzan's siddur*?" asked the *Rebbe*.

R' Mordechai didn't reply.

"Do you realize," continued the *Rebbe*, "that when you

use that *siddur*, not only do you give the man who donated it pleasure, but there is also merit to the soul of the person in whose name it was donated? Why should you hold back the joy of those individuals both in this world and the next?"

R' Mordechai got the message, went back to the *amud*, closed the *siddur* he had brought up to the *amud* and reopened the *chazzan's siddur...*

Now years later, holding the table *shtender*, R' Mordechai made an about-face and returned to his seat. He put the *shtender* back where it had been before, placed his *siddur* on it, and prayed with a special intensity, thanking Hashem for having blessed him with the opportunity to learn Torah-sensitivity from a great man.

⋖ξ Chicken Soup Therapy

R av Sholom Eisen (1917-1988), a member of the *beis din* in Jerusalem, was known for the insights and innovations he expressed in his judicial rulings. He sat on the *beis din* for close to fifty years, and throughout his life he answered thousands of *she'eilos* (religious questions) — those brought before the *beis din* as well as those posed by people who came to his home seeking his counsel and wisdom.

One Friday night a young man came to Rav Eisen's home in the Meah Shearim section of Jerusalem, visibly upset. Recognizing his state of mind, Rav Eisen asked the gentleman to sit down and offered him a glass of tea. Then the *Rav* asked him what the problem was.

It seems that during the Friday night *seudah* the young man, who was recently married, noticed a chicken bone in his soup that he thought might be *halachically* questionable. The position of the break in the bone along with its unusual bluish color concerned him. Was it possible that the bone had pierced the chicken's lung prior to *shechitah*, thus rendering the chicken, and all that was cooked with it, *treife*? (See *Yoreh Deah* 53:2.) To make matters worse, the young man's wife had not put the entire chicken into the soup. Part of this same chicken was, at that very moment, simmering in the *cholent*, waiting to be served at the Shabbos *seudah* the next morning.

Rav Eisen discussed the *she'eilah* with the young man for a few moments, and then the sage and the student began "talking in learning." He was very impressed with the young man's grasp of various *sugyos* (Torah topics) and shared with him a *chiddush* (innovative Torah thought) that he had recently thought of.

By the time they had talked for more than half an hour, a relationship of mutual admiration was beginning to evolve. Finally Rav Eisen said, "I would really like for you and your wife to join us for the *seudah* tomorrow after *davening*."

The young man was startled by the unexpected invitation but replied that he would be honored to accept. As he was about to leave he asked the *Rav*, "What about the *she'eilah* that we discussed earlier. Is the soup kosher or not?"

"Oh, that," Rav Eisen smiled warmly. "You really don't have to worry. The soup and the *cholent* should not be eaten, but it's no longer a problem because you will be eating with us tomorrow anyway. We agreed to that already, didn't we?"

The young man smiled to himself as he realized the cleverness of the *Rav*. He had shrewdly made sure that the young man and his wife had a place to eat before telling him that the food they had was prohibited.

The *Rav* had provided the רְפוּאָה קוֹדֶם לְמַכָּה, the remedy before the affliction (see *Megillah* 13b), and it was therapeutic.

Part B:

The Master's Plan

The following story is wondrous because it is multi-faceted. It contains elements of friendship, family heritage, inspiration, intrigue and surprise. However, for me personally, there is an additional component that makes this story memorable.

A number of years ago, after having performed a *bris* in my neighborhood of Kew Gardens, I entered into a discussion with the *sandek* (person who holds the child during the *bris*), Rabbi Shmuel David Walkin (1905-1979), a *rav* in the community. What he told me that Shabbos morning, as interesting as it was, merely became a nugget of information regarding *bris milah* which became hidden in the recesses of my mind. However, upon hearing the following story, I suddenly recalled Rabbi Walkin's words of years ago. What he had taught me that Shabbos now illuminated this story in an incredible fashion.

In the winter of 1985, Rabbi Yitzchak Mayer Schorr, a *Rosh Yeshivah* at Yeshiva Torah Vodaath in Brooklyn, received a call from a personal friend. Unbeknownst to Rabbi Schorr and his friend, that call was to trigger a chain of events which, linked together, affected and changed the lives of numerous individuals.

Rabbi Schorr was told that in an apartment across the street from his home, there lived a young married couple, the Panzers,* who were very special people. Both Mr. and Mrs. Panzer were highly intelligent, but not religious at all. The friend suggested that perhaps he should make it a point to get to know them so that he and his family could inspire and motivate them towards genuine *Yahadus*.

Rabbi Schorr assured the caller that he would establish contact with them. A few days later he noticed a young couple coming out of that home, who fit the description given by the caller. He approached them and asked if they were indeed the Panzers.

When they said that they were, he introduced himself and

---

* Name has been changed by personal request.

explained that a mutual friend had suggested that he get to know them. After a short conversation Rabbi Schorr invited them to join him for a Shabbos meal. The couple seemed curious as to what a Shabbos meal in an Orthodox home might be like, and so they accepted the invitation. A few days later they came to the Schorrs for the Friday night *seudah*.

It became apparent, almost immediately, that these people were not ordinary, as their quest for knowledge seemed endless and their curiosity about authentic *Yiddishkeit* seemed genuine. The Schorrs and the Panzers became very friendly, and the Panzers' visits grew more frequent.

A while later, on a spring afternoon, Rabbi Schorr suggested to Marc Panzer that perhaps he might want to spend a few days at Yeshivah Ohr Somayach in Monsey, New York. Rabbi Schorr assured Marc that Ohr Somayach catered to people with little religious background, and that most likely he would find the environment and the *shiurim* there stimulating.

Marc and his wife, Arlene, decided that he would try Ohr Someyach for a week in the summer. The week they spent in Monsey with the Ohr Somayach community was fascinating, as it opened before them new vistas of wisdom and insight they had never imagined. After they returned to the city, Marc and Arlene decided that they would soon visit Ohr Somayach again, but for a longer period of time.

Before *Rosh Hashanah*, Marc gave notice to his employers that he would be leaving his job and told his friends that he would be enrolling in Ohr Somayach for the upcoming *zman* (semester). He soon found that he was happier and more content than he had ever been before. It wasn't long before Marc was being called by the name he had been given at his *bris* — Moshe David. Similarly, Arlene began to use the name Chana, the name she remembered was given to her in honor of a beloved grandmother.

Moshe David and Chana became a regular part of the Monsey community, and within a year they were Torah-observant Jews in the fullest sense of the word. Soon they took up permanent residence in Monsey.

They had been in Monsey for two years when one day the

Panzers came back to Brooklyn for a talk with Rabbi Schorr. "When I was growing up," Moshe David said to Rabbi Schorr, "I was led to believe that all my relatives were deranged and peculiar. My parents did not have anything to do with any of their brothers and sisters, and I didn't see my grandparents for years. However, now I realize that my relatives were probably not 'insane' or 'crazy' as my father always said they were. It was just that they were religious, and this was abhorrent to my parents. That is why they raised me with feelings of enmity towards them."

R' Yitzchak Mayer could only feel sad for the young man who had been deprived of family warmth for so many years. Moshe David took a deep breath and continued, "I would like to find some of my relatives, but I don't know where they live. However, I do know that I have a distant relative who is a *Chassidic Rebbe* living in Boro Park. Would you mind calling him for me to make an introduction so that he and I could get acquainted?"

Rabbi Schorr was only too happy to oblige, and made the call immediately. The *Rebbe*, an elderly gentleman, told him that he would welcome these guests, although he didn't know exactly who they were.

Moshe David and Chana made plans to be in Boro Park. A few weeks later, during *Chol HaMoed* (the intermediate days of) *Sukkos*, the couple made their way nervously to what they feared could be an awkward and embarrassing meeting. Moshe David was convinced that he was related to the *Rebbe*. The only question was: Could he get the *Rebbe* to realize it?

Chana relates that when she walked into the *sukkah* where the *Rebbe* was sitting, and took one look at his exquisite appearance — at his immaculate long white beard, radiant *kapote*, elegant *shtreimel* and soft facial features — she started to cry. She sat down in a corner and tried to compose herself, but she continued to sob uncontrollably. She had cried that way only once before — on the day she had made her commitment to become an Orthodox Jew.

[Chana explains that she cried on both occasions because each time she suddenly realized how close she had been to losing an enormous opportunity. Had a different chain of events taken place in her life, she would never even have known what she was missing

— first in being Orthodox, and now in getting to know this holy man.]

Moshe David and the *Rebbe* became engaged in a warm conversation. After a while the *Rebbe* took out old manuscripts and explained that they were texts of *sefarim* that Moshe David's great-uncle had written in Hungary. "You come from a family of *talmidei chachamim* (Torah scholars)," the *Rebbe* assured Moshe David. No words could have been sweeter.

The *Rebbe* reflected quietly for a moment and then asked Moshe David, "Don't you have an Aunt Martha?"

"Yes," came the reply. "But why do you ask?"

"I think I recall that I was at the *bris* of Aunt Martha's son," the *Rebbe* said.

"No, I'm sorry," said Moshe David, "but Aunt Martha has only two daughters and no sons."

The *Rebbe* was puzzled because he seemed to vaguely recall attending a family *bris* years ago where no one but he and the *mohel* were religious. Suddenly the *Rebbetzin*, who had been listening to the conversation, turned to Moshe David, pointed to him excitedly and exclaimed, "Wait, are you the Moshe David who was born in the Bronx?"

"Yes," replied Moshe David, somewhat startled.

"*Rebbe*," she cried out, "this is the one whose *bris* you went to!"

And then it all came back to him. The dilemma, the debate and the decision.

"Now I recall the whole story," the *Rebbe* proclaimed, astonished at how pieces of a historical puzzle were beginning to fall into place.

"The night before your *bris*, your father called me and asked me to be *sandek*. By then, most of the family had cut off relations with him. For many years before he was married, he was irreligious, and people in the family tried to influence him to return to *Yiddishkeit*. However, when he became serious about your mother, and her total lack of commitment to *Torah* and *mitzvos* became clear to our family, we all tried to dissuade him from going through with the marriage. He wouldn't listen to anyone and they got married anyway. It was a defiant act on his part, and because of it not one of the religious relatives showed up at the wedding. From then on we lost contact with him.

"When he called me a few years later to tell me that he had a son and that he wanted me to be *sandek*, I was surprised that he would even contact me. My first reaction was not to go to the *bris*. I didn't know what type of *mohel* he would take, I was quite sure the food wouldn't be kosher, and I wondered what value my going would have altogether. But when the *Rebbetzin* heard about his call she insisted that I go to the *bris*. 'Don't go for the father's sake,' she advised. 'Go for the sake of the newborn infant, and when you are holding him during the *bris*, pray that some day he will grow to be an *ehrlicher Yid* (religious Jew).'

"And that is exactly what I did," the *Rebbe* continued. "I went for your sake, and while I was holding you during the *bris*, I indeed prayed that you should be an *ehrlicher Yid* and now, twenty-eight years later, I see that my prayers have been answered. How wondrous are the ways of Hashem!"

The story in itself is remarkable, but when I heard it, I remembered my encounter with Rabbi Walkin.

It was Shabbos morning and I was performing a *bris* in Rabbi Shmuel Walkin's *shul* in my neighborhood of Kew Gardens. Rabbi Walkin was honored with being *sandek*, and just as I was about to begin the actual *bris*, he began to cry softly to himself. By the time the *bris* was over his crying had reached a crescendo, and his weeping seemed to be without control.

I knew Rabbi Walkin to be a caring and friendly man, and I felt bad for him. At times people will shed tears at a *bris* as bittersweet memories are evoked due to the child being named after a dear departed family member. Others cry at a *bris* (or any other *simchah*, for that matter) if a particular family member is noticeably absent because he or she has recently passed away. However, neither explanation was applicable in this case. The infant was not being named for anyone that Rabbi Walkin knew, and the *baalei simchah* (people hosting the affair) were not related to him in any way. I couldn't help but wonder why he seemed so moved.

Afterwards, when most of the gathered had already left, I

approached Rabbi Walkin and asked if everything was all right. He understood that I was inquiring about his crying during the *bris*. He put his outstretched hand on my shoulder and said in bewilderment, "You mean you don't know?"

"No," I replied. "I'm sorry, but I don't know what you are referring to."

"Bring me a *Gemara* (Tractate) *Shabbos*," he said.

I brought it to him and he turned to the back of the *Gemara* to the commentary of Rabbi Eliyahu Gutmacher of Graiditz (1796-1875). "Read what it says here," Rabbi Walkin said.

❦   ❦   ❦

I read where Rabbi Gutmacher writes (*Shabbos* 130a) that it is known that David *HaMelech* wrote a chapter in *Tehillim* that refers to *bris milah* (ritual circumcision). (See *Tosefos Shabbos* 130a.) Many are under the impression that this is Chapter Twelve, which begins: "לַמְנַצֵּחַ עַל הַשְּׁמִינִית מִזְמוֹר לְדָוִד" — To the One Who grants victory; regarding the eighth, a song to David," in which the word הַשְּׁמִינִית (lit., the eighth) is a reference to the day on which a *bris* is usually performed. However, notes Rabbi Gutmacher, there is nothing in the rest of that chapter that makes any other reference to *bris milah*. Therefore, he concludes, it can not be Chapter Twelve.

Rather, he claims it is Chapter Six that refers to *bris milah*. There, too, the first verse in the chapter contains the word הַשְּׁמִינִית (the eighth), a reference to *bris milah*: "לַמְנַצֵּחַ בִּנְגִינוֹת עַל הַשְּׁמִינִית מִזְמוֹר לְדָוִד — To the One Who grants victory; [sing this] with musical instruments, regarding the eighth, a song to David." In this chapter Rabbi Gutmacher, citing *Olilos Efrayim* (Chap. 415), finds numerous references to *bris milah*.*

Then, citing *Olilos Efrayim* again, he adds that when one is at a *bris*, one should think about his problems and pray to Hashem for assistance at the exact moment that the child is crying from the pain of the *bris*. This is because the cry of the child is holy and pure and

---

* In verse 3, David *HaMelech* writes, "חָנֵּנִי ה' כִּי אֻמְלַל אָנִי — Favor me, Hashem, for I am unfortunate." The word אֻמְלַל, Rabbi Gutmacher notes, is actually a contraction of two words "אֲנִי מָל — I am circumcised." Thus, one who is ill should pray "חָנֵּנִי ה' — Favor me, Hashem [and heal me] — כִּי אֲנִי מָל — for I am circumcised."

goes straight up to Heaven, unhindered, carrying with it the prayers of individuals as well.

This is alluded to in the ninth and tenth verses in this Chapter (6) which state: "כִּי שָׁמַע ה׳ קוֹל בִּכְיִי — For Hashem has heard the sound of my weeping" — this is a reference to the cries of the child during the *bris*, "שָׁמַע ה׳ תְּחִנָּתִי ה׳ תְּפִלָּתִי יִקָּח — Hashem has heard my plea, Hashem will accept my prayer."

Rabbi Gutmacher concludes by saying that this is an incredible bit of advice.

❧ ❧ ❧

Rabbi Walkin smiled at me and said, "You see, it is very special to pray at a *bris*, and because it is such an opportune moment, I feel it is only right to pour one's heart out to Hashem at that time. That is why I cried the way I did."

❧ ❧ ❧

Years ago, when the *Rebbe* was praying at Moshe David's *bris* in the Bronx, for the sake of the infant he was holding, it was indeed the most propitious time to appeal to Hashem. No wonder his prayers were answered.

⋖§ Celebrations

When the book *Around The Maggid's Table* was completed, I made a *seudas hoda'ah* (a festive meal of appreciation) to thank Hashem for allowing me the opportunity to complete that work. Wishing to celebrate with those who helped put the book together, I invited the staff of ArtScroll/Mesorah Publications to the *seudah*, as well as friends who reviewed and commented on each of the stories and parables.

My mother, Mrs. Hindy Krohn, too, had just completed a book of her own, also published by ArtScroll. Entitled *The Way It Was*, it described her early years growing up in Philadelphia. When I told her about the *seudah*, she asked if she and those who had helped with her book could join with me to celebrate the publication of her work as well. Naturally, I welcomed the idea.

Among my mother's guests was her editor, Chavi Willig Levy. Chavi has published many books, has edited major works and manages her own communications consulting firm. What makes Chavi's accomplishments extraordinary is that as a child she had contracted polio, which left her with paralyzed muscles in both arms and legs. Because of the resultant impeded mobility she uses a motorized scooter to get around.

❧ ❧ ❧

Few people thought that Chavi would ever get married. However *Chazal* (Talmudic sages) wrote (*Bereishis Rabbah* 68:4): "הקב״ה יושֵׁב וּמְזַוֵּוג זוּוּגים — Hashem ponders and matches couples." Thus it was part of Hashem's master plan that in 1982 Chavi, wheelchair and all, met a young man named Michael Levy. Aside from his many talents, Michael has a special empathy for people enduring life's difficulties for he, too, must deal with a handicap on a constant basis. Michael is blind. He and Chavi discovered that they shared mutual interests for, despite what life had handed them, both were deeply committed to *Yiddishkeit* and had a keen appreciation for music and words. They eventually married and after six long years they had their first child, a daughter named Tehilah.

To watch the remarkable ways in which Chavi and Michael compensate for each other's disabilities is inspiring. With great sensitivity they graciously complement and compliment each other. All who find themselves in their presence are simply awed.

❧ ❧ ❧

Present at our *seudah* was a personal friend of mine, Dovid Stein* from Stamford,* Connecticut, and his wife. Dovid had spent countless hours over the past two years giving me his reactions to the stories in the book. Like most others at the *seudah*, this was the first time he had met the Levys, and he was overwhelmed by how

---

* The name and city have been changed.

the two of them seemed to manage. He couldn't help but be amazed at the way Michael held his daughter Tehilah (because Chavi found it difficult) so that Chavi could feed the little girl (because Michael found that difficult).

The Steins and the Levys chatted amiably, and as the evening drew to a close, Dovid said to Michael and Chavi, "My wife and I would be delighted to have you spend a Shabbos with us. Would you honor us by coming?"

Dovid felt that aside from fulfilling the *mitzvah* of *hachnasas orchim* (hosting guests), the lessons that his children would learn from spending a Shabbos with this extraordinary couple would be everlasting.

The Levys replied that they would be happy to come to Stamford, but explained that because travel was difficult for them they would have to be picked up by car from their apartment in Manhattan. The Steins were only too happy to oblige. It was agreed that three weeks from the upcoming Shabbos the families would be together.

The week before the Levys were to visit Stamford, Michael's father passed away. Michael called to tell the Steins the sad news and explained that he would remain at home throughout the whole week of the *shivah* (mourning period of seven days). Their Shabbos visit would have to be postponed.

After the *shivah* period, new plans were made. Thus it was two weeks later than originally planned, on a Friday afternoon, that Dovid showed up at the Levys' front door. He helped them into the elevator and, once outside, into his car, and drove them to join his eager family for Shabbos.

Friday, before sunset, Dovid explained to Michael that they had a choice of two different *shuls* in which to *daven* on Shabbos morning. The one Dovid usually attended was about a mile away; the other — where they would *daven Kabbalas Shabbos* — was merely across the street. "I imagine," Dovid said, "that it would be much easier for us to walk to the *shul* across the street. However, there is a *bar mitzvah* there this Shabbos and *davening* might end quite late because of the Rabbi's speech, the *bar mitzvah* boy's *leining* (reading the Torah) and the extra *aliyos* (people that are called to the Torah) for the many guests. Which *shul* would you prefer?"

Michael answered that it would be easier for him to *daven* in the *shul* across the street, and he didn't mind if it took a bit longer, so Dovid decided to *daven* in the *shul* across the street too. Michael, as usual, took, his Braille *chumash* and *siddur* to *shul* before candle lighting.

❦   ❦   ❦

Shabbos afternoon, as Dovid and Michael were making their way across the street to *shul* for *Minchah*, the *rebbi* (teacher) of the *bar mitzvah* boy came running toward them. "Dovid," he called out with great excitement, "you won't believe what a miracle happened in *shul* this morning!"

Dovid couldn't imagine what the *rebbi* was talking about. He had not seen or heard anything unusual in *shul* that morning except that a boy had celebrated his *bar mitzvah*.

"It is unbelievable!" the *rebbi* exclaimed once again. "I had been working with this boy on his *leining* (reading of the Torah) for over a year and a half. He had such trouble with it and, to make matters worse, his parents went through a bad divorce this year, which only added pressure to everything that was going on. We had reviewed the *leining* so many times, yet I was never really sure that he would come through. The boy's father had promised him that he would come to *shul* this morning, and as the boy was getting ready to walk up to the *bimah* (central podium) to *lein*, he looked around for his father — but he was nowhere to be found. This made the boy so anxious that I was sure he would barely make it to *sheini* (the end of the first *aliyah*), or worse — that he would faint.

"But instead, he got up there and he *leined* so well and so beautifully that I was shocked. I have never heard him *lein* so well. Afterwards, I turned to him and said, 'Ezra,* how did you *lein* so well? I never heard you *lein* like that before!'

"He turned to me and replied, 'Remember what you told me

---

* Name has been changed.

when we first started learning the *sidrah* (portion of the week) together?'

"Frankly, I didn't recall what I had told him," the *rebbi* said. "But then Ezra said, 'You told me, right at the beginning, that I have to *lein* so well and so clearly that if there were a blind man in *shul* he would be able to follow. I was so nervous — because of the *leining* in general, and because my father hadn't come. But then as I looked up near the *bimah*, I saw a blind man sitting there with a Braille *chumash*. I decided to block everything else out of my mind and concentrate on *leining* well, just so that the blind man would be able to follow perfectly!' "

> The meeting at the *seudah*...the invitation for Shabbos...the delay in the visit...the choice of *shul*...the blind man's seat...Dovid *HaMelech* wrote, "מַה גָּדְלוּ מַעֲשֶׂיךָ ה'" — How great are Your deeds, Hashem" (*Psalms* 92:6).
>
> Indeed, as the Master of the Universe orchestrates so many events to coincide in perfect harmony, it is music to the ears of those wise enough to listen.

◆§ *Crash Course in Yiddishkeit*

> Shlomo *HaMelech* writes (*Koheles* 3:1) that all things have their proper time. Citing examples of contrasting and conflicting elements, he notes that there is a time to talk and a time to be silent, a time to love and a time to hate, a time for war and a time for peace. Essentially, man must use his maturity and intelligence to guide him as to how and when to act.
>
> Yet there is much that transpires both in our personal lives and in world events that seem beyond our control. At times events seem to occur randomly, without any forethought regarding time or reason. In this story, retold by Mr. Daniel Sukenik of Kew Gardens, New York, we come to realize, among other things, that events indeed happen at specific times because whether we realize it at the time or not, there is a Master Plan.

For Gadi Biton,* the beauty of life was personified by the rip-roaring rides he took on his motorcycle every opportunity he had. Gadi lived in the Galil, the northern part of *Eretz Yisrael*, and every afternoon, or whenever time allowed, he would race along the rolling ribbon of black-topped roadways that laced the magnificent mountains of the Galil. He knew every little town and hamlet in that part of the region, and people in each one of them had seen and heard him thunder by in a blur of metal and chrome.

One afternoon, as he was riding through a small town, Gadi made his way towards an approaching intersection and decided to turn right at the upcoming corner. Coming out of his turn at a fast pace, he was startled to see a little girl directly in his path. There was no time to stop, nor could he swerve to avoid her. He slammed into the poor child and she went hurtling across the street, right into a brick wall. In a moment she was knocked unconscious.

Gadi screeched to a halt, jumped off his motorcycle and, surrounded by the hysterical screams of the child's mother and other pedestrians, quickly ran to the child. Everyone started giving everyone else orders as the little girl lay unconscious. After several excruciatingly long minutes an ambulance appeared on the scene. As there was no hospital in that particular small town, the ambulance rushed the mother and child to the nearest medical center, a few miles away.

At the hospital, the little girl remained in a coma for days. The parents of the child were beside themselves with grief, and Gadi himself went about his business troubled and bewildered. He was deeply sorry about what had happened, but he rationalized that it wasn't really his fault because, as he had been told, the little girl had let go of her mother's hand and scampered into the middle of the road. Over and over Gadi kept repeating to anyone who would listen that he too was a victim of this horrible accident. He could neither sleep at night nor concentrate by day. All he thought about was the condition of the poor, innocent child.

One afternoon the child began to awaken from her coma. First

* Name has been changed.

she recognized her parents, and then slowly her memory returned, and soon she could talk and think normally, just as she had before. A few days later, the doctor announced to the child's mother that the little girl would suffer no permanent damage, and that she would be released from the hospital shortly.

The last day that the girl was in the hospital, Gadi made his way to her room. As he approached the room he noticed the girl's mother sitting outside. Gadi went over to her and began to speak softly. He knew that the mother recognized him and so he got straight to the point.

"I want you to know," he said, almost inaudibly, "how terrible I feel about what happened. I know that it was not my fault completely, as your daughter ran out into the middle of the street. However," he continued, "I feel terrible about the accident and I do want to do something for you and your daughter. I myself don't know what I can do. I am not a wealthy person, but whatever you tell me, I am ready to do for the benefit of either one of you."

The young mother looked up at Gadi and said softly, "The day that you were riding that motorcycle was Shabbos. Promise me that you will never ride your motorcycle on Shabbos again."

Gadi was stunned! It never even occurred to him that the day of the accident was Shabbos and besides, what did that have to do with anything? "Is that all you really want of me?" he asked.

"Yes," the mother replied in her quiet manner. "If you promise me that, it will mean everything to both me and my daughter."

Gadi nodded his head in the affirmative and then turned away. He left the hospital in a daze. Of all the things he had imagined that she would tell him, the thought about Shabbos had never even crossed his mind.

The following Shabbos, as he was about to mount his motorcycle, Gadi remembered the promise he had made. He went back into his apartment building and knocked on the first door that he noticed had a *mezuzah*. A child came to the door and invited him in. As he entered, he saw a family sitting together at a table eating their Shabbos *seudah* (meal).

"I was wondering. . ." Gadi began haltingly, as he addressed the man seated at the head of the table. "Perhaps you could explain to me why I am not allowed to ride a motorcycle on Shabbos?"

"Shabbos is a day of rest," the man answered pleasantly.

"But that is my form of rest and relaxation," Gadi protested. "Riding in the mountains is both exhilarating and calming."

A conversation ensued as the two men verbally fenced with each other. Finally the gentleman got up and said to Gadi, "Look, I am not the most learned of men, but I do know that down the block from us lives a very nice rabbi. You should go to him and he will explain to you why you can't ride your motorcycle on Shabbos."

That seemed reasonable enough, so Gadi made his way to the rabbi, who cordially greeted him. He invited Gadi to join in his Shabbos seudah, and throughout the meal they spoke about many different topics. The rabbi did not lecture nor admonish Gadi, and invited him to come back another time.

Gadi began to visit him regularly, and soon they were having study sessions together twice a week. After a few months, though, Gadi announced that he was going on vacation. "I can't stay around here right now," he announced. "I need a change."

"Where are you headed?" the rabbi asked.

"No place in particular," Gadi replied. "I just want to travel throughout the country."

"Listen," the rabbi said. "Today is Thursday. Why don't you go to Jerusalem for Shabbos and stay at a yeshivah called Ohr Somayach (a yeshivah which specializes in reaching young men who have little religious background)? If you stay in that particular yeshivah for one Shabbos, you will understand forever why you can't ride a motorcycle on Shabbos. I will make all the arrangements for you."

Gadi thought that it might be an interesting experience and consented to go. He came to Yeshivah Ohr Somayach and didn't leave for two weeks! He spent his entire vacation there.

Gadi returned to live in his hometown in the Galil. A few months later he went to his friend the rabbi and told him that he had decided to leave the town for good. His two weeks at Ohr Somayach had opened up a vista to the world he never knew before. From now on the driving force in his life would be the study of

Torah and the observance of *mitzvos*. He enrolled in Ohr Somayach, where he applied himself to his learning full throttle. He stayed on for a number of years, became a *talmid chacham* (Torah scholar) and changed the course of his life forever.

> We cannot know the reason Hashem deemed it necessary for the little girl and her family to suffer the pain and anguish they did. However, the timing of the incident, Shabbos afternoon, seems almost obvious. It was the catalyst for a young man to take a road he had never taken before — the road home.

◆§ Divinely Synchronized

Rabbi Shimon Gutman,* a well-known *talmid chacham* who served for many years as a *rav* in New York and then as dean of a *yeshivah* in Jerusalem, is today the *mara d'asra* in a community he founded in a city in Israel.

In 1986, a young woman living in *Tsefas*, Mrs. Adina Efrat,* came to visit Rabbi Gutman following a lecture he had given in Moshav Chilkiyahu. She had been married for eight years and had only one child. She was coming now to ask for a *berachah* (blessing) that she be able to conceive.

Rabbi Gutman, who has taught thousands of men and women throughout his life, explained to the young woman that giving a *berachah* for something of this nature was not within his parameter. "I am a teacher. I study Torah with people. I discuss *hashkafah* (Jewish philosophy) with those who seek guidance," He said to the woman. "But for what you seek, you must go to a very holy person — a *tzaddik* — someone known for his blessings and prayers, someone known to have been answered from Above."

The distressed young woman would not be put off. She insisted that because she had heard so much about Rabbi Gutman from his students, she wanted a *berachah* specifically from him.

Again and again he explained that *berachos* are a serious matters laden with holy intensity and sincere prayers by those who offer

---

* Due to personal nature of this story, names were changed by personal request.

them. "*Berachos*," Rabbi Gutman explained, "are not merely flippant wishes for good fortune and attainment."

His arguments were to no avail. Mrs. Efrat, who was a *baalas teshuvah* (one who had come to Torah Judaism of her own volition), said that she didn't know any *tzaddikim*, *Rebbes* or any other prominent *Roshei Yeshivah* whom she could easily relate to or speak openly with. That is why she desired to receive a *berachah* from Rabbi Gutman.

He thought quietly for a few moments and then said to Mrs. Efrat, "I want you to know that I feel your anguish and I share your pain. I myself have a daughter living in Milwaukee, who has been married for more than ten years and has never borne a child. The *Gemara* (*Bava Kamma* 92a) instructs us: 'כָּל הַמְבַקֵּשׁ רַחֲמִים עַל חֲבֵירוֹ וְהוּא צָרִיךְ לְאוֹתוֹ דָבָר הוּא נַעֲנֶה תְּחִילָה — If one has a problem and prays for another who has the identical problem, he who has prayed will be answered first.' Let us make an agreement between us. You pray for my daughter and I will pray for you."

Now it was Mrs. Efrat who was struck by another's anguish. The personal pain that Rabbi Gutman had unexpectedly shared with her, and the unique suggestion he proposed, bonded the young woman with the renowned individual who sat before her. She felt an inner serenity and knew that regardless of what the future held, her trip had been worthwhile.

Mrs. Efrat left the *moshav* and went back home to *Tzefas*. In the ensuing months Rabbi Gutman did not hear from her, nor did he discuss the matter with his own daughter, Mrs. Devorah Shain,* in Milwaukee. In the course of time Rabbi Gutman's daughter and son-in-law adopted a child.

Five years went by, but the incident with the young woman was on Rabbi Gutman's mind almost daily. And then he heard that his own daughter was expecting a child! The Gutman and Shain families were ecstatic as they anxiously awaited the great event. One day Rabbi Gutman unexpectedly received a letter from Mrs. Efrat. She wrote that she heard the good news that Rabbi Gutman's daughter was expecting a child. She wished to tell Rabbi Gutman that she, too, *b'ezras Hashem* was going to give birth in a few months.

The doctors in Milwaukee had given Mrs. Shain the date they thought she would give birth, but her little girl was born two weeks later than the "due" date. Little Faige Elisheva arrived on the 15th day of *Shevat* (1991).

A few days later Rabbi Gutman received an excited call from Mrs. Efrat. The doctors had given her a "due" date but her infant son arrived earlier than expected. "He was born just a few days ago," she said excitedly. Rabbi Gutman asked her the exact date of birth, and was stunned by her reply. The boy's birthday was the 15th day of *Shevat!* Incredibly, the infant girl in Milwaukee and the newborn boy in Israel had been born on the same day!

According to human calculation the baby girl had come late and the baby boy had come early, but in reality their arrivals had been Divinely synchronized. Because of the prayers that had been offered, the children would forever be united by time of a different standard.

⊷§ A Moving Experience

One afternoon in 1971, Mrs. Leah Trenk, then of Brooklyn, entered a taxi to go from Boro Park to her home in Flatbush. During the short trip she was surprised to notice a leather-bound volume of *Shas* lying behind her, beneath the rearview window.

She took a close look at the driver, checked his name on the identification sticker affixed to the bulletproof glass plate separating the back from the front seat, and realized that there was no chance that he was Jewish. "Excuse me," she said, "but I noticed this big book here. Is it yours?"

"No, Ma'am," the taxi driver retorted. "One of the people I drove earlier today must have left it there."

"Would you mind if I take it?" Mrs. Trenk asked. "I think I might have a way of returning it to its owner."

"Go right ahead," the driver replied.

When Mrs. Trenk came home she called her husband, R' David, who was then a *rebbi* in the Mirrer Yeshivah in Brooklyn. "What *masechta* are the boys learning in the *yeshivah*?" she asked. "I was in a taxi today and found a *Shas Gemara Yevamos*. Maybe it belongs to one of the boys in your class or one of the boys in the *beis hamidrash.*"

R' David told her that the *yeshivah* was not learning *Yevamos*, they were learning *Masechta Kiddushin* and therefore, most likely the *Gemara* did not belong to any of the students.

For the rest of the afternoon Mrs. Trenk made numerous calls to various *yeshivos*, but none of them were learning *Yevamos*. She checked to find out where the people who were learning *daf yomi* were up to, but they too were nowhere near *Yevamos*. She called various *shuls* and inquired whether *shiurim* were being given in that *masechta*, but to her dismay no one seemed to be learning *Yevamos* that year.

Over the next few days Mrs. Trenk had notices hung in various schools and *shuls* in the neighborhood as she tried to notify people about the beautiful *Shas Gemara* she had found. However, despite her efforts to find its owner, no one seemed to be missing the *sefer*.

Disappointed, she put the *Gemara* away in a safe place, content with the knowledge that at least in her home it would be treated with dignity. There was no telling what the gentile taxi driver might have done with it.

Eight months later, Rabbi Shlomo Green* came to see his friend R' David Trenk in the Mirrer Yeshivah. R' Shlomo, a mathematician by profession, wanted to start an afternoon learning *seder* (session) and was looking for a *chavrusa* (study partner). He approached R' David and said, "I am looking for a *chavrusa*. Do you think you can find one for me?"

"I just happen to know of someone like yourself, also looking for a *chavrusa*," he said. "Let me introduce you to him. He happens to be learning here right now."

As they walked towards the potential *chavrusa* in the *beis hamidrash*, R' David asked R' Shlomo, "What *masechta* do you want to learn?"

"I would like to learn *Yevamos*," came the reply.

"Do you have a *Gemara*?" inquired R' David as they wended

---

* Name has been changed by personal request.

their way through the chairs, tables and *shtenders* in the *beis hamidrash*.

"I used to have a beautiful one," he said sadly, "but a few months ago I left it in a taxi."

R' David stopped in his tracks, absolutely astounded. Exuberantly, he did a little dance and embraced the baffled R' Shlomo.

[It seems that several months earlier, R' Shlomo was moving from one home in Brooklyn to another. All his *sefarim* were packed away in boxes, all but this particular *Gemara* which he kept with him, so that he would have it available even during the days of transition. On the day of the actual move, he had been so preoccupied with a myriad of details that he inadvertently left the *Gemara* behind in the taxi.]

That afternoon, even before the first *mishnah* was learned, the *Gemara* was returned to its incredulous owner.

Chazal (Shabbos 104a) teach: "בָּא לִיטַהֵר מְסַיְּיעִים אוֹתוֹ — If one comes to cleanse himself, he is [Divinely] helped." If one sincerely wishes to do a *mitzvah*, Hashem will see to it that he gets it done. Eventually.

❧ Walk Before Me and Be Perfect

The following story was told by Rabbi Arye Meletzky, *Rosh Yeshivah* of Kollel Zichron Reuvain in Jerusalem. Rabbi Arye is the son-in-law of Rabbi Sholom Schwadron, the *Maggid* of Jerusalem, and thus has had the good fortune of hearing hundreds of fascinating stories from R' Sholom over the last decades. This particular story, though, is his favorite.

Shortly before World War II, a young woman in Jerusalem, the mother of four young children, found herself facing a serious problem. Her third child, Chaya, who was already three years old, had not yet started to walk. The child born after Chaya was already walking, and although Chaya seemed to be a bright child in every way, her mobility was impaired and her family was extremely worried.

Fewer than twenty years earlier, it had been said, a *tzaddik* was revealed in Jerusalem. He came to Israel in 1925, just before the Russians ravaged his town in Eastern Europe. He quietly settled in Jerusalem without fanfare and would daily go off to learn by himself in a small *shul* in the Old City. His name was Rabbi Shlomo Goldman, but he had been known in Eastern Europe as the Z'vihler *Rebbe*, or Rabbi Shlomka Z'vihler (1869-1945).

One day a wealthy man from Z'vihl had come looking for his *Rebbe*. No one seemed to know where he was or who he was. When the gentleman found his *Rebbe* in a remote corner of an ancient *shul* in the Old City, he was beside himself with anguish. He turned to the people in the *shul* and cried, "Do you know who you have here? This man is a *tzaddik*, a *baal mofeis* (one who can accomplish wonders). How could you have let him sit here alone?"

The secret was out and in no time people began flocking to the *Rebbe*, telling him their problems and seeking his advice and counsel.

Now, years later, the young woman with the daughter who couldn't walk wanted to see the *Rebbe* to get his blessing. She had already been to doctors, who gave her little hope for the future, but she felt that a *tzaddik* could surely intervene with Hashem on her behalf.

It was a time of great poverty in Israel and much of the food available was being rationed. This young woman knew the Talmudic teaching (*Kesubos* 105b) that "One who brings a present to a *talmid chacham* is credited as though he brought the *bikkurim* (first fruits) offering [to the *Kohen* in the *Beis HaMikdash*]." Scraping together whatever money she could, she went to the market and bought a selection of the fruits, breads and spices that were available.

She made her way to the Z'vihler *Rebbe's* home and presented her gift to the *Rebbetzin*. Although the *Rebbetzin* appreciated it greatly, she could not possibly have imagined the cost and sacrifice endured by the poor woman and her family.

When she saw the *Rebbe*, the young woman began to cry. Through her tears she explained that she had a three-year-old daughter who was not walking, and that the doctors gave her little hope for the future. The *Rebbe* listened to her carefully and sympathetically until she finished speaking. Then he said sadly, "But what can I do? There is nothing that I can do."

His words only served to increase the woman's anguish. "*Rebbe*," she pleaded, "my daughter needs your blessing. I know in my heart that if you bless her she will be fine. Please, *Rebbe*," she begged, "for the sake of my husband who learns Torah day and night, for the sake of my family, please bless the child."

The *Rebbe* was quiet for a few moments and then he told the woman, "There is a *kabbalah* (tradition) that a person who has a problem and *davens* at the *Kosel* (the Western Wall) for forty days in a row will be answered. The only thing I can suggest is that you do just that. Go to the *Kosel* for forty days in a row, pray for the resolution of your problem, and Hashem will answer your plea."

"But *Rebbe*," the woman replied, "I have four children at home. I can't get away. There is no way that I can go to the *Kosel* for forty consecutive days without missing even one day."

She sat there crying softly to herself, her face buried in her hands. Then, hoping that the *Rebbe* would not consider her rude, she cried out as a last resort, "*Rebbe*, please, you be my *shaliach* (messenger). You go for me."

The *Rebbe* thought for a moment and then benevolently said, "All right, I will be your messenger. I will go for you."

The young woman could not thank the *Rebbe* enough. She went home and began to mentally count the days. Every day she would count the days that had gone by and enumerate those days that were left. She wasn't really sure that the *Rebbe* had started to go to the *Kosel* the very day after her visit, but she counted from that day anyway.

On the fortieth day she was standing in her kitchen when she heard a shriek from her child's room. She ran to the room and was amazed to see that her daughter, Chaya Schwadron, had taken her first step and was attempting another. She called her husband, R' Sholom, who was in the other room. Standing there together, R' Sholom and his wife, Leah (the sister of Rabbi Shlomo Zalman Auerbach), thanked Hashem, "הַמֵּכִין מִצְעֲדֵי גָבֶר, Who prepares the footsteps of man," for the miracle that had been wrought.

Chaya Schwadron eventually married Rabbi Arye Meletzky who, understandably, considers this his favorite story.

◄§ A Decree Defined

In our day and age, when yeshivos are flourishing in every major Jewish metropolis, it is perhaps difficult to imagine or identify with the hardships and adversity encountered by yeshivah bachurim in Eastern Europe before and during World War II.

The following story, told by the Rosh Yeshivah of Yeshiva Emek Halacha in Brooklyn, Rabbi Tuvya Goldstein, is one of sacrifice, tragedy and heroism. As war thundered in Europe, the daily turmoil of events caused the yeshivos there to be in a constant state of flux. This story took place amidst turmoil which made concentration on learning extremely difficult. Yet, by extraordinary perseverance and strength of will, yeshivah learning flourished, and R' Tuvya himself was there to witness and be part of it.

The legendary figures involved in this story, and the perspective that R' Tuvya lends to the events, are remarkable and inspiring. I feel fortunate to have heard this episode from him personally.

On erev Rosh Hashanah in the year 1939, the bachurim in the Kamenitzer Yeshivah in Poland heard that Germany had invaded the country. Many of them had indeed anticipated Poland's occupation by a foreign power and their own subsequent need to escape to another country. They understood that no matter where they ran, their Polish currency would be worthless. With this in mind they stocked up on commodities they felt they could sell or barter in order to sustain themselves in their new surroundings. The decision was made to buy sacks of sugar and hundreds of pairs of winter socks, both of which were in constant demand throughout Eastern Europe.

Once these treasured goods had been purchased, someone in the *yeshivah* always knew exactly where they were hidden. Everyone realized that their future survival could depend on this cache.

On *Yom Kippur*, German soldiers entered the *beis hamidrash* (study hall) and demanded that the *bachurim* turn over the entire stockpile. The Germans threatened to kidnap and kill the *Rosh Yeshivah*, Rabbi Baruch Ber Leibowitz (1870-1941), if their demands were not met.

The *bachurim* surmised that most likely a Polish anti-Semite had seen them buy items in large quantities and had informed the German authorities. The *bachurim* had no choice but to hand over all they had bought. They could not be sure of the informant's identity; it might even have been the salesman, who knew the precise amount purchased and passed this information along to the Nazis. Nothing was worth risking the life of their beloved *Rosh Yeshivah* for, so, regretfully, they handed over everything they had stored away.

The Germans were in Poland for only eleven days when Russia invaded the same territory and took it over. Rabbi Chaim Ozer Grodzenski (1863-1940), who was living in Vilna, Lithuania, had been urging all the *yeshivos* in Poland to escape and travel (even on Shabbos if necessary) to Lithuania at once. Now, faced with the new occupation by the Russian communists, many of the *yeshivos* — such as those in Radin, Grodno, Baranovich and Mir — did indeed come to Vilna and its environs.

On a Shabbos night, the *bachurim* of Kamenitz, among them the twenty-year-old R' Tuvya Goldstein, escaped by train and set out on the day-and-a-half-long journey to a small section of Vilna named Lukashkeh.

The frigid winter had already arrived in Lithuania, and the Kamenitzer Yeshivah in Lukashkeh lacked firewood for heat. The *bachurim* sat huddled in their coats and learned as the biting cold pierced through the walls of the building they occupied.

It was during these weeks in Lukashkeh that Rabbi Reuvain Grozovsky (1896-1958), R' Baruch Ber's son-in-law, who periodically gave *shiurim* to the *bachurim*, gave a rousing *shmuess* (talk) that still rings in R' Tuvya's ears today, fifty years later.

In his powerful talk he cited the *Rambam* in *Hilchos Talmud Torah* (1:8) which details one's obligation to continue his Torah studies even under the most adverse conditions. "The *Rambam* writes," cried R' Reuvain, "that every Jew is obligated to learn Torah regardless of whether he is poor or rich, regardless of whether he is in perfect health or suffers from pain, regardless of whether he be young or old and weak ..." R' Reuvain urged the *bachurim* to withstand this test of Hashem as a sign of their determined and relentless perseverance.

"His powerful words gave *chizuk* to so many of us for so many months afterwards," recalls R' Tuvya.

The Kamenitzer Yeshivah stayed in Lukashkeh only a few weeks, for its members feared that Vilna, too, would eventually be overtaken by the Russians. They traveled northwest to another community in Lithuania, called Rassain. There, things were a bit improved because the *baalei battim* (Jewish lay people) were very supportive of the *yeshivah*.

There was a rule, though, that any refugee entering Rassain with the intention of living with a local family had to be registered with the local government. As there were no dormitories for *yeshivah* students at the time, the *bachurim* stayed with individual families. Hence there was a record of the names and addresses of eighty-six of the boys learning in Yeshivas Kamenitz. More than a hundred other *bachurim*, however, managed to avoid being recorded.

After a year of unrestful quiet, the surface tranquility was shattered forever. On a Sunday night, as the *bachurim* were learning in their *beis hamidrash* in Rassain, a member of the Russian Communist party came into the *beis hamidrash* with an urgent warning. The Soviet Union had annexed Lithuania and there was a good chance, he told the startled *talmidim*, that they would all be rounded up soon. Joseph Stalin (leader of the Soviet Union) had ordered that all clergy and capitalists in Lithuania be taken in for questioning and possible deportation because they were considered adversaries of the Communist party.

The Jewish communist revealed that his mother, an old Jewish woman, had prevailed on him to alert the *yeshivah* boys about what was going on. He warned them, however, that he could not and would not accept any responsibility for what might happen to any of them. All he knew, he claimed, was that the roundup could happen any time within the next few days. His warning duly delivered, the soldier left the *beis hamidrash* and headed on his way.

The *bachurim* were terrified by the news. Should they hide? Did they have a day or two in which to make plans? Was the situation really serious? No one could be sure. Later that evening, shortly after midnight, came the answer. Officers from the NKVD (Soviet secret police) swooped through the neighborhood, waking people and demanding that all clergy (in this case, *yeshivah* boys) come with them.

R' Tuvya was one of the boys registered by name and address. He was picking up his clothes from a woman who did the laundry for the *bachurim* when he heard the frightening knock on the door. In a moment the soldier was ordering him to get his things together and follow him out.

"His laundry is still wet," the woman protested. "Can't you wait a while?"

The soldier just laughed and replied, "In Siberia it will have plenty of time to dry."

R' Tuvya ran to get his *tefillin* and a treasured *sefer*, the newly printed edition of Rabbi Chaim Soloveitchik's commentary on the *Rambam*. As he packed everything together under the watchful eye of the Russian soldier, the cruel soldier confiscated both the *tefillin* and the *sefer* and remarked snidely, "You won't have time for study where you're going. You'll be working all the time."

The other eighty-five boys who were registered were rounded up that night as well, and by morning they had been taken to stables where they were sequestered in animal stalls for three days.

[It was during these three days of total havoc throughout Lithuania that Rabbi Elchanan Wasserman (1875-1941) was brutally murdered by Lithuanian thugs in Slobodka, while delivering his nightly *shiur* to eleven young men. Rabbi Yonah (Minsker) Karpilov, one of the finest *bachurim* of the Mirrer *Yeshivah* was among those tragically killed with R' Elchanan that night.]

On the morning of the fourth day, the *bachurim* held in the stalls were herded into three wagons. R' Tuvya and twenty-one others were shoved into one of them. Suddenly a young man, R' Tuvya's night-*seder chavrusa*, came running towards him. Crying, he reached out to touch R' Tuvya and gave him a *"peltz"* (heavy winter coat), a package of bread and a small sack of sugar. "I swear to you," he said, his voice breaking, "that I won't get married until I bring you out of Siberia alive."

With that the wagon left. R' Tuvya feared that he would never see his *chavrusa* again. Siberia was certain death for the weak, the elderly and the frail. He was young — but how would he handle the frost? How would he survive the heavy labor? If only he hadn't registered, he thought to himself. If only he had the freedom that his night-*seder chavrusa* now had. The unregistered boys would remain for the time being in Rassain, with the possibility of fleeing elsewhere. There would be no escaping, however, the clutches of the Russian "bears" in Siberia.

But somehow, for five-and-a-half years in Siberia, R' Tuvya did survive. Despite the cold, the labor, the hunger, the beatings, the agony of witnessing death before his eyes and the frightful prospect that he could be put to death at any time, he managed to survive. It was the will of Hashem that he live to tell about his experiences, and therefore he was among the fortunate who came home again.

After the war, R' Tuvya was repatriated to Lodz, Poland, where he was met by Vaad Hatzolah representatives, who had brought food and clothes for the survivors. There he heard the terrible news that the Russians, under Stalin's orders, had attacked Lithuania and thousands had been killed. Among them were more than half of the *talmidim* of Kamenitz, including R' Tuvya's night-*seder chavrusa*.

It was then that R' Tuvya thought about the *mishnah* in *Berachos* (54a) that teaches "חַיָּיב אָדָם לְבָרֵךְ עַל הָרָעָה כְּשֵׁם שֶׁמְּבָרֵךְ עַל הַטּוֹבָה" —

One is obligated to bless [Hashem] for the bad that occurs to him just as he is obligated to bless [Hashem] for the good that occurs." R' Tuvya says that the experiences in Rassain and Siberia made him see this *mishnah* in a different light. Conventionally, this *mishnah* is understood to mean that even though what occurs is in fact "bad," one must learn to take the bad with the good. However, R' Tuvya explains that he realized that for him the *mishnah* meant that one must be indebted to Hashem for the "bad," because man, in his finite understanding of things, may perceive as "bad" something which, viewed from the perspective of the Infinite One, is actually "good."

In retrospect, R' Tuvya now realizes, his having registered with the local municipality — the act which caused him to be rounded up in the first place — was actually the best thing that could have happened to him, because it was that very same act which led to his being spared.

◆§ Baltimore Bound

Rabbi David Kronglas (1910-1973), the *Mashgiach* in Yeshivah Ner Yisroel in Baltimore for more than twenty-five years, and author of the *sefer Divrei David,* was known for the practical and penetrating *mussar* he gave in his *shmuessen* (lectures on ethics), and for the depth of his Torah knowledge. A *talmid* (student) of Rabbi Yeruchem Levovitz (1874-1936), the noted *Mashgiach* of the Mirrer Yeshivah in Europe, R' David epitomized for all who knew him the way one should live according to the precepts of *Mussar.*

The following story, first told to me by Rabbi Meyer Birnbaum of Baltimore, took place many years ago. Rabbi Yosef Wolk, who was a principal of Ner Yisroel for thirty years, was kind enough to fill in the pertinent details. He should know them — for the story actually involved him and the revered *Mashgiach.*

One morning in 1967, when Rabbi Wolk picked up R' David to take him to *shul* as he did every day, he asked the *mashgiach* if he could borrow a particular *sefer* — the classic *Mussar* work, written by Rabbi Yeruchem Levovitz, *Daas Chachmah U'Mussar*.

The *Mashgiach* told Rabbi Wolk that he would be happy to lend it to him, but added, "Please be especially careful with it. I have a great deal of sentimental attachment to that particular *sefer*."

When the *Mashgiach* noticed that Rabbi Wolk was surprised by his request, he told the following incredible story.

In 1939, he was learning in the Mirrer Yeshivah in Europe, R' David and the other *bachurim* in the *yeshivah* were told that they would have to relocate quickly to another city because of the impending onslaught of the Nazis. The *bachurim* could take only a few of their personal belongings, as they had to leave at once. They, together with the *rebbeim* of Mir, began their strenuous and exhausting journey through Europe, which eventually led them to Shanghai, China, where they found refuge for six years. (See p. 152)

Throughout the war, after the Jews had been chased or deported from the cities in which their families had lived for hundreds of years, the Nazis collected Jewish books and memorabilia for a museum they wished to establish someday to recall the "[Judaic] society that once existed." They filled many warehouses with such material.

After the war, when the Nazis had been decisively defeated, American officials brought many of these Jewish artifacts to the United States where they were distributed to Jewish societies and organizations. Truckloads of Jewish books and memorabilia made their way to *yeshivos* and Jewish libraries throughout America.

> Rabbi Wolk adds that he can still vividly picture in his mind the tragic tears that his *Rosh Yeshivah*, Rabbi Yitzchak Hutner, shed when some of these boxes came to Yeshiva Rabbi Chaim Berlin.

Cartons of *sefarim* were also shipped to Yeshivah Ner Yisroel, in Baltimore. When they arrived, the *Rosh Yeshivah*, Rabbi Yaakov Yitzchak Ruderman (1900-1987), called in R' David and said benevolently, "I came to America [in 1931] before the war, but you suffered through the war. I therefore feel that you deserve to take for yourself any of these *sefarim* that you desire."

It was a gesture of sensitivity and greatness, and the *Mashgiach* was deeply touched. R' David anxiously opened the first box and in it was the classic *sefer* of R' Yeruchem, *Daas Chachmah U'Mussar*, which had been printed just a few months before the war. Only a limited number of copies had been available when the *sefer* first appeared, and R' David was thrilled that at least one copy of his *Rebbe's* work had survived.

He smiled to himself, pleased that he would have the opportunity to learn from R' Yeruchem's words. However, when he opened the cover he was shocked! There, on the inside cover, was his own name in his own handwriting!

By an absolutely incredible act of *hashgachah pratis*, (Divine Providence), R' David's own copy of the *sefer* had made its way back to its rightful owner!

No wonder he wanted Rabbi Wolk to be careful with it! Rabbi Wolk kept the *sefer* for one day and returned it the next morning.

◆§ Disguise, Deception and Deliverance

In this harrowing story of intrigue, betrayal, human suffering and unexpected heroism, we witness both the compassion and the cruelty of which man is capable.

The tragedy and turmoil that befell European Jews in the late 1930s and 1940s have left severe scars until this very day. This tale is worth retelling because when night was at its darkest, dawn suddenly appeared for a family of faith.

It has been noted that the words following the recital of *Krias Shema* in the morning are "אֱמֶת וְיַצִּיב" — It is true and certain," whereas the words following the evening recital of *Krias Shema* are "אֱמֶת וֶאֱמוּנָה" — It is true and faithful." A reason suggested for the different wording is that in the morning — when things are obvious and clear — one can easily exclaim that the role of

Divine Providence in the world is certain. However, in the evening when darkness abounds — one can only declare Divine Providence as an act of faith.

This noted family, of Rav Elie Munk of France, kept their faith during their time of darkness. They and their descendants have therefore merited to proclaim aloud today that Divine Providence is certain, established and enduring יַצִּיב נָכוֹן וְקַיָּם.

I am grateful to the family members who shared their thoughts with me, particularly *Rebbetzin* Amelie Jakobovits of London (daughter of Rav Munk), Mrs. Tova Lehman of Brooklyn (a granddaughter of Rav Munk), and Rabbi Nosson Scherman, the noted editor of Artscroll/Mesorah Publications (whose wife, Chana, is Rav Munk's niece).

In 1940, France, a country weakened by an inferior army and a floundering defense system, depended on the British Royal Armed Forces to protect it. However, when Germany invaded France, the British army escaped and the Nazis occupied the northern part of France. Paris, situated in the north of France, was overrun by Nazis. Jews, especially prominent ones, knew they would have to escape before they were caught and deported to Germany, from where they would be sent to concentration camps.

Rav Elie Munk, the noted *talmid chacham* and author of the widely acclaimed book, *World of Prayer*, who was also the chief *Rav* of Paris and *Rav* of the Parisian Rue Cadet *shul*, realized that his family's life was in jeopardy. He escaped with his wife and four children southward. They wandered through various towns and villages, living in Toulouse for a while. Eventually they settled in Nice, a town on the Mediterranean coast which was primarily inhabited by Italians and Frenchmen but controlled by the Italian army.

When they first arrived, Nice was beyond the reach of the claws of the Nazi regime. Every day, however, the situation throughout France became more perilous as Germany now began to spread its web of terror and control over the southern part of the country. Eventually, no area was safe. Hatred for Jews in the country became more rampant, and when *Rebbetzin* Fanny Munk gave birth to twins, she was scorned by her gentile neighbors who thought it ludicrous for Jews to bring children into a world of turmoil.

One Monday morning, as Rav Munk was *davening* with a *minyan* in Nice, a young man approached him with some startling news. Just yesterday, he informed the *Rav*, he had been arrested for teaching Judaic studies to children. He was taken to Nazi headquarters where he underwent extensive interrogation and endured repeated warnings. When the officers walked out of the interrogation room for a moment, he noticed a file on the desk which had the word MUNK emblazoned on its cover.

With full knowledge of the great risk to his life if he were caught, the young man opened the file. "At the top of the first page," he said, "I read that the Munks are to be arrested Wednesday morning and deported to Germany."

That night the Rav disappeared. His wife was frantic; she had long suspected that as a prestigious Jew, her husband might be a priority on the Nazis "wanted" list. The Munks had a nasty neighbor. A woman who lived on the second floor, in the apartment directly beneath their own, would often bang with her broomstick on the ceiling as a protest against the constant noise from above. The crying of the twins bothered her, she said, as did the incessant chatter of the other youngsters as they played the usual games children play. Again and again she threatened to turn the Munks in to the authorities. Now *Rebbetzin* Munk feared that she had indeed done so.

The next morning a man knocked on the door of their home. He was filthy, dressed in clothes that were several sizes too big, and he wore a cap indicating that he worked for the sanitation department.

The younger Munk daughter, Francoise, opened the door. "Is your Mommy home?" the caller asked.

The little girl called out to her mother, "There's a man at the door who wants to see you."

By the time *Rebbetzin* Munk came to the door, the man had already taken a few steps into the house — and he was crying! The "stranger" was Rav Munk himself, and his own daughter had not recognized him!

His beard had been shorn off, and his disguise was so perfect that his own child did not know who he was. He explained to his anxious and incredulous family that yesterday, after hearing the news in *shul* that they were all to be arrested, he made contact with the Maquis — the French underground resistance organization — who were expert at smuggling people out of the country, albeit for a very large sum of money. In one day, the Maquis had procured for the family of eight, passports, visas, birth certificates and food ration cards. The family now had a new name as well. They were no longer the Munks; courtesy of the Maquis, they were now the Martins.

The plan was for the Martins to travel by train to a small town on the southern border of France. In a small farmhouse near the Swiss border they would be met by another group of Maquis, who would take them across the border to freedom in Switzerland. For these services Rav Munk had paid the astronomical sum of five thousand francs.

In order not to arouse suspicion, it was decided that the family would not travel together. Amelie, the oldest child (merely twelve years old!), was given the awesome responsibility of caring for her two younger sisters and brother on one train, while the Rav and his wife traveled with the twins on another.

The six-hour train ride was harrowing and nerve wracking, as the train sputtered on its way, stopping and starting unpredictably. Despite the ever-present menace of Nazi soldiers on the lookout for fleeing Jews, the confident young girl managed to shepherd her siblings through all the checkpoints, calmly dealing with all inquiries without problems.

Meanwhile, on another train, Rav Munk, his wife and the twins also went undetected. To their vast relief, the documents provided by the Maquis proved to be excellent forgeries.

From the train station, each of the two groups hitchhiked to the farmhouse near the border. At night the exhausted family was reunited. They had very little food with them, and the only clothes they had were those they were wearing. They knew they would need help soon in order to survive.

They waited throughout the autumn night for their Maquis contacts to arrive and lead them to freedom. But they never came! The Munks had been double-crossed! Rav Munk had paid a fortune to get out of Nice, but now they were left stranded. By the next morning, which was Friday, he and his wife decided that they could remain in the farmhouse no longer. They would have to make their way to a nearby town. Once again they thumbed a ride, this time to Aix-le-Bains.

He hoped that they would soon find someone who might be able to assist them. On Shabbos morning Rav Munk took a walk through the town of Aix-le-Bains with his son Yakky. They saw someone who was obviously Jewish. *"Gut Shabbos,"* Rav Munk ventured.

The gentleman returned Rav Munk's greeting and said, "If you are looking for a place to *daven*, there are a few of us getting together this morning. Would you like to join us?"

As Rav Munk and his son fell into step with the gentleman, Rav Munk smiled to himself. The gentleman was actually a member of Rav Munk's Rue Cadet *shul* in Paris, but Rav Munk's appearance was so greatly altered that even someone from his own *kehillah* did not recognize him! Rav Munk introduced himself as Monsieur Martin and explained that he wanted to contact the members of the French resistance organization, the Maquis, so that he and his family could be smuggled across the border.

After *davening*, the men who had come together greeted their new guest and asked him where he was staying. "In a hotel downtown called 'The Plaza,'" he replied.

"That's preposterous!" they exclaimed. "That hotel is the headquarters of the Nazi party in the area!"

"Wonderful!" replied Rav Munk. "That's all the more reason to stay there, for the Germans will never suspect that there are any Jews in that hotel."

The tiny Jewish community of Aix-le-Bains helped Monsieur Martin contact a branch of the Maquis. The Maquis assured the family that for a considerable fee they would escort them across the border. Once again they were told to meet the French guides at the small farmhouse near the border, from where they would be led to safety and freedom.

The Munks made plans to travel to the farmhouse. So as not to arouse suspicion, they would once again split up into two groups, with Rabbi and Rebbetzin Munk taking the twins, and Amelie taking her three younger siblings.

And so it was on a late afternoon in 1943, the day before *Erev Rosh Hashanah*, that Amelie walked along the road with her siblings and flagged down a truck carrying a load of hay. She told the driver they were going to an orphanage, and asked for a lift. The driver smiled and welcomed them in. Was he a member of the resistance? Was his smile one of understanding and empathy for a wandering family? Or was it a smirk on his face, a warning that he would betray them and alert the authorities? Amelie could not be sure, but she had no choice. It was a question of survival, and she had to take the chance. Later that afternoon the entire family was reunited at the farmhouse.

As the sun was about to set, they huddled together. They knew they would have to wait until dark for only then would the French soldiers come. The Maquis' guides, too, had to be sure they arrived undetected by the Nazi sentries who patrolled the border with guard dogs. The Munks said *Tehillim*, made small talk and waited.

At a quarter to eleven at night, two huge men approached the farm. They were, indeed, the anxiously awaited French guides, and they were well armed. The guides issued strict orders as to how they would proceed.

"We will walk ahead of you through a forest to the frontier, and you will all follow behind. If we turn around, lie down flat and don't say a word. Don't even whisper! We will give you a signal when it's time to resume walking. The Nazis and their dogs can appear at any time and at any place."

The guides explained that at the end of the half-hour's walk to the border, they would lead the family to a barbed-wire fence into which they would cut an opening large enough for all of them to fit through. "Now," they said, "let's get moving."

Each of the guides took one of the twins on his shoulders and turned to go. Rebbetzin Munk could feel the knot in her stomach tighten. What if these guides were also frauds? What if they kidnapped the children and demanded a ransom? They had the guns, the Munks didn't. These thoughts were too painful to consider and she brushed them aside. In all of life's excursions, the

Munks had always placed their ultimate faith in the *Ribono Shel Olam*. This half-hour's journey would be no different.

They walked for a while and suddenly the guides turned around. The Munks threw themselves down, flat on their faces. No one — not parents, nor children, nor infants — uttered a sound. The rustling of little animals was loud in the stillness of the night, but still no one moved.

After a short time they resumed their trek. The guides led them along paths and through open fields and then again, suddenly, turned around. Once again the Munks fell to the ground, hardly breathing as they listened for the telltale barking of dogs. They heard nothing. They walked for ten minutes more until the guards stopped, retraced their steps where the Munks stood and handed back the twins. Then they disappeared.

Was this the end? Were they to be left here as defenseless prey to any passing German? For five long minutes the Munks wondered what lay in store for them. But the guides eventually reappeared. "We checked the fence," they said. "You can all get through. It is only two hundred meters ahead. On the other side you will see a hill. You must all get down that hill."

Without warning, the guides whipped out their guns and pointed them at the Munks. To the utter disbelief of the already frightened family, they barked, "Get your hands up!"

How could this be? Were they serious? Yes, they were! The despicable French guides proceeded to rob the Munks of everything they had. Their documents, their money, Rebbetzin Munk's wedding ring, even the little box of matches that Rav Munk was carrying — all were stolen. They even had the unmitigated gall to force the Munks to open their mouths so they could check for gold teeth!

The guides ran off into the night, leaving the Munks shocked, drained, confused — and still in danger. No one said a word. They were all too stunned to speak. Finally Rav Munk said softly, "We have nothing left but our faith in the *Ribono Shel Olam*. Let us proceed."

Slowly, quietly, gingerly, they made their way to the barbed-wire fence. Did another betrayal await them there? If those monsters could rob them at this stage, they might double-cross their helpless charges in other ways as well.

But the Munks had no choice but to continue. To their relief, the fence was indeed cut open. At least the guides had done that, and in essence that was more important than anything else.

They crept through the hole in the fence, one by one, and finally all were assembled on the other side. The Nazis had not come after them, the dogs had not sniffed them out. *Rebbetzin* Munk was overjoyed. She touched the grass and exclaimed in ecstasy, "We are at the Greenlawn Hotel. *Baruch Hashem* we are free!"

Her joy was shortlived. They started to descend the hill carefully, one step at a time, making their way down through tall grass and wild shrubbery that scratched their skin. Amelie could hear the words of *Tehillim* once again emanating from her father's lips. But then they encountered another shock. They had reached flat land, but the ground felt cool and wet. They all stopped. There was a river before them!

How long was it? How deep was it? Not all of them could swim. If this was indeed a river, then they were not over the border. Then they were still within the clutches of the Nazis after all. How could they possibly have been the victims of yet another heartless hoax?

Rav Munk was trembling. The guides had stolen the matches he had taken for just such an eventuality, so there was no way to visually assess the situation. Again they were stuck. They would have to wait until dawn before moving. They ached from the exertion of the trip, and although they had been wearing two sets of clothing, their bodies were scraped and bruised.

Suddenly one of the one-and-a-half-year-old twins, Maxi (Nusson), started to cry. He had been quiet all along. When he had been held by the French guides, who were total strangers, he had been still. When he was squeezed through the hole in the fence, he had been silent. Throughout the long night he had been quiet, but now he was crying uncontrollably. His parents tried to calm him, but to no avail. The older children tried to talk to him, cuddle him, rock him, feed him — but nothing soothed him.

A cry in the still of night carries a long distance. If they were still in French territory, the child's cry would surely alert the Nazi patrol to the family's whereabouts.

And then Amelie saw a light in the distance. It flashed once and then stopped. Her father told everyone to get down. They all lay on the wet grass, pressing their bodies as close to the earth as they could. Maxi was still crying, and the light scanning the area was coming closer. The children could hear their father's heart thumping. The light subsided, and suddenly something toppled on all of them.

They let out a shriek. But then they heard a soft, pleasant voice and saw a man in uniform picking himself up off the ground, after tripping over the prone family. "I am a Swiss soldier," he said, brushing himself off. "Come. Follow me."

"But what about the river?" Rav Munk asked.

"We can wade right through. It's not deep."

The soldier took the twins over his shoulders and carried them across the river as the others waded behind him in the waist-high water. The soldier led them up a hill to a road, and across a field into a small building. The light in the building temporarily blinded this family that had just journeyed through the darkest of nights.

The soldier sat down and said to Rav Munk, "I am a father of a large family. I heard your baby, and his cries touched my heart and made me think of my own children back home. I went to my commanding officer and asked if I could save you, and he said, 'Yes.' "

The Munks found out that they had actually been in no-man's land. "If your child had not cried," the gentle soldier said, "the Nazis would have found you. Night after night they have arrested hundreds of people in that area. But they didn't catch your family. Welcome to Switzerland!"

❊   ❊   ❊

The Munks stayed in Switzerland until after the war, and during that time *Rebbetzin* Munk had her seventh child. In 1946 the Munks returned to Paris, where the Rav resumed his duties in the Rue Cadet *shul*. He worked feverishly to release Jewish children from the gentile homes in which they had been hidden during the war; he assisted people in the DP (displaced persons) camps; he tried to enhance *kashrus* standards and gave frequent *shiurim*.

And soon the time came to celebrate the *bar mitzvah* of Maxi. After the Torah reading in the *shul* to which he thought he would never return, Rav Munk stood at his lectern near the *aron kodesh* and said, "My dear son Maxi: Since the day you were born I waited for this special moment, the moment I often feared would never come, the *simchah* of your becoming a *bar mitzvah*. I thank you, dear child, for crying when you did, not only because you saved the life of your mother, my life and the lives of your brothers and sisters. I thank you, dear son, in the name of all the future generations that will be born into our family. Someday they will know that it was your crying that saved them as well, and they will thank you too."

As Rav Munk wiped away his tears, there was not a dry eye in the *shul*.

◆§ *The Mother of All Commitments*

On a recent trip to London, I was fortunate to become acquainted with Rabbi Mayer Roberg, dean of the Hasmonean School in Golders Green. Both R' Mayer and his wife, *Rebbetzin* Miriam, have been involved in the Torah education of London's children for more than three decades.

As we discussed matters of *chinuch*, the *Rebbetzin* told this touching story that involved her brother, Rabbi Shlomo Nager, who now lives in Jerusalem. The story actually took place years ago, when Rabbi Nager was living in Holland. I am grateful to both *Rebbetzin* Roberg and Rabbi Nager for the details they provided for this story.

In the 1960s, Rabbi Shlomo Nager was appointed by the Dutch Ministry of Defense to be a chaplain in the armed services of the Netherlands. It was his duty to be available to counsel and guide the young Jewish soldiers in Holland's military. Enthusiastically taking on his new role, Rabbi Nager made it a point to visit army bases around the country and seek out the Jewish soldiers, offering them any assistance they might require.

As there are no major *yeshivos* in Holland, the religious background of the average Jewish boy in the country is limited. However, in his office in The Hague, the capital city of Holland, Rabbi Nager had a library of *sefarim* and books on Jewish subjects which he made available to any of the armed forces personnel wishing to utilize them.

One day Rabbi Nager received a call from a Protestant serviceman who was stationed in Amersfoort, a small town southeast of Amsterdam. The soldier, Wim (pronounced Vim) van Kampen, requested an appointment with Rabbi Nager. The latter was surprised by this request from a Protestant boy. The military provided chaplains who were either Jewish, Roman Catholic, Protestant or Humanistic. Why would a Protestant boy choose to talk with the Jewish chaplain?

When Wim came to the office, he attempted to explain his seemingly strange behavior. As a child, he confessed, he had harbored an interest in Judaism. However, both in school and at home with his strict Protestant parents he could never openly display his curiosity about another religion. Therefore, his stint in the army held the promise of answering some of his long-standing questions. At the military orientation, when the soldiers were told of their obligations during their fourteen-month tour of duty, they were also informed about the availability of chaplains. Wim therefore decided to take the initiative at this time.

Wim had an endless number of questions, and Rabbi Nager was surprised by the intensity with which this young man was pursuing the philosophies of *Yiddishkeit*. Rabbi Nager gave Wim numerous books and told him to call again when he had a whole list of questions. Four days later, Wim called with a list that was two pages long. He had read all the books that Rabbi Nager had given him in their entirety, and was now prepared to read more.

After studying the second group of books, Wim came back to The Hague with questions that surprised and even startled Rabbi Nager. This highly intelligent young man was pondering Jewish values that were discussed in such noted *sefarim* as *Chovos HaLevavos* (*Duties of the Heart*) by *Rabbeinu* Bachya ibn Paquda, and *Shaarei Teshuvah* (*Gates of Repentance*) by *Rabbeinu* Yonah!

"The topics you discuss and the problems you concern yourself with," said Rabbi Nager to Wim, "are those with which the greatest Jewish thinkers of the past have grappled. It is remarkable that in so short a time you are getting to the essentials of our beliefs."

"They are my beliefs as well," replied Wim. "Someday I would like to make them an integral part of my life."

Rabbi Nager felt his stomach tighten. The *Rabbanim* of Holland, as most traditional *Rabbanim*, did not look favorably upon gentiles who sought to convert to Judaism. More often than not, those who wished to convert had ulterior motives. However, as time went on and Rabbi Nager grew to know Wim better, he became less apprehensive. This boy, he realized, was someone special.

It is said (see *Shabbos* 146a) that the *neshamos* of all future converts were actually at *Har* (Mount) *Sinai* when the Torah was given. Rabbi Nager wondered whether Wim possessed one of those sacred *neshamos*.

"Did it ever occur to you that you would actually have to discard the religion in which you were brought up and exchange it for a totally different way of life as a Jew?" Rabbi Nager asked.

"I would love nothing more," Wim replied, "but I know that it would kill my parents."

"It's just as well that you remain as you are," Rabbi Nager replied. And then, following the procedures mentioned in the *Shulchan Aruch* (*Yoreh Deah* 268:2), Rabbi Nager began trying to dissuade Wim from undertaking the mantle of *Yiddishkeit*. "Being a committed Jew is difficult, Wim. You will be looked down upon by all your friends. Additionally, living as a Jew is an ordeal that encompasses one's entire day from the moment one gets up until one goes to sleep. You might as well just continue being the honest, dedicated person you already are, and enjoy your intellectual stimulation with Judaism as a passing fancy."

Wim, however, was not one to be cast aside so easily. "I know deep inside me that one day I will make that commitment," Wim said with conviction. "It's in my heart."

"But life is so easy for you now," Rabbi Nager persisted. "There are few obligations burdening you. In Judaism they are numerous."

Wim responded, "Because I believe there is a G-d in Heaven, I believe that He has ordained specific instructions about how He is to be served on a daily basis. Not just on Sundays!"

Rabbi Nager couldn't argue with the young man's logic.

Wim came from the small town of Haarlem, a suburb of Amsterdam. Rabbi Nager called the *beis din* (religious court) that had jurisdiction over that area, and to his surprise they informed him that Wim had already petitioned them to be a candidate for *giur* (conversion). The *beis din* had also tried to dissuade him from converting, explaining that the procedure could take years. Wim, however, insisted that he would be ready much sooner.

Throughout his metamorphosis, Wim had hardly discussed his thoughts and feelings with his parents. However, now that he was about to take the first irrevocable step, that of *bris milah*, he realized that he would have to tell them of his intentions. As he was a twenty-year-old, the procedure would have to take place in a hospital, and, although he could return home the evening after the *bris*, he did not want to undergo an operation without his parents' knowledge.

At first Wim had considered telling his parents that he needed to be circumcised for medical reasons, but after giving the matter some more thought, he decided that the time had come to reveal the truth.

Wim's first step was to go to the *beis din* and arrange for Rabbi Nager, who is also a *mohel*, to come to the Willemina Gasthuis Hospital in Amsterdam to perform the *bris*. The procedure was scheduled to take place on a Wednesday morning.

Sunday night at the family dinner table, Wim began by telling his parents about the nature of his discussions with Rabbi Nager over the last few months. He told them about the books he had been reading and about his application to the *beis din* in Haarlem regarding *giur*.

Wim's father was thunderstruck. He knew his son to be a man of intense commitment who, once having made up his mind about something, would not retract for anyone or anything. At first the queries about Wim's new life came slowly, but soon, like a torrent roaring down a mountainside, the impact of his father's anger packed a wallop that made even Wim retreat. He looked to his mother, who had remained silent, for support, but she seemed to be sweating profusely and becoming pale as he watched. She returned her son's stare with vacant eyes and then abruptly teetered and fainted.

As he helped revive his mother, Wim blamed himself for his lack of sensitivity, believing that it was the thought of an adult undergoing what was an uncommon (in Holland) operation — one that would mark her son for eternity with the symbol of Judaism — that was so disturbing to her.

The next morning, Rabbi Nager received a frantic call from Wim. He was crying so hysterically that he could hardly speak. All Rabbi Nager was able to understand was that Wim desperately wanted to see him, but could not obtain permission to leave the military base. He pleaded with Rabbi Nager to come to Amersfoort.

Rabbi Nager drove out to the military post and there he met Wim, who was by then somewhat more composed. They went to a private office where Wim again began to cry.

"Last night I told my parents about my decision to convert," he began, "and my mother literally collapsed. However, when she was revived she began to weep. Later that evening she took me aside and told me that she herself was born Jewish! She had forsaken everything relating to Judaism because of all the terrible things that happened to Jews during the Nazi regime. Some of her distant family members actually perished in the concentration camps.

"When she met my father, and they decided to get married, they agreed never to reveal her true origin. He is indeed from the Netherlands, having been born in Zevenbergen, but my mother was actually born in Brussels, Belgium."

Rabbi Nager embraced Wim, still not believing what he had just heard. In reality, then, Wim was Jewish. There was no need for *giyur* and no need to persuade a reluctant *beis din* that he deserved to be accepted as a Jew.

The *bris* was performed, and Rabbi Nager hosted a small *seudah* in Wim's honor. He encouraged Wim to move to *Eretz Yisrael*, maintaining that not only would it be difficult for Wim to pursue his Jewish studies in Holland, but also the probability of finding a suitable *shidduch* in Holland was very remote.

"Go to Israel," Rabbi Nager insisted. "There you will grow in your learning. Go to the land of our Fathers," Rabbi Nager said, stressing the word "our."

"Yes," Wim added, "and to the land of my mother."

Every morning we proclaim, "אֱלֹקַי נְשָׁמָה שֶׁנָּתַתָּ בִּי טְהוֹרָה הִיא — My G-d, the soul You placed in me is pure." A soul that is G-dly sheds a light that is eternal. Its glow must someday burst forth and shine. Though it may be covered for years by layers of darkness, the illumination, because it is Divine, can never be totally extinguished. It surfaces eventually and then its radiance becomes a beacon for others.

Part C:

Deeds of Distinction

Youth is so impressionable that *Chazal* (Talmudic sages) state (*Shabbos* 21b; see *Rashi)* that גְּרְסָא דְּינָקוּתָא (learning during childhood) is significantly superior to learning as an adult. This is so because knowledge acquired in the early years of life is usually retained much longer, since it was initially embedded in a fresh, vibrant mind.

The following incident, which took place about seventy years ago, is a case in point. It involved Rabbi Yitzchak Eisenbach then an eight-year-old boy growing up in Jerusalem. The incident left an indelible impression that remained with him all his life. The story was retold by his son R' Avraham, who lives in the Givat Shaul section of Jerusalem.

R abbi Yitzchak Eisenbach came from a prominent, pious family. As a youth he was an active, feisty little fellow who made the streets and alleyways of Jerusalem his personal playground.

One Shabbos afternoon, Yitzele was walking to the *Kosel HaMaaravi* through the Jaffe gate, in a section of the city which was densely inhabited by Arabs. As he walked through the narrow, unpaved streets he passed numerous Arab-owned cafes in which young and old folks were milling around. Suddenly Yitzele noticed a gold coin on the sidewalk. The value of the coin was such that it could support a family the size of his own for two weeks. The poverty in his home was wrenching, and he was thrilled at the prospect of being able to help his parents in their struggle for their family's survival.

However, because it was Shabbos (and the money was *muktzeh* [forbidden to be handled]), he would not pick up the golden coin. He immediately put his foot on the coin to hide it from view, and decided to stand there until nightfall (after Shabbos), when he would take the coin home to his family. For another child his age, the time element might have posed a problem, but for the determined Yitzele there would be no difficulty, even though there were four hours left to Shabbos!

After Yitzele had been standing immobile in the Arab street for more than an hour, an Arab teenager approached him and asked, "Why don't you move on? Why are you standing here like a statue?"

At first Yitzele didn't answer, but when the larger and stronger boy persisted, he replied innocently, "I have something under my foot that I can't pick up because it is Shabbos today. I'm watching it this way, so that after Shabbos I can take . . ."

Before the last words were out of Yitzele's mouth, the Arab boy shoved Yitzele to the ground, swiftly bent down, plucked up the coin and ran off. Yitzele lay in the street, stunned. By the time he got up, the culprit had long since disappeared over a fence, and Yitzele knew it would be hopeless — perhaps even dangerous — for a Jew to chase an Arab in that neighborhood.

Late that afternoon a dejected Yitzele made his way back to the *shul* of the Chernobyler *Rebbe*, Rabbi Nachum Twersky (1840-1936), where his father *davened Minchah* and ate *shalosh seudos*. Yitzele usually helped set up the chairs and tables and put out the food for the men who sat down to eat with the *Rebbe*, but today he sat in a corner by himself.

The *Rebbe*, who loved little Yitzele, realized that something was amiss because the chairs and benches were in disarray. He looked around for a moment and then saw Yitzele sitting in a corner by himself, downcast.

The Chernobyler *Rebbe* approached the child and asked, "What's wrong? You look so unhappy. We all need you at the table."

Yitzele told the *Rebbe* what had happened earlier that afternoon, and explained how he felt about the opportunity he had lost. The *Rebbe* listened intently, then, taking Yitzele by the hand, he said, "Come to the table with me now, and after Shabbos come into my house."

After Shabbos, Yitzele followed the *Rebbe* into his home which was connected to the *shul*. The *Rebbe* opened a drawer and removed from it a golden coin similar to the one Yitzele had seen near the Jaffe gate that afternoon. "Here, this is yours," said the *Rebbe*. "However, I am giving it to you on one condition: that you give me the *sechar* (reward) of the *mitzvah* that you did this afternoon."

The startled young child looked up at the *Rebbe*. "The *Rebbe* wants the *sechar* in exchange for the coin?"

"Yes," the *Rebbe* said. "You made a great *Kiddush Hashem* (sanctification of Hashem's name) by not picking up the money because it was Shabbos. The coin is for you, though. I just want the *sechar*."

Yitzele was astounded. Was the *mitzvah* that great? Was it really worth so much? He looked at the coin and thought fleetingly about what it could buy for his family. He looked up at the *Rebbe* and said, "If that is what the *mitzvah* is worth, then the *mitzvah* is not for sale."

The *Rebbe* bent and kissed the boy on his forehead.

Years later, R' Yitzchak would tell his children and grandchildren that it was this lesson he learned from the Chernobyler *Rebbe* in his youth, more than anything else learned in his later years, that made him keenly aware of the significance of *mitzvos*.

❧ The Heart of the Matter

Rabbi Shmuel Rubenstein (1934-1982) was a gentle, soft-spoken man who wrote many pamphlets and booklets on a variety of Torah topics. I remember how he came to Mesivta Torah Vodaath in 1962 to inform the *bachurim* (young students) about his very first work, a forty-page manual on the component parts of *tefillin*.

That pamphlet was a pioneering effort, as it included many pictures and detailed original drawings of the construction, forming and writing of a kosher pair of *tefillin*. Since then, many people have followed Rabbi Rubenstein's lead, as similar books and pamphlets containing laws, drawings and pictures abound. Subsequently, Rabbi Rubenstein authored similar equally informative works on *tallis, mikvah, beis haknesses, mezuzah, tzitzis* and the *arbah minim* (Four Species — *lulav, esrog, hadassim* and *aravos* — used on *Sukkos*).

This remarkable story, told by his wife, bespeaks Rabbi Rubenstein's love for *mitzvos* and the reverence with which he regarded his esteemed *Rebbe*.

As a young boy R' Shmuel lived in the Bronx, from where he would travel by train every day to Brooklyn to attend Yeshiva Torah Vodaath. During his childhood, however, he contracted rheumatic fever, a disease affecting the heart and the central nervous system. His doctors then suggested that the two hours spent commuting, on top of his long hours in school, overtaxed the child. They advised his mother to find him a school closer to home.

It was at that time that the Bobover *Rebbe*, Rabbi Shlomo Halberstam, started a small *yeshivah* for sixteen boys in the West Side of Manhattan. Shmuel's mother felt that the trip to Manhattan from the Bronx would be less strenuous than the one to Brooklyn, and because she had a *chassidic* background she enrolled her son in the new *yeshivah*.

Shmuel excelled in his learning and soon became very fond of the *Rebbe*. With his mother's approval he began dressing in *chassidic* garb, as he tried to absorb as much as he could from the *Rebbe*.

One day during *Chol HaMoed* (the intermediate days of *Sukkos*), Shmuel went to visit the *Rebbe*. As they were talking, amicably, Shmuel mustered up the courage to ask the *Rebbe* something that he knew very few people his age would ask. "Would the *Rebbe* allow me to use his *lulav* and *esrog*?" he asked shyly.

The *Rebbe* smiled and replied, "Shmuel, didn't you make a *berachah* (blessing) on your own *lulav* and *esrog* today?"

"Yes," replied Shmuel. "But it would be a *zechus* (deed of merit) to shake the *lulav* and *esrog* that the *Rebbe* used during his *tefillos* (prayers)."

The *Rebbe* went to his desk, where he had his precious *esrog* in a silver box, unwrapped the *esrog* and handed it to the young lad. Shmuel trembled slightly as the *Rebbe* passed it to him. Fleetingly, he remembered the terror that had gripped him the night before when he had thought of the moment the *esrog* would be given to him. What if he dropped it? No humiliation could be worse than that.

Shmuel first held the esrog with its *pitam* facing downward. The *Rebbe* then handed him his *lulav*, which the boy held in his right hand. Wishing to observe the *mitzvah* properly, Shmuel attempted to turn over the *esrog* so that its *pitam* would be upright and he could then shake the *lulav* and *esrog* together. (See *Orach Chaim* 651:5.)

Nervously, he slowly rotated the delicate *esrog* upward. Suddenly, to his utmost horror, the *esrog* began to slip from his grasp! He tried desperately to hold onto it but it rolled right over his outstretched fingers and escaped from his grasp, tumbling downward. Shmuel felt his heart tumble with it as the *esrog* bounced off the floor and rolled a few feet away. Shmuel felt as if the whole world had dropped from his hands.

He wanted to cry but he couldn't; he wanted to speak but no words came forth. He was too terrified to look down, convinced as he was that the *pitam* had surely snapped off, thereby rendering the *Rebbe's esrog* invalid.

The *Rebbe* bent to pick up the *esrog* that was now resting against the leg of a table. Shmuel's eyes were closed for what seemed an eternity. He could not bear to see the *Rebbe's* face or the *esrog*.

After what seemed like a very long time, Shmuel heard the *Rebbe's* gentle voice saying, "Shmuel, don't worry. The *esrog* is in perfect shape. Nothing happened. The *pitam* is intact." Shmuel's relief was akin to that of a man receiving a life-saving reprieve.

"My dear one," the smiling *Rebbe* continued, "this is a sign from Heaven for you. *Chazal* tell us (see *Vayikra Rabbah* 30:14) that the Four Species represent different parts of the human body. The *lulav* represents the spine, the *hadas* (myrtle) represents the eyes, the *aravah* (willow) represents the mouth and the *esrog* represents the heart of a man.

"This *esrog* is obviously a strong one. Your heart, too, will be a strong one. I know you have been ill, but Hashem will grant you a vigorous heart."

Shmuel was overjoyed when he heard the blessing. A potential disaster had turned into a dream! Shmuel stayed on for a little while longer and then returned home.

Time passed, and Shmuel continued his studies in the Bobover Yeshivah. He eventually married and raised a family. Even after becoming a *sofer* (scribe) and a well-respected author who lectured often on the art and methods of writing *Sifrei Torah, tefillin* and *mezuzos*, R' Shmuel kept his connection with the Bobover *Rebbe* and periodically took his children for personal visits to the *Rebbe*.

R' Shmuel never told anyone the story of the *esrog* until one year, when he was sitting with his children in his *sukkah* on *Chol HaMoed Sukkos*, he said, "You know, today is the anniversary of an incident that happened to me many years ago."

He went on to describe the episode in vivid detail, reliving the event as though it had only happened the day before. His family listened with fascination to every aspect of the story. When R' Shmuel finished, he added, "The *gematria* (numerical equivalent) of the word לֵב, *heart*, is 32. (ל [30] + ב [2] = 32.) Today it is thirty-two years since the *Rebbe* blessed me by saying that I would have a strong and vigorous heart."

Within weeks R' Shmuel died of coronary failure. His heart, like the *Rebbe's esrog*, had been resilient. But like even the most fragrant *esrog* after *Sukkos*, it withered with time. Thirty-two years of blessed time.

◈§ Lulava

R abbi Shammai Parnes* is the head of the *Chevra Kadisha* (Burial Society) of the Israeli army. He is a deeply religious man who comes from a long line of Yerushalmi families. His job is not a pleasant one, but it is, unfortunately, a very essential one. Among R' Shammai's responsibilities is to be near the battlefronts in order that he be able to retrieve the remains of soldiers killed in the line of duty. Once retrieved, the bodies are returned to family members who then accord their loved ones proper and dignified burial.

---

* Names have been changed by personal request.

R' Shammai does not talk to many people about the tragedies he has seen, for he would rather forget them. This story, though, is one he enjoys retelling because of the emotional and spiritual uplift it gives to whoever hears it.

The story took place during the Yom Kippur War in 1973, when the Israelis were caught by surprise and attacked by Arabs on all fronts. One of the critical points of battle was near the Suez Canal. For days after *Yom Kippur* and throughout *Sukkos*, R' Shammai and his assistants traveled throughout the Sinai desert and southward towards Suez, where they cautiously and caringly gathered the bodies of those who had fallen in battle.

Throughout the days of *Sukkos* R' Shammai traveled in his jeep, taking with him his *siddur, Tehillim, tallis, lulav* and *esrog.* In every army camp where he stopped, soldiers approached him, begging for permission to use his *lulav* and *esrog.* Infantrymen who were irreligious would pick up his *siddur*, caress it gently and say, "R' Shammai, let us pray from your *siddur* . . . R' Shammai, let us say the *Shema* . . . R' Shammai, could we say some *Tehillim* . . ."

He would help as many as he could and at times he was detained from his work for more than an hour. Much to his regret, though, he eventually had to say to the young men, "I can't stay any longer. I've been summoned elsewhere."

R' Shammai says that in certain areas there were times when he did not tell the soldiers that he had his *siddur*, or *lulav* and *esrog* with him, for fear that he would be endlessly delayed.

On *Hoshana Rabbah* (the last day of *Sukkos*), R' Shammai and his assistants were near the Suez. It was late morning, and as he drove towards a newly constructed army base in the wide open desert, the thought occurred to him that because he had already *davened* and used his *lulav* and *esrog* for the last time this *Yom Tov,* he could leave them in the army base if he were summoned away, as he would no longer need them.

Shortly after R' Shammai's arrival at the base, a long line of soldiers began to form, waiting to use his *lulav* and *esrog.* As a crowd began to assemble, a young non-religious soldier, Arik Shuali,* driving an ammunition truck, was making his way southward. Looking through his powerful binoculars he noticed a large crowd of fellow servicemen gathered in one area. Curious, he got out of his truck and made his way on foot to where the soldiers had assembled.

As he came closer, he asked someone, "What is all the commotion about?" They explained to him that R' Shammai from the *Chevrah Kadisha* had come, and people were waiting for an opportunity to use his *lulav* and *esrog*. Arik didn't seem interested in waiting around. However, when one of his friends mentioned that it was the last day to do this *mitzvah*, he agreed to wait his turn.

Eventually Arik's turn arrived. Just as he was holding the *lulav* and *esrog* a bomb hit his truck. The vehicle exploded and set off multiple explosions of the ammunition on board. The blasts were so intense that a crater was formed in the ground where the truck had been parked. R' Shammai says, that later, when they investigated the spot where the truck had been, the soldiers couldn't find even a shard of metal remaining from the shattered vehicle.

❀ ❀ ❀

Three months later, R' Shammai read a short notice in the Israeli army newspaper. It was an announcement stating that the wife of serviceman Arik Shuali had given birth to a little girl. The announcement included a statement by the new father. "I believe with every fiber of my being, that I am alive today and that I merited to see my new daughter only because of the *mitzvah* that I was doing at the time my truck was bombed."

To remember Hashem's goodness, he named his daughter Lulava.

◆§ The Warmth of a Father's Love

Many well-intentioned people find themselves caught in a web of conflicting demands on their time. As responsible members of *Klal Yisrael* they feel obligated to take part in events such as parlor meetings, dinners, teas, bazaars and auctions to benefit local institutions (*shul*/school/*mikvah*) or charities in other Jewish communities outside their own.

But that is not all. There are other noble community endeavors which require volunteers, groups such as Bikur Cholim, Tomchei Shabbos and the Chevrah Kadisha. Additionally, *shiurim* must be given, lectures attended, classes created and *kiruv* efforts generated. Each of these worthwhile ventures takes time, effort and financial support. Quite often, involvement in a number of these projects comes at the expense of family life, as time that should be spent at home with one's spouse and children is used for these outside activities.

If we, at times, feel overwhelmed, we can only imagine the pressures a *gadol hador* (a generation's prominent Torah sage) must experience as he is constantly besieged by countless members of *Klal Yisrael* who seek his time, advice and involvement in a myriad of matters. The *gadol's* balancing of public and private life is therefore exceedingly difficult.

Rabbi Moshe Feinstein (1895-1986), whose time and attention were in constant demand by Jews throughout the world, was faced with this dilemma on a daily basis. The *Rosh Yeshivah* maintained close family ties with each of his children and grandchildren. The following episode, told to me by R' Moshe's son, R' Reuvein, the *Rosh Yeshivah* of Yeshivah Staten Island, reveals a father-son relationship worthy of emulation.

The *bar mitzvah* Shabbos of one of R' Reuvein's sons coincided with the Shabbos of the annual convention of Agudath Israel of America. Understandably, R' Moshe, as the *gadol hador*, was designated to be the primary speaker at the convention. His personal participation at the convention gave stature and motivation to the world-wide efforts of Agudath Israel, and his absence would have been glaringly obvious.

On the other hand, it was his *grandson* that was celebrating his *bar mitzvah*! How could a beloved, caring grandfather not attend such a significant family *simchah*?

The conflict was resolved in the following manner. On Thursday morning, with R' Moshe in attendance, the *bar mitzvah* boy received an *aliyah* at R' Moshe's *yeshivah*, Tifereth Yerushalayim, in the Lower East Side of Manhattan. All the family members then participated in a modest *seudah*. On *Shabbos*, however, R' Moshe attended the Agudah convention.

Years later, R' Reuvein, the father of the *bar mitzvah*, was asked, "Didn't you mind that your own father did not attend your son's *bar mitzvah?*"

R' Reuvein smiled and said, "Of course every person would love nothing more than to have his father at such a special family *simchah*. But I was able to accept the fact that my father didn't attend the *bar mitzvah* because deep in my heart I knew that he really loved me."

R' Reuvein then gave three reasons for his certainty.

When he himself was a child, R' Reuvein reminisced, his father used to get up very early in the morning to learn. At six o'clock in the morning R' Moshe would come into his little son Reuvein's room, take the boy's clothes and put them on the radiator. A half hour later he would return and remove the clothes that were, by then, nice and warm, and dress his son while the child was still under the covers. That way, when he got out of bed he would already be warm and not be chilled by the freezing New York winters!

A second memorable indication of R' Moshe's understanding love for his son would occur in the Connecticut bungalow colony where the Feinstein family spent its summers. There were not many facilities to keep the children of the guests occupied. Therefore, when the owner of the colony would take his pick-up truck into town to purchase supplies for his guests, all the children were allowed to sit in the hay-lined back of the open-ended truck, where they frolicked happily as the truck made its way into town along the bumpy roads.

R' Moshe used to spend quite a bit of time learning with his son Reuvein. However, when he noticed that the truck was about to leave, he would tell his son to close the *sefer*, get on the truck and enjoy the ride. "He assured me that we would make up the learning at another time," R' Reuvein explains, "However he knew what was important to a child, so he encouraged me to go."

The third indication of his father's love manifested itself every Shabbos. R' Reuvein was always seated at his regular place at the table, on his father's right side, regardless of which guests were at the table (unless a *gadol hador* was present).

"My father" said R' Reuven, "used to quote *Pirkei Avos* (1:5) and say, 'יִהְיוּ עֲנִיִּים בְּנֵי בֵיתֶךָ' — Treat the poor as members of your household,' and then he would add, 'but they shouldn't take over!' "

[R' Moshe obviously felt that a child feels a sense of security and confidence in knowing that his or her place at the family's table is significant. The place is only meaningful if it is permanent]

Thus, the undeniable love of a father for his son created a sense of security that shouldered all situations.

> There are opportunities in every household for parents to show their unequivocal love and concern for their children. If they do so, they can then take time for community needs as well, for their children will not feel threatened. Showing responsibility for others is also an aspect of *chinuch habanim*. It is the wise and discerning parent who knows where to draw the line between public commitments and private [family] concerns.

◄§ Sensitivity at Sunset

> Each of us understands that we must be sensitive to people in need. The hungry, the lonely, the bereaved — all deserve our care and concern. In this story about the Klausenberger *Rebbe*, Rabbi Yekusiel Yehudah Halberstam, we learn of a sensitivity of a different nature. It is the combination of the *Rebbe's* scholarship and perception that makes this episode so remarkable.
>
> This story is recounted in the *sefer Tiferes Banim* (p. 300) by Rabbi Bunim Yoel Toisig of *Yerushalyim*.

In 1954, the Klausenberger *Rebbe* made his first trip to *Eretz Yisrael*. Coming to the Holy Land after years of terror and tragedy in the concentration camps in Europe, the trip was a deeply emotional one for him. Every *Rebbe*, every town, every *yeshivah* and every *kever* (gravesite) of a *tzaddik* that he visited left an indelible impression on him.

In the monthly publication *Tzanz* (*Kislev* 5752), Rabbi Sholom Shtemir records that the first time the Klausenberger *Rebbe davened Shacharis* in *Yerushalayim* — the holy city still bereft of the *Beis HaMikdash* — the *Rebbe* was torn by such intense emotion that he cried uncontrollably when he recited the words "אֵיזֶהוּ מְקוֹמָן שֶׁל זְבָחִים" (What is the location of the offerings?)."

Still in Jerusalem the next morning, *Rosh Chodesh Kislev*, the *Rebbe davened Shacharis* for close to four hours. He sang *Hallel* for nearly an hour, concentrating on the verse "בְּחַצְרוֹת בֵּית ה' בְּתוֹכֵכִי יְרוּשָׁלַיִם הַלְלוּיָהּ" (In the courtyards of the House of Hashem, in your midst, O Jerusalem, Halleluyah!)."

One late afternoon the *Rebbe* and a group of *chassidim* traveled to the *Galil HaElyon* (upper Galilee) near the holy city of *Tzefas* to visit the *mekomos hakedoshim* (lit., holy places) there. On the side of the road leading to Meron, they came to the *kever* of the *Tanna* (Mishnaic scholar) R' Yehudah bar Ilai. The sun had already set by the time they all gathered near the *kever*, and it was there that the *Rebbe davened Minchah*. (There are those who *daven Minchah* even after sunset. See *Orach Chaim* 233:1 and *Mishnah Berurah* note 14, also 261:2 with *Mishnah Berurah* note 23 and *Biur Halachah*.)

From there the *Rebbe* and his entourage continued on their way to *Tzefas*. That evening, the *Rebbe*'s mood seemed to change, as he appeared disturbed and upset. No one could understand why he seemed so troubled, and the *Rebbe* himself would not reveal the reason.

Early the next afternoon the *Rebbe* went back to the *kever* of R' Yehudah bar Ilai and once again *davened Minchah* there. The *Rebbe davened* with unusual fervor, crying throughout his recitation of the *Shemoneh Esrei*. Afterwards, when he stepped away from the *kever*, he appeared relaxed and content.

Rabbi Shmuel Unsdorfer (then the *Rosh Yeshivah* of Yeshivah

Reishis Chachmah in Montreal, and today the *Rav* of the Klausenberg community in Petach Tikvah) approached the *Rebbe* and respectfully asked why his mood seemed to change so radically, and why he had insisted on coming back to *daven Minchah* in the same place as the day before.

"Last night when we came to *Tzefas*," the Klausenberger *Rebbe* explained, "I made a *cheshbon hanefesh* (a spiritual accounting) of everything that I had done that day. I suddenly remembered the *Mishnah* (*Berachos* 26a) in which R' Yehudah bar Ilai states that one must complete *Minchah* before *plag haminchah* (an hour and a quarter before sunset; see *Orach Chaim* 233 and *Mishnah Berurah* note 3). I had *davened Minchah* at the *kever* of the great *Tanna*, at a time that he himself ruled that *Minchah* was invalid! I could not believe that I had been so insensitive!

"It was as though I were as audacious as Haman, whom Achashveirosh reprimanded by saying, 'הֲגַם לִכְבּוֹשׁ אֶת הַמַּלְכָּה עִמִּי בַּבָּיִת — Would he actually capture the queen while I am in the house?' (*Megillas Esther* 7:8).

"That is why I was so disturbed last night. I made up my mind to return to the *kever* and ask Hashem that the holy *Tanna* forgive me. And so today I came back here and *davened Minchah*, with a repentant and broken heart, at a time which is in consonance with R' Yehudah bar Ilai's view. Now I feel that I have been forgiven."

> Sensitivity is an attribute of kindness. Here it revealed a quality of greatness.

✦§ Hands of Purity

> For untold thousands of people who experienced the unspeakable horrors of the Nazi concentration camps, the pain, even after fifty years, is still with them. Though they hardly speak about the unimaginable atrocities they witnessed and suffered, their anguish and grief are no less real.
>
> The following is a case in point.

A Belgian Jew, Rabbi Zisha Rotberg,* recently went back to the city of Oswiecim (Auschwitz) in Poland to see the concentration camp where he had been interred as a child. Upon his return to Belgium, he was asked how he could possibly have gone back to the site where such bestial acts had been committed by the Nazis against him and his fellow Jews.

R' Zisha replied, "For more than four decades I have not had one restful night. The frightening screams of death I constantly heard during those years have been ringing in my ears every evening. I had to go back and see with my own eyes that the gas chambers were no longer operative. In my mind I knew they were shut down after the war, but my heart could not accept it. I had to see for myself that they were totally abandoned and inactive. Now, finally, I can sleep at night."

It is with such trauma and pain that many survivors of the Holocaust still live.

During a recent trip to London, an elderly woman came to tell me a story that had been tormenting her. "For years I have felt," she said, "that this story should be recorded. No one, unless they were in the concentration camps, can know of the heroism and *mesiras nefesh* that certain individuals manifested under the most trying circumstances. I can never forget this particular incident, and although it is painful to relive, I feel there is much to learn from it."

I am grateful to both her and Mrs. Miriam Gottesman, who lived through the episode as well, for having willingly supplied the details of that dreadful and tragic time of their lives.

We, in turn, can only be inspired.

❧ ❧ ❧

During the last two weeks in the notorious Bergen-Belsen concentration camp, there was no water to be had. Located in a forest, the barracks, housing thousands of women, were terribly cramped. Illness, specifically typhus, was rampant, the temperature was a stifling one hundred degrees and now, with almost no food

---

* Name has been changed.

and nothing to drink, women were dying wretched deaths from thirst and starvation. The women who could talk were begging those who could walk to get them some water. Countless women requested that if they died during the night, those who remained alive should at least carry them out of the barracks so that others would not trample on them.

There was a swamp nearby that had polluted, putrid green water, but no Jewish women could get near it because it was guarded by vicious Russian female soldiers who had been captured by the German army and were now being sequestered in separate barracks in Bergen-Belsen. Because these communist women were trained and fit for the Russian army, they were strong enough to mercilessly beat anyone who tried to approach the swamp to get water. The Russians were saving whatever was left in the swamp to aid in their own survival.

The atmosphere in the barracks was one of desperation and hopelessness, but when twenty-year-old Leah Kaiser from Serdehele, Slovakia perished, everyone was crushed. If she could die, then few felt they would be spared. Leah had been the one who took the pieces of black coal that were distributed daily to supply heat in the winter and marked the days of the Jewish calendar on the wooden beds so that the women would know when it was Shabbos or *Yom Tov*.

The women in London interrupted themselves to further describe the life of Leah Kaiser.

One year, as the evening of *Tishah B'Av* approached and the women were waiting desperately for their daily ration of food — a small piece of turnip — to be delivered, Leah realized that by the time she would finally get her share it would be after sunset. She hadn't eaten anything that day, but because her food did indeed come after sunset — which meant that *Tishah B'Av* had started — she put the food aside and fasted the rest of the evening and the entire next day — going without a morsel of food for two days!

That night of *Tishah B'Av*, Leah gathered the women in the barracks and, to the sad, haunting tune of *Eichah*, chanted a poem that she had composed in Yiddish, in which she begged the *Ribono Shel Olam* to look down at his poor and tormented nation and redeem His people from their travails. That evening, women cried themselves to sleep.

However, it was nineteen-year-old Esther Fleischman, also from Serdehele, that the women in London wished to talk about. A cousin of Leah Kaiser, Esther was so weak and frail that in those last weeks at Bergen-Belsen she was a mere skeleton of herself. "I can't go on much longer," she moaned to anyone who could possibly help her. "Someone, please get me some water. . ."

For two days she begged and pleaded and often fell into a semi-conscious sleep. Finally, one night, Leah Tzvia Krauss (Stern) heard that the taps had been turned on and that there might be some drops of water available. Risking her own life, Leah Tzvia left and in the dank darkness of night she collected the precious liquid, drop by drop, until she had a quarter of a cup of water.

When Leah Tzvia returned with the little bit of water that she had managed to garner, she bent over the frail Esther Fleischman and said tenderly, "Here, my dear, wet your lips."

"That's not why I wanted the water," Esther replied faintly. "It's too late for me. I can't make it. I just wanted the water to wash my hands so that I should be able to say a '*Yiddish vort*' (an expression for 'words of prayer')."

With that, she took the water, poured it slowly over her hands and began to recite the *Shema Yisrael*. She managed to say the first verse, and when she came to the word "*Ve'ahavta*. . .(And you shall love. . .)," she closed her eyes, collapsed, and passed away — going to her eternal rest.

In Talmudic times (see *Eruvin* 21b), the great sage R' Akiva was faced with a similar dilemma while in prison. He, too, chose to use the meager amount of water he was given, to wash and purify his hands rather than refresh himself by drinking it.

R' Akiva survived that incident only to die later in a vivid manifestation of *Kiddush Hashem* (sanctification of G-d's name; see *Berachos* 61b). Esther Fleischman didn't survive, but her memory lives on because she, too, perished while performing an act of *Kiddush Hashem*.

⋑ *A Stamp of Approval*

Rabbi Yitzchak Dwek, the noted *Rav* of the Syrian Sephardic community of Deal, New Jersey, explained a Talmudic teaching in a unique manner during his address to a National Convention of Agudath Israel of America.

"*Chazal* (Sages of the Talmud) (*Gittin* 7a) instruct us," he said, "אִם רוֹאֶה אָדָם שֶׁמְּזוֹנוֹתָיו מְצוּמְצָמִין יַעֲשֶׂה מֵהֶן צְדָקָה" — If a person sees that his livelihood is barely sufficient, he should give charity from the money that he does have.' That seems puzzling," claimed Rabbi Dwek, "for by giving charity, one reduces his material assets even further. Why are *Chazal* giving us advice that seems counter-productive?"

Rabbi Dwek explained this enigmatic teaching with a beautiful parable he heard as a child growing up in Syria.

> There was once an unsophisticated, poverty-stricken man who lived in a small village. He wished to mail a letter and was told that he would have to go to the central post office in the large city.
>
> He made his way to the big city, found out where the post office was and handed over the letter to the clerk behind the counter. "I would like to send this to a friend," he announced proudly.
>
> The clerk picked up the letter, placed it on a scale, then turned to the villager and said, "I am sorry, but this letter is too heavy."
>
> "Too heavy?" the villager cried out. "What am I supposed to do now?"
>
> "Put on another two stamps," replied the perturbed clerk.
>
> The puzzled villager looked up at the clerk and said, "But sir, listen to what you're saying. If I put on another two stamps, that will make the letter even heavier!"

The idea, of course, is that although technically the letter becomes heavier with the addition of the stamps, it is the stamps (and the money paid for it) that actually enables the letter to reach its destination. So is it, too, with the distribution of charity. Although a donation technically reduces the amount of money one possesses, it actually is the catalyst for increasing one's fortune. As *Chazal* teach (*Taanis* 9a): "עַשֵּׁר בִּשְׁבִיל שֶׁתִּתְעַשֵּׁר —Tithe so that you will become wealthy."

⋰§ Four Me and Four You

In today's pale economic climate many people feel pressured by heavy demands on their limited funds. Family obligations combined with business responsibilities are so great that, when one is approached for donations to charitable causes, one's response tends to be lukewarm. This story, however, with its insight from the Satmar *Rebbe*, Rabbi Yoel Teitelbaum (1887-1979), could well serve as a blueprint for behavior.

A man who lived in the Midwest once came to the Williamsburg section of Brooklyn to discuss a problem with the Satmar *Rebbe*. The man, a well-to-do individual who lived comfortably, graciously supported many Torah and *tzedakah* institutions.

Every year without fail, the various organizations would contact him by phone, mail, or personal visit, and every year he would give each of them a sizable donation. However, as his family grew, so did the size of his financial obligations to his children and grandchildren.

His grown sons were learning in *kollelim* both in Israel and America, and his daughters had married young men who were still studying in *yeshivos*. It seemed as if everyone in his large family was depending on him for financial support! School tuitions, summer camps and children's clothes for *Yom Tov* were all expenses that he and his wife had thought they were finished with years ago. But now that cycle of expenses, on an even larger scale, was starting all over again.

Yet the organizations' representatives still came knocking at his door, looking at least, for the same amount of money they had received in previous years. They, too, had increasing fiscal burdens, and with more people becoming hard pressed financially, there were fewer individuals willing to make long-term financial commitments.

"What shall I do?" the concerned gentleman asked the *Rebbe*. "I feel very bad, but it just doesn't seem possible to help everyone the way I used to."

The Satmar *Rebbe* told the man to take out a *chumash*. The *Rebbe* turned to a *passuk* (verse) in *Devarim* (16:11) and told the gentleman to read it. The *passuk* details the obligations a man has when rejoicing during the festival(s) of (*Pesach*,) *Shavuos* (and *Sukkos*).

The man read, "וְשָׂמַחְתָּ לִפְנֵי ה' אֱלֹקֶיךָ אַתָּה וּבִנְךָ וּבִתֶּךָ וְעַבְדְּךָ וַאֲמָתֶךָ וְהַלֵּוִי אֲשֶׁר בִּשְׁעָרֶיךָ וְהַגֵּר וְהַיָּתוֹם וְהָאַלְמָנָה אֲשֶׁר בְּקִרְבֶּךָ — You shall rejoice before Hashem your G-d, along with your son, daughter, servant, maid, the Levite from your settlements, the convert, the orphan and widow among you..."

The *Rebbe* pointed to the *passuk* and said, "Count how many people the Torah tells you to rejoice with."

The man counted each of them and said, "Eight." (Son, daughter, servant, maid, Levi, convert, orphan and widow.)

"No," said the *Rebbe*, "you counted wrong. Count again."

Bewildered, the man once again counted the individuals named in the *passuk*, and though he counted more carefully this time, he again came up with the number eight.

"Now look at Rashi's commentary," instructed the *Rebbe*. "See his calculation and you'll learn a great lesson."

Slowly the man's eyes gazed over the words of Rashi as he tried to comprehend the *Rebbe's* intention. Rashi (ibid.) writes, "The Levi, the convert, the orphan and the widow — [Hashem says] these four types of people are Mine and they correspond to the four types of people that are yours — son, daughter, servant and maid. If you gladden Mine, then I will gladden yours."

"Rashi is teaching us that mankind falls into two distinct categories," said the *Rebbe*, "your people and Hashem's people. Rashi is informing us of Hashem's promise and assurance. You take care of His people and He will take care of yours. And that has to be your attitude," concluded the *Rebbe*. "See that you help others, and Hashem will provide for yours."

Thus, in difficult financial times, one must remember that helping those who need assistance outside the home is actually an investment whose dividends pay off inside the home.

⋙ Watch Your Step

A number of years ago I had the wonderful opportunity to be in *Eretz Yisrael* for *Sukkos*. After *Yom Tov,* on the night that I was to return home, I went to say good-bye to a new friend and acquaintance, Rabbi Avraham Shmulevitz, son of the noted *Rosh Yeshivah* of Mir, Rabbi Chaim Shmulevitz (1902-1978).

As we walked along on this cool Jerusalem night in the Ezras Torah section of the Holy City, my eyes were focused on the magnificent view of thousands of lights glittering in homes nestled in the distant hills. R' Avraham's eyes, however, lingered on the partially taken-down *sukkos* that lined the *mirpesot* (porches) of his beloved neighborhood. Now that *Yom Tov* was over, every remaining *sukkah* was dark, and *schach* (long stalks of furry willows used as ceilings in every *sukkah*) lay strewn along the sidewalks and curbsides.

Suddenly he stopped, turned to me and said, "I have a good story for you."

And this is what he told me.

Many years ago, two *bachurim* (students) came to the *yeshivah* of the Chasam Sofer (Rabbi Moshe Schreiber [1763-1839]) in Pressburg, Hungary to take a *farher* (test), to determine whether or not the boys qualified for admission as *talmidim* in his prestigious *yeshivah*.

It was right after *Sukkos*, just a few days before the new *zman* (semester) was to begin, and the *bachurim* were anxious to become part of the world-renowned Torah institution. One of the boys had the reputation of being an *iluy* (genius), whose understanding and perception of *sugyos* (Torah topics) was outstanding. The second boy also had the reputation of being an exemplary scholar for his age, but he was not known to possess the sharp mind that the first boy had.

Both boys took the *farher* and afterwards the Chasam Sofer announced that he would be accepting only one of them — the second boy, the one with the fine reputation — but not the outstanding *iluy*.

Staff members who had observed and overheard the boys being tested were surprised. Both had done well, and the *iluy* certainly had done better. "Why," they asked the Chasam Sofer, "are you taking only the second *bachur*?"

The Chasam Sofer peered at those who questioned him and answered sternly, "I was sitting by the window and noticed the two *bachurim* as they made their way from the street into this building. There was some *schach* on the sidewalk from one of the *sukkos* that had just been taken down after *Yom Tov*. The first *bachur* did not make it a point to avoid the *schach*, but nonchalantly stepped on it as he was walking. The second boy, however, walked around the *schach*.

"I maintain," continued the Chasam Sofer, "that a *bachur* who can step on *schach* two days after *Sukkos* does not have the appropriate sensitivity to *kedushas hamitzvos* (holiness of *mitzvos*). Such a *bachur* I don't want in my *yeshivah*. He will find someplace else to learn" (See *Mishnah Berurah Orach Chaim* 638 note 24).

As Rabbi Avraham Shmulevitz and I resumed walking, the *schach* strewn on the sidewalks took on a new significance. I realized that although I had been concentrating on the lights in the distance, it was R' Avraham's view that had brightened the night.

Rabbi Tuvya Goldstein, the *Rosh Yeshiva* of Yeshivah Emek Halacha in Brooklyn (see p. 93), recently recalled an interesting event that occurred when he was learning in Yeshivah Ohel Torah in Baranovich, where Rabbi Elchanan Wasserman (1875-1941) was the *Rosh Yeshivah*.

One evening R' Elchanan had a very sore throat and wasn't feeling well. When it came time to *daven Maariv* (the evening service), he asked that a group of students come from the *yeshivah* to his home so that he could *daven* with a *minyan*.

R' Tuvya was among the group that came that evening. When it was time to begin, a *bachur* who had just joined the *yeshivah* was asked to be the *chazzan*.

The *bachur* was not accustomed to the slow and steady pace at which the *yeshivah* boys *davened*. Rather, he was used to a *baalei battim's* (laymen's) *minyan* back in his home town, where they *davened* at a quicker pace.

As the *bachur* sped through the *davening*, R' Elchanan looked up at him numerous times, surprised and annoyed. It was obvious that this boy had no idea how *yeshivah bachurim* (and the rest of us) are supposed to *daven*.

When the *davening* was over, R' Elchanan called the young man over. He first asked him his name, and then inquired as to where he came from. Then R' Elchanan told him gently, "Young man, I want you to know that the verse 'וְנַסְתֶּם וְאֵין־רֹדֵף אֶתְכֶם — You will run away even when no one is chasing you' (*Vayikra* 26:17) is part of the *tochachah* (section of rebuke and admonishment given by Moshe *Rabbeinu* to *Klal Yisrael*)!"

❈ ❈ ❈

R' Elchanan's gently stated criticism made an indelible impression on R' Tuvya and the older students who understood his intent. Thoughtlessly running through the *davening* just to be finished with it is as dreadful in Hashem's eyes as the horrifying paranoia of fleeing from an enemy that does not exist. The running in both cases is unjustified and uncalled for.

·§ Entebbe Entreaty

It was June of 1976, and the news hit the people of *Eretz Yisrael* like a thunderbolt! An Air France flight from Tel-Aviv, filled almost to capacity with Jews, had been hijacked by Palestinian terrorists after a stopover in Athens, and taken to an airport in Entebbe, Uganda. Israeli flights had been the targets of hijackers before, but this incident was more frightening, for the Jewish hostages now in Entebbe were at the mercy not only of the Palestinians, but also of one of the world's cruelest dictators, the president of Uganda, Idi Amin, who was known for his frequent ruthless mass killings.

The hijacked plane was the main subject of conversation throughout *Eretz Yisrael*. In every city, town, village and *moshav*, people were glued to their radios, desperate for news of the Jewish hostages. Jews all over the world were congregating in *shuls* and *yeshivos* to learn Torah and fervently say *Tehillim* on behalf of the unfortunate kidnap victims. Thousands of people gathered at the *Kosel HaMaaravi* in prayer.

In the Mirrer Yeshivah in the Beis Yisrael section of Jerusalem, worried *bachurim* filed into the *beis hamidrash*. As their *Rosh Yeshivah*, Rabbi Chaim Shmulevitz was expected to join them there, the *talmidim* did not begin to recite *Tehillim* in unison immediately, but waited for the *Rosh Yeshivah* to arrive. The mood of the crowd was sullen and the air was thick with nerve-racking tension. Any minute, they knew, word could come that the Jews in Entebbe had been shot and killed in cold blood. It seemed as though everyone knew someone who knew someone on that plane.

The *bachurim* and *baalei battim* in the huge Mirrer *beis hamidrash* crammed into every inch of available space. Everyone waited anxiously for the *Rosh Yeshivah* to make his entrance. R' Chaim had been ill, they knew, but had decided to participate in the collective outpouring of pain being felt and expressed by Jews everywhere.

Walking slowly, R' Chaim entered the hallway and began to

make his way up the stairs. As he reached the third step he began whimpering to himself as his mind filled with images of frightened people trapped far away in the darkest of situations.

A hush fell over the *beis hamidrash* as the *Rosh Yeshivah* was about to enter. R' Chaim stopped for a moment at the back door of the *beis hamidrash*, took one look at the huge tense crowd — and suddenly the impact of the dangerous situation hit him with an intensity that he hadn't felt before. Reeling from the impact, he grabbed onto a chair for support as he stepped into the *beis hamidrash*. Unable to go any further, he sat down slowly in a seat in the back of the large hall, lowered his head onto his arm and wept uncontrollably.

A sense of shock prevailed, and for several moments no sound could be heard other than the tortured sobs of the *Rosh Yeshivah*. Soon, moved by R' Chaim's obvious anguish, the *bachurim* joined him in his wordless expression of grief and tears rolled unchecked down the faces of dozens of *talmidim*.

After a few moments, R' Chaim got up and was helped to the front of the *beis hamidrash*. Approaching with his head down, he walked up to the *Aron Kodesh*, kissed the *paroches* and turned slowly back to the *bachurim* ready to speak.

He said two words, then stopped, unable to force his words out past his muffled sobs. He wiped his eyes and tried again. In a barely audible voice that was choked with pain, R' Chaim said, "Imagine how you would be saying *Tehillim* if it was your father or mother, your brother or sister, who was there."

And with that he sat down.

The *Rosh Yeshivah* had uttered only one sentence, but it had extraordinary impact. The *Tehillim* recited afterwards was so powerful and so awesome and so intense that it still sends chills up and down the spines of those who were there when they think about it today, more than fifteen years later.

Two days later, in a legendary daring rescue operation, Israeli forces attacked the Entebbe airport and saved the one hundred and three hostages confined there. However, for those like Rabbi Moshe Zucker, a noted *mechanech* from Brooklyn, who was in the Mirrer Yeshivah at that time, it was not only the perilous liberating venture but the magnitude of concern for fellow Jews manifested by the *Rosh Yeshivah* that remains with him to this day.

✍ Bullish Behavior

The *Gemara* (*Bava Metzia* 58b) teaches כָּל הַמַּלְבִּין פְּנֵי חֲבֵירוֹ בָּרַבִּים כְּאִילוּ שׁוֹפֵךְ דָמִים — whoever embarrasses someone publicly it is as though he kills him. To humiliate another person is to deny his צֶלֶם אֱלֹקִים, his G-dliness. (See *Tiferes Yisrael* Avos 3, note 72.) Thus, by shaming an individual, one diminishes his existence to the level of a mere animal. Perhaps for this reason *Chazal* equated humiliation to murder, for in essence humiliation nullifies the humanity in man.

In this light, the following story told by Rabbi David Soloveitchik, the *Rosh Yeshivah* of one of the Brisker *yeshivos* in Jerusalem, is remarkable.

One afternoon the Brisker *Rav*, Rabbi Yosef Dov Ber Soloveitchik (1820-1892), author of the *Beis HaLevi*, was in the *beis hamidrash* (study hall) learning with his son, R' Chaim (1853-1918). It was a hot summer day and the two Torah luminaries were sitting in their shirtsleeves, deeply involved in a *sugya* (Torah topic).

Suddenly the local butcher burst into the *beis hamidrash*. Still out of breath, he ran over to the *Beis HaLevi*, pointed an accusing finger and began to yell. "I know why you ruled against me yesterday at the *din Torah* (religious adjudication). You were bought off! You were paid a fortune by the other side to rule in their favor! But you know in your heart that I was right. What a disgrace!" He stomped on the floor with indignation.

The *Beis HaLevi* and his son were shocked by this outburst. However, with measured movements, the *Beis HaLevi* stood up, put on his jacket and bowed his head respectfully to the butcher. "I understand your feelings," he said softly. "I forgive you. I forgive you."

But the tirade continued. The butcher relentlessly spewed his anger and fury at the *Rav*, claiming the *Rav* was biased and unfair. Yet, throughout the attack the *Beis HaLevi* absorbed his accusations quietly, nodding his head slowly and repeating calmly, "I forgive you. I forgive you."

The butcher's tirade finally ended and he turned to leave. The Brisker *Rav* followed behind him, telling him again that he held nothing against him, that he wasn't upset by his words and that he understood his bitterness.

The two Torah scholars then resumed their discussion, but the *Beis HaLevi* was visibly shaken.

The next morning, the butcher was leading some bulls on a path going downhill to the *beis hashechitah* (ritual slaughterhouse). Suddenly, one of the bulls in the back charged forward, violently pushing aside the animals blocking its way as it tried to run ahead of the others. Startled, the other animals panicked, and pandemonium ensued as the lumbering beasts stampeded, uncontrollably, forward.

Before the butcher could get out of the way, he was trampled. Terrified, he lay sprawled on the ground right in the path of the raging bulls. He was crushed to death almost instantly.

When the townsfolk heard of the dreadful mishap, tremendous commotion and confusion gripped the area. People ran immediately to the *Rav* to tell him what had happened.

When the *Beis HaLevi* heard the news, he was beside himself with grief. He started to cry, fearing in his heart that perhaps, in an indirect manner, he was responsible for the terrible destiny that had befallen the disrespectful butcher. (See *Tosafos Bava Basra* 22a ד"ה אנא.) When R' Chaim saw his father's anguish, he tried to console him. "Father," R' Chaim exclaimed, "this was not your fault, it was not your doing! You forgave him. You told him numerous times that you were not angry with him."

"Do you remember specifically that I forgave him?" the *Beis HaLevi* asked his son, still concerned. R' Chaim assured his father that he had indeed acted nobly, in a manner far beyond the call of duty.

Nevertheless, the *Beis HaLevi* went to the butcher's funeral and wept bitter tears at his gravesite. For the next eleven months the *Beis HaLevi* said *Kaddish* for the sake of the butcher, and every year he learned *mishnayos* on his *yahrtzeit!*

In retelling this incident, R' David (R' Chaim's grandson) pointed out that the *Beis HaLevi* could justifiably have perceived the sudden turn of events as "proof" that the butcher's actions the day before were improper and inappropriate. He could have seen himself as being vindicated.

Instead, because of his humility and genuine love for a fellow Jew, the *Beis HaLevi* sought to either find fault with himself or, failing to do so, at least show concern for the soul of the butcher. The *Kaddish* and *mishnayos* were indications of his concern.

✑§ Chews, Shoes and a Pocketful of Quarters

Often we find ourselves responding in a sensitive fashion to the feelings and requirements of prominent people or individuals who, we feel, may somehow affect our lives. A law in the Torah, which at first seems to have a limited application, actually — in the context of the *Daas ZeKeinim's* explanation — broadens the scope of just whose feelings we should be sensitive to.

In a terse, five-word sentence the Torah (*Devarim* 22:10) tells us: "לֹא תַחֲרֹשׁ בְּשׁוֹר וּבַחֲמֹר יַחְדָּו" — Do not plow with an ox and donkey together." Although no reason is given, the *Daas Zekeinim* (ibid.) offers: "Because an ox chews its cud [it brings up the food it has already swallowed and chews it again], a donkey who is harnessed together with an ox would feel anguish when it hears how the ox is [apparently] eating [a second time], while he, the donkey, [now] has nothing to eat!"

If the Torah is concerned about the sensitivities of a simple-minded donkey (see *Rabbeinu Bachya, Bereishis* 2:19, regarding the origin of the word חֲמוֹר), how much more so should we be concerned about human beings, regardless of their status or stature!

In light of the above, the routines of two particular individuals shed light not only on their own character, but on their approach to fellow Jews as well.

Rabbi Leibish Pincus of Brooklyn was a very kind, quiet, unassuming man who had survived the *churban* of Europe and come to America in his early teens. In his new country *parnassah* did not come easily, and he struggled all his life to make a living as a furrier.

When he was older, R' Leibish always carried a roll of quarters in his pocket. No one ever seemed to know why, but after he passed away, someone revealed the reason.

Every morning as he *davened* in *shul* he would be approached by itinerant poor people who went from *shul* to *shul* with outstretched hands, asking for money. R' Leibish felt that if he were to take out a dollar bill with the intention of asking for change, for a fleeting moment the man might experience a surge of joy at the thought of actually getting the entire dollar. That momentary hope would instantly be transformed into disappointment when R' Leibish asked for change. Therefore, to avoid launching anyone on this split-second, roller coaster ride of emotions, he would always carry a roll of quarters. That way he would always have exact change for those who sought money every day!

❦ ❦ ❦

In the Borough Park home of Rabbi Michael L. Munk, the eminent educator, author and *askan* (community activist) in Europe and America, a beautiful silver *pushka* (charity collection box) was displayed among his other treasured items. Rabbi Nisson Wolpin, the noted editor of *The Jewish Observer*, once visited Rabbi Munk and asked what — if anything — was the significance of the *pushka*.

"Oh," smiled the dignified *Rav* with a twinkle in his eye. "This *pushka* was presented to my great-grandmother, who was known in her community as Chana *Klapperpantofil*."

Sensing Rabbi Wolpin's curiosity and interest, Rabbi Munk proceeded to relate the following noteworthy story.

In the early 1800s, *Rebbetzin* Chana Munk lived in a small town outside Danzig together with her husband, Rabbi Michael Leib Munk, who was the *Rav* in the community. The *Rebbetzin*, a very caring woman, was always attentive to the needs of the Jewish citizenry. In this town as in every other neighborhood, funds were constantly needed for the indigent. To meet this necessity, *Rebbetzin* Munk would walk around the town and its environs almost daily, collecting charity for the needy.

Everyone knew how dedicated and devoted she was, and hardly anyone ever refused her requests for funds. She would knock on a door and if the people living in the house were home, they would slide open a wooden slat in the door to see who was there. When they realized it was *Rebbetzin* Chana Munk, they would let her in and give her a contribution.

One day it occurred to the *Rebbetzin* that very few people ever declined to give her money. Everyone always seemed to donate something when she approached them. Perhaps, she thought, people feel pressured to contribute because it was the *Rav's* wife who was collecting. In a sense, then, she was taking money from people who might really not want to give it.

Rebbetzin Munk wanted to alleviate whatever shame or discomfort might be felt by any person who was not able or did not wish to give her charity, for whatever reason. She therefore bought a pair of heavy wooden clogs and wore them every time she went collecting. The shoes would make loud thumping noises as they struck the cobblestones of the streets. Thus, as she would approach a home, its inhabitants knew even before she knocked on the door, by virtue of her creative and clever method of announcing herself, that it was *Rebbetzin* Munk outside. This way, anyone who did not wish to donate charity at that particular time would simply not come to the door, and after a few moments she would leave. She lovingly became known as *Chana Klapperpantofil*, German for "noisemaking house shoes."

In 1841, on her seventieth birthday, *Rebbetzin* Chana "*Klapper-pantofil*" Munk was presented with a silver *pushka* honoring her noble work. It was this precious commemorative *pushka* that R' Munk displayed in his home in Brooklyn.

The *pushka* has become a family heirloom. When Rabbi Michael Munk, the gentleman who told this story, passed away, the *pushka* was given to his daughter, Mrs. Chana (Munk) Mandelbaum of Philadelphia, who was born on the *yahrtzeit* of her illustrious great-great-grandmother and was therefore named after her.

> Unsung acts of kindness and sensitivity performed without pretensions indicate people of true eminence. *Klal Yisrael* has these types of people in every generation. It is not easy to find them, but the search is well worth the effort, for it is these wonderful people who are truly worthy of emulation.

✑§ Understood in a Different Vein

> I recently had the opportunity to spend time with Rabbi Moshe Mordechai Shulsinger of Bnei Brak, Israel, a prominent *talmid chacham* and the author of numerous popular *sefarim*. Among the stories he was kind enough to share with me from his seemingly endless flowing fountain of narratives, was this precious gem.

It happened one time that the Amshinover *Rebbe*, Rabbi Mayer Kalisch (1901-1976) who lived in Bayit Vegan, Jerusalem, was very ill and had to be taken to a hospital. While there, he was given a blood transfusion. A *yeshivah bachur* (young student) who heard about this went to a friend and neighbor of the *Rebbe*, Rabbi Yechezkel Abramsky (1886-1976), who was the *Rosh Yeshivah* of the Slabodka Yeshivah in Bnei Brak, and told Rabbi Abramsky that the Amshinover had just been given a transfusion.

Rabbi Abramsky expressed his concern for the welfare of the

Rebbe and then said, "I pray every day that I should not have to be given blood."

The *bachur* seemed perplexed. "When does the *Rosh Yeshivah* say that *tefillah* (prayer)?" he asked.

"We say in *Bircas HaMazon* (Grace after meals), וְנָא אַל תַּצְרִיכֵנוּ ה' אֱלֹקֵינוּ לֹא לִידֵי מַתְּנַת בָּשָׂר וָדָם—And please make us not needful, Hashem our G-d, of the gifts of human hands." The words מַתְּנַת בָּשָׂר וָדָם can also be taken to mean 'the gift of flesh and blood,' causing us to imply in our prayers that we never require either transplant or transfusion.

"But *Rebbe*," the *bachur* protested, "that is not the *pshat* (elementary meaning) of the words!"

He smiled at the boy and offered him an insight worth remembering. "Any time a Jew is pressed by a problem for which he needs Hashem's assistance, he may fit his request for help into the words of his *tefillah*, regardless of whether it is the conventional *pshat* or not. Hashem in Heaven understands his intentions and He will surely be attentive."

It is for this reason, adds Rabbi David Cohen, that it took individuals such as the *Anshei K'nesses HaGedolah* (the Men of the Great Assembly) to write our significant prayers. For it is only their words, written with *ruach hakodesh* (a Divine spirit of holiness), that can encompass all the requests and supplications of mankind.

⊷§ A Plea and a Place

The *Gemara* (*Berachos* 6b) tells us: כָּל הַקּוֹבֵעַ מָקוֹם לִתְפִלָּתוֹ אֱלֹהֵי אַבְרָהָם בְּעֶזְרוֹ — Anyone who sets aside a fixed place for prayer [will merit that] the G-d of Avraham [*Avinu*] will be his helper." The *Gemara* further explains that we know that Avraham *Avinu* had a specific place where he prayed, for the Torah writes (*Bereishis* 19:27): וַיַּשְׁכֵּם אַבְרָהָם בַּבֹּקֶר אֶל הַמָּקוֹם אֲשֶׁר עָמַד שָׁם — Avraham arose [to pray] early the next morning to the place where he had stood."

"The significance of this narrative about Avraham *Avinu*," suggests Rabbi David Cohen, "is that although Avraham *Avinu* was not answered the first time he prayed [for the city of Sodom to be saved from destruction], he still went back to pray at the same place where he had prayed before. The fact that his request had been rejected did not cause him to try a different approach, perhaps praying at another place. Rather, he demonstrated a faith and a trust in Hashem by continuing to pray in the same manner and at the same place as he did the day before."

This, perhaps, is one of the virtues of having a specific, set place for *davening* rather than hopping from one *shul* to the next, or even from one place to another within the same *shul*. [See *Rabbeinu Yonah* ד"ה כל, and *Shiltei Giborim* (on *Berachos* 6b)]. It shows Hashem that all our prayers are directed to Him in the same manner, with the same intensity, with the same loyalty — regardless of whether the prayers are responded to, or not.

❀ ❀ ❀

In this light, an anecdote told by Rabbi Avraham Kabalkin of *Morasha L'Hanchil* in Jerusalem is noteworthy.

A man once approached the Ponevezher *Rav*, Rabbi Yosef Kahaneman (1886-1969), and complained (in Yiddish), *"Ich daven tzu der Ribono Shel Olam, und Ehr enfert nisht.* (I have been *davening* to Hashem and He doesn't answer me.)"

The Ponevezher *Rav* thought for a moment, then he replied in Yiddish, *"Ehr enfert: 'Nisht!'* (He is answering: 'No!')"

Just because our requests are not granted does not mean Hashem has not heard our prayers. He indeed has heard them; however, for reasons that only He knows, He has decided that what truly is best for us at this particular moment is that our request be shelved. We must then continue to pray.

May we come to know His ways.

⋑§ A Tallis Travelogue

The time, effort and significance that parents lavish on *mitzvos* and *minhagim* leave indelible impressions on their children. Dovid *HaMelech* wrote (*Tehillim* 126:5): "הַזּרְעִים בְּדִמְעָה בְּרִנָּה יִקְצֹרוּ — Those who plant with tears will reap with song." This story, told by Rabbi Mordechai Schwab, the *Mashgiach* of Yeshiva Beis Shraga in Monsey, New York, is a case in point. The incident involved a prominent, prosperous German Jew who lived in Lucerne, Switzerland, whom Rabbi Schwab knew very well.

R' Zevulun* was in the sewing accessory business. When his son Daniel became seventeen years of age, he was brought into the family business. Daniel was blessed with a keen, enterprising mind, and within a short time he was being given great responsibility on the job.

As Daniel grew older he began to take business trips for his father. These usually were one-day excursions, and he would usually manage to be home the same evening. One day R' Zevulun asked him to travel to Locarno, a small town in the Italian part of Switzerland, to clinch an important business deal. The journey itself would take more than five hours, and the plan was for Daniel to remain in Locarno for a week.

The morning after Daniel left, R' Zevulun happened to go to his son's room, where he noticed that Daniel's *tallis* was still on the shelf. The German custom is for young men, even before they are married (and some even before they are *bar mitzvah*), to wear a *tallis* for *davening* every morning. (See *Orach Chaim* 8:2, *Mishnah Berurah* 4.)

R' Zevulun realized that Daniel had taken his *tefillin* but had left his *tallis* behind. He could not be sure whether the *tallis* had been forgotten inadvertently or intentionally. On the one hand, Daniel could have overlooked the *tallis* because his mind was preoccupied

---

* Names in this story have been changed at the request of the family.

with remembering to pack his business material. On the other hand, he had taken his *tefillin*, so it was possible that he had deliberately neglected to take the *tallis* because he accorded the custom little significance — for only German and Sephardic young men wear *talleisim* before they are married, whereas the rest of *Klal Yisrael* does not.

R' Zevulun made arrangements for someone to tend his business, then caught a train and made the same long, five-hour trip that his son had made the day before. He went to the hotel where his son was staying and knocked on his door. Daniel was startled to see his father.

"Father, is everything all right at home?" Daniel asked.

"Yes, my son, everything is fine," replied R' Zevulun. "I came here because it seems you may have forgotten something. Can you remember what it was?" R' Zevulun asked.

"No, not really," Daniel stammered. He could not imagine why his father had taken such a long, arduous trip. "Did I forget to take some of the important samples or some of the vital papers?" he asked.

"No, not quite," said R' Zevulun. "I believe you forgot your *tallis!*"

Daniel was embarrassed. Indeed, he had forgotten his *tallis* at home. "I can't believe you made this whole trip just to bring me the *tallis*," Daniel said in amazement.

The father handed over the *tallis*, kissed his son good-bye and returned at once to the train station for his ride back home to Lucerne.

❦ ❦ ❦

Years later, Rabbi Schwab told this incredible story to the *Mashgiach* in the Kamenitzer Yeshivah, Rabbi Naftali Zev Leibowitz [(1890-1954) a brother-in-law of Rabbi Baruch Ber Leibowitz]. When he finished the story, Rabbi Schwab commented, "Isn't it remarkable that a man would make a trip like that just for a *tallis?*"

"You have it wrong," answered the *Mashgiach*. "R' Zevulun did not make that trip for the *tallis*. He made the trip for generations!

Not one of his descendants will ever forget the *minhag* of the *tallis.*"

❁ ❁ ❁

As I was completing my research for this story I was privileged to speak with one of R' Daniel's grandsons, who is today a *Mashgiach* in a major *yeshivah.* "I can't say if what I am about to tell you has any relevance," he said, "but a number of years ago my grandfather returned from a trip to Israel with gifts for his grandchildren. He bought each of his grandsons the same gift — a *tallis.*"

> May the toil of all parents merit a harvest of blessing in their children and grandchildren.

✍§ *A Visa and a Master*

The Gemara (*Avodah Zarah* 17b) notes that when Rav Chanina Ben Teradyon and Rav Elazar ben Parta were seized by the Roman authorities for defying governmental edicts prohibiting them from teaching Torah in public, the two *tannaim* worriedly discussed their future. Rav Chanina ben Teradyon said to Rav Elazar ben Parta, "You are more fortunate than I, because although they arrested you on five counts and me on only one, you have the merit of *gemilus chassadim* (acts of kindness) to go along with your merit of Torah study. I merely have the merit of Torah study and that will not be enough to save me."

The Chofetz Chaim in his *sefer Ahavas Chessed* (2:4) writes that for an individual to merit that Hashem protect him from any tragedy he must fulfill his potential not only in Torah study but in *chessed* as well. Obviously every person has a different level he can reach and it is the duty of each one of us to strive to attain that plane.

In the following story, first told to me by R' Meir Zlotowitz, founder of ArtScroll/Mesorah publications, we witness a world renowned *gadol b'Torah* striving to achieve magnificence in *chessed*. The story was retold to me in detail by both Rabbi Zevulun Schwartzman and Rabbi Yankel (Kviat) Perach from Jerusalem. Rabbi Alter Pekier provided important background information.

In 1985 when Rabbi Zevulun Schwartzman, the grandson of Rabbi Aharon Kotler was sitting *shivah* for his mother (*Rebbetzin* Sarah Pesha, the daughter of R' Aharon), many of the people who came to be *menachem avel* related stories of the esteemed Kotler family, particularly episodes about R' Aharon. An older gentleman was sitting among the group listening intently. Suddenly he spoke up, "You are all talking about R' Aharon's *gadlus* (greatness) and *gaonus* (brilliance) in learning but let me tell you what kind of *mensch* R' Aharon was."

The gentleman, Rabbi Yankel (Kviat) Perach from Givat Mordechai in Jerusalem, then went on to tell this amazing story.

❀　❀　❀

At the end of 1940 the world of *yeshivah bachurim*, particularly those who had learned in Kletzk, Poland, where R' Aharon was the *Rosh Yeshivah*, was in turmoil. A month after the Germans invaded Poland in September of 1939, R' Aharon and his talmidim fled Kletzk and took up residence in Vilna, then under Lithuanian control, at the behest of Rabbi Chaim Ozer Grodzensky.

Vilna was at the time, a haven for *yeshivah bachurim* from the great *yeshivos* in Lithuania and central Poland such as Mir, Kamenitz, Radin, Grodno and Bialystok. (See page 93.) After a short time, R' Aharon, wishing that his students not be distracted by the hustle and bustle of the big city, moved the yeshivah to a small town (on the highway between Kovno and Riga) named Yanova.

Everyone feared that the Russians would soon invade Lithuania and when they would, the Jews in the country would be trapped. Thousands of people were trying desperately to get visas, certificates or immigration papers so that could safely and legally escape from Lithuania. When Soviet tanks rolled into Lithuania in June of 1940, people became even more frantic in their attempts to get out.

It did not take long for Russian authorities to crack down on *yeshivos* in Lithuania, and they soon demanded that R' Aharon's *yeshivah* in Yanova disperse. The *yeshivah* divided into three groups. R' Aharon himself went with a group to the Latvian town of Salock. Yankel Kviat from Piesk (known as Yankel Pieskover) was in the second group which settled with the *Mashgiach* (dean of students), R' Yosef Leib Nenedick, ten miles west of Salock in Dushat, and a third group of older *bachurim* established themselves in Dukst.

Yankel wanted to leave the country as soon as he could. He ran from embassy to embassy trying to get an exit permit but to no avail. Embassies were closing, the lines at those that remained open were impossibly long and no *yeshivah bachurim* (except those of the Mirrer Yeshivah) believed that the Japanese visas for sale were worth anything.

Yankel made his way to the British embassy and procured a letter stating that they might possibly grant him a visa. He was buoyed by the letter and began making plans to leave the country. However, a few days later the embassy closed and he was left holding a letter that had little, if any, value. Still he thought that he would make his way to Memel, the Baltic seaport, and from there try to make his way out of the country.

He went to Salock to say goodbye to his *Rosh Yeshivah*, R' Aharon. R' Aharon was aghast that Yankel would try and get out on the basis of that worthless piece of paper. "If they catch you in the port with this letter they will ship you to Siberia for attempting to escape illegally. What you are holding is insufficient. They won't give you permission to leave. You need other documents. Do not take a chance," the *Rosh Yeshivah* insisted, "stay and try something else."

But Yankel was frightened and overwrought with terror. Under no circumstances did he wish to stay in Lithuania. "I have been told that there is a chance that papers may be waiting for me at the port. I realize it is a small chance but it is the only chance I have."

R' Aharon was adamant. "It is not worth the chance," he said.

"They can cart you off to Siberia and then who knows how long you will be there? Who can even be sure that you will get out alive?"

Yankel Kviat was determined and no one was going to stop him. Realizing that, the *Rosh Yeshivah* gave Yankel a *berachah* and wished him well.

Yankel took a bus in Salock for the long ride to the train station in Kovno where he attempted to purchase a ticket to Memel. The mob scene in Kovno was stifling as the terminal was in pandemonium. Everyone was trying either to get information on scheduled departures, say tearful goodbyes to family and friends, or get a ticket and a place on the next train out. Somehow, Yankel managed to get a space on the train to Memel. In his heart he knew that the trip to Memel might be his last ride in freedom. The next few hours would be harrowing.

It was now hours after he met with his *Rosh Yeshivah* but that did not stop R' Aharon. Shortly after Yankel had left Salock, R' Aharon himself made the same long trip and was now at the train station frantically looking for Yankel Pieskover. R' Aharon was yelling at the top of his lungs, "Yankel, Yankel Pieskover. . .Yankel Kviat. . .Yankel!"

R' Aharon ran through the lines searching for his *talmid*, his eyes darting in every direction scrutinizing the throngs as he kept calling out "Yankel!" From booth to booth and from line to line R' Aharon unabashedly screamed, "Yankel Pieskover, Yankel Kviat. . ."

People were already getting on the train. R' Aharon realized that Yankel could very well have gotten on already. If Yankel didn't make the train, R' Aharon reasoned, he could always search for him after the train left, but once the train pulled away, with Yankel on it, it would be too late.

R' Aharon ran towards the train and began banging on the windows, calling out, "Yankel, Yankel Kviat," as he knocked on each one of them. As his fist hammered on a window, the people inside turned to see who was pounding so hard. Rav Aharon ignored all the stares and incredulous looks of the passengers and kept running along the stationary train banging on every window as he made his way towards the front car. Finally, as he pounded on one of the windows he caught the attention of Yankel Kviat.

From inside the train, Yankel ran towards the window and called out, "*Rosh Yeshivah*, why are you here? What is the matter?"

R' Aharon held up a paper and said, "*Zorgt zach nisht* (Don't worry), Yankel, *zorgt zach nisht*" R' Aharon screamed over the din, "You may go in *simchah* (with happiness). After you left, a telegram came saying that papers will indeed be waiting for you at the port! Make sure to ask for your visa. *Fuhr l'chaim u'l'shalom* (go in life and peace)."

❈   ❈   ❈

Now at the home of R' Zevulun Schwartzman, Rabbi Yankel (Kviat) Perach turned to his spellbound audience and said, "R' Aharon in his greatness understood that my long trip to Memel would be filled with fear and worry. By the time I was on the way to Kovno he knew very well that a visa and immigration papers would be waiting for me and that I would be able to leave the country legally. But in his great kindness and consideration R' Aharon didn't want me to suffer those hours of anxiety on the train and so he made the trip from Salock to Kovno himself just to find me and reassure me not to worry."

R' Yankel shook his head in disbelief as he relived that scene once again. "R' Aharon was truly a *gadol*," he said. "No smaller a *gadol* in *chessed* than a *gadol* in Torah."

◄§ A Foundation in Yiddishkeit

Rabbi Elchanan Zohn of Kew Gardens, New York, director of the *Chevra Kadisha* (Burial Society) in Queens, and a recognized authority in his field, has lectured extensively on the dignity and holiness involved in the *mitzvah* of *kavod hames* (honor to the deceased), and has been instrumental in the formation of local *Chevra Kadisha* societies in accordance with *halachah*. The following story is one that he tells often. Its lesson is applicable to all *mitzvos*.

R abbi Alexander Ziskind from Horodna, Lithuania (1740 - 1794), author of *Yesod V'Shoresh HaAvodah*, was known for his great piety and for the passion and intensity with which he performed every *mitzvah*. In his *sefer* he outlined in great detail the intentions one should have during every part of the *davening*. In addition, he dealt with the attitude one should have towards food and its consumption, the holiness of Shabbos and the solemn days of *Elul*. He also presented his perspective on the various stages of the Jewish calendar year. Much of what the *Yesod V'Shoresh HaAvodah* wrote is based on *kabbalah* (the mystical literature of Judaism such as the *Zohar* and the writings of the *Arizal*).

Rabbi Alexander Ziskind also wrote a very lengthy (forty-six chapter) ethical will to his family, in which he described his punctiliousness in his adherence to *mitzvos*. In a loving manner he exhorted his family to follow in his ways. Furthermore, he wrote a will to be given to the *Chevra Kadisha* containing exact orders in regard to the handling of his body after death, the burial process and the set of prayers to be recited at his funeral. He specified what may and may not be said at his eulogy, and gave directions as to what should and should not be written on his tombstone.

One of the items mentioned in his will to the *Chevra Kadisha* baffled its members. He wrote that he wanted to be buried in a *tallis* on which there were valid *tzitzis* that a *talmid chacham* (Torah scholar) had made. This is in direct contrast to the generally accepted custom among *Klal Yisrael* which is that when a Jewish man is buried, he is interred in his *tallis* with the *tzitzis* intentionally made defective (See *Rama, Yoreh Deah* 351:2).

The *Chevra Kadisha* brought this question before the *Chamudei Daniel*, R' Daniel of Horodna, the *Rav* and *posek* of the town, who ruled that no one should tamper with anything that the eminent *tzaddik* desired. Undoubtedly, the *Yesod V'Shoresh HaAvodah* had his reasons for requesting to be buried with kosher *tzitzis*, and so the *Chamudei Daniel* ruled that the *Yesod V'Shoresh*

HaAvodah should be buried with his *tallis* and its *tzitzis* intact. [See *Tosefos Bava Basra* 74a ד״ה פסקי.])

After the crowded funeral, those carrying the body (who had been instructed to immerse themselves in a *mikveh* beforehand) began to lower the remains of the *tzaddik* into his grave. As they did so, an incredible thing happened. One of the four corners of the *tallis* caught and became entangled on a piece of stone jutting out from the side of the newly dug grave. Before anyone realized it, the *tzitzis* from one corner of the *tallis* ripped off and remained dangling on the rock — thereby invalidating the *tallis*!

In the ensuing commotion the people once again sought out the *Chamudei Daniel* for advice. "This," he said, "is obviously a sign from Heaven."

The people of Horodna then buried the great *tzaddik* with a renewed respect for the rituals of *Klal Yisrael* as they realized that it was the custom that had remained intact, and not the *tallis*.

Thus, in his passing, the *Yesod V'Shoresh HaAvodah* was instrumental in teaching people one more thing — the veracity of that which *Tosefos* in *Menachos* (20b ד״ה נפסל) writes "מִנְהָג אֲבוֹתֵנוּ תּוֹרָה הִיא — The custom of our forefathers is [as binding] as the Torah itself."

✑§ Ripples

No one lives in a vacuum. Everything we do and say can have an effect on someone else, even though we may not realize it. This was always the case, and in our era of worldwide instant communication it is even more so. Since one can never know what effect his actions or inactions will have, it pays to take into consideration our every word and deed.

A recent incident, in which I was only peripherally involved, demonstrates the ripple effect of a man's deeds.

A while ago, a young couple with no real religious commitment called me to their "out-of-town" community to perform the *bris* of their first son. The child was born on a Thursday morning and thus, the *bris* should have been scheduled to take place on the eighth day, the following Thursday.

On the phone, however, the mother of the child explained that she wished to have the *bris* delayed until the following Sunday, which would be the eleventh day. Although I tried to explain to her the importance of having a *bris* done on its proper day (the eighth day after the child's birth), she said that because her family could not come in the middle of the week, and because she had just experienced a difficult childbirth, having the *bris* on Sunday would be more convenient.

"Besides everything else," she added, "I am not religious. Having the *bris* a few days later doesn't bother me or my husband."

I saw that I could not convince her to change her mind, so I began to give her a list of items to prepare for the *bris*. Near the end of our conversation I asked her how, so far from New York City, she had gotten my name.

"Oh, I have a very religious cousin, Rabbi Yoel Gartner,* who lives in your neighborhood," she said. "He told me months ago that if I had a boy I should call you."

"Do you realize," I said, "that if Rabbi Gartner knew that his cousin was having the *bris* delayed merely for the sake of convenience he would feel very badly about it?"

She was surprised by that. "Do you really think it would make a difference to him?" she asked.

When I assured her that it would, she decided that in deference to him and out of respect to all that he stands for she would relent and have the *bris* on Thursday — the proper day.

I was positive that when I came that Thursday to perform the *bris*, Rabbi Gartner would be there. He wasn't.

The following Shabbos, when I saw Rabbi Gartner at *Minchah*, I told him that I was surprised not to have seen him at the *bris* the past week.

---

* Name has been changed by personal request.

"What *bris?*" he asked.

"You don't know?" I replied. "Your second cousin had a boy and they even told me that you were the one who told them to call me."

Rabbi Gartner just shrugged and smiled. "That was months ago," he said.

"Don't you realize," I said to Rabbi Gartner, "that when you eventually stand before Hashem on your final Day of Judgment, He will mete out reward to you for a *bris* that was done on the eighth day — and you won't know what He is talking about."

"I have no idea what *you* are talking about," Rabbi Gartner exclaimed in exasperation.

I recounted the whole episode to him and told him that only in deference to his being an observant Jew did his second cousins even consider having the *bris* on time. It seems, though, that the family decided to make a very small gathering and called only a few of the relatives. Being a second cousin, Rabbi Gartner wasn't called. However, even though he had known nothing about it, his being an observant Jew had caused the *mitzvah* to be done properly and therefore the merit of having the *bris* performed on time will surely be his.

Thus, like widening ripples in a pond caused by a pebble flung on its surface, the effects of good deeds (and, unfortunately of bad ones as well) spread far beyond their immediate arena.

Rabbi Moshe Feinstein (1895-1986) once asked, "We say in our daily morning prayers, 'וְתֵן בְּלִבֵּנוּ בִּינָה לְהָבִין וּלְהַשְׂכִּיל לִשְׁמוֹעַ לִלְמוֹד וּלְלַמֵּד לִשְׁמוֹר וְלַעֲשׂוֹת וּלְקַיֵּם אֶת כָּל דִּבְרֵי תַלְמוּד תּוֹרָתֶךָ בְּאַהֲבָה — Instill understanding in our hearts, so that we may understand and elucidate [Your Torah], to listen, learn, teach, safeguard, perform and fulfill all the words of Your Torah's teaching with love.' Each of us," said R' Moshe, "has the opportunity every day לִלְמוֹד, to learn [Torah], and לְקַיֵּם, to fulfill [*mitzvos*], but where do we have the daily opportunity לְלַמֵּד, to teach? Most of us are not teachers.

"The answer is," continued R' Moshe, "that we do indeed teach others every day — by our example. What we do and say instructs others, for good or for bad, whether we realize it or not."

Perhaps, then, there can be a new understanding of the well-known Talmudic teaching (*Pirkei Avos* 4:2), "מִצְוָה גּוֹרֶרֶת מִצְוָה — One *mitzvah* leads to another *mitzvah.*" It is not merely that the performance of one *mitzvah* mitigates the *Yetzer Hara* somewhat so that the performance of another *mitzvah* will be more easily forthcoming on the heels of the first one, but also, the performance of a *mitzvah* by one person will eventually lead to the doing of another *mitzvah* by another person.

Our words and deeds — whether at home or in the office, in the presence of family or co-workers (religious and not religious) — always set an example.

⋖§ Respect, Reverence and Reward

Seemingly insignificant acts are often more meritorious than they appear to be. *Chazal* (*Midrash Rabbah Ruth* 2:9) teach that because Eglon, the king of *Moav,* rose from his throne as a sign of respect when the *shofeit* (judge) *Ehud* told him that he had a message for him from Hashem (*Shoftim* 3:20), Eglon merited the reward of having, as one of his descendants, Ruth, the great-grandmother of David *HaMelech* (see *Rashi,* ibid.).

Similarly, Nebuchadnezzar, the murderous Babylonian king, was rewarded with victory in his attempt to destroy the first *Beis HaMikdash* for having taken three steps in honor of Hashem (see *Sanhedrin* 96a). [Interestingly, one of the reasons that we take three steps backward at the end of *Shemoneh Esrei* and then pray for the rebuilding of the *Beis HaMikdash* is to negate the effect of Nebuchadnezzar's three steps forward in homage to Hashem (see *Maharsha, Sanhedrin* 96a and *Mishnah Berurah Orach Chaim* 123 note 2).]

Every act a man does is weighed and accounted for in the Heavenly Courts in accordance with his station in life. What is his background? Should he have known better? Could he have known better? Was his deed routine or extraordinary? No two people are judged identically, and only Hashem in His infinite wisdom can be the final Judge.

In light of the aforementioned, we can appreciate all the more the following story, told by Rabbi Shimon Goldstein of Brooklyn, regarding an insight he gleaned from Rabbi Yitzchak Hutner (1904-1980), *Rosh Yeshivah* of Yeshivah Rabbi Chaim Berlin.

In May of 1973 Rabbi Hutner had to travel from Brooklyn to the Bronx to attend the *bris* of a son of one of his *talmidim*. Rabbi Shimon Goldstein, who was then learning in the *beis hamidrash* of Yeshivah Rabbi Chaim Berlin, arranged for a taxi to take the *Rosh Yeshivah*, and together they traveled to the *bris*.

When both Rabbi Hutner and Rabbi Goldstein noticed the driver's identity plate which had his name, Sol Yanofsky,* in bold letters, they understood that he was Jewish. Meanwhile, in the front seat, the cab driver realized that one of his passengers was a prominent rabbi. Without saying a word he reached over to the right, picked up a cap and, as an act of respect, covered his bare head.

Rabbi Hutner turned to R' Shimon and said to him in Hebrew so that the driver would not understand, "מִי יוֹדֵעַ כַּמָּה עוֹלָם הַבָּא יֵשׁ לוֹ עַל תְּנוּעָה זוֹ — Who knows how much *Olam Haba* (merit in the World to Come) he will get for this act."

R' Shimon was surprised by the *Rosh Yeshivah's* comment, for he didn't think that putting on a cap in the presence of the *Rosh Yeshivah* was an act of such great significance.

"Does it merit *Olam Haba?*" R' Shimon asked.

"Let me tell you a story," the *Rosh Yeshivah* replied. "The *Chidushei HaRim*, Rabbi Yitzchak Mayer Alter (1789-1866), used to go to the *mikveh* (ritual bath) every day. However, he never took the shortest route to the *mikveh*. Instead, every day he would take a long, roundabout way to reach his destination. For a while his *shammash* (attendant) did not inquire about it until finally one day he became so curious that he did indeed ask the *Rebbe* why he purposely seemed to go the long way to get to the *mikveh*.

" 'I'll tell you,' said the *Chidushei HaRim*. 'When we go this way, we pass the station where Jewish porters unload the heavy packages

---

* Actual name has been changed.

for travelers. These porters are very simple non-religious people. They do not *daven*, nor do they learn Torah. However, when they see me, they stop what they are doing, straighten up and call to each other, "Reb Itcha Myer is coming! The *Rebbe*, Reb Itcha Myer, is coming!"

" 'As I pass by they nod their heads respectfully and acknowledge my presence. For this (their display of *kavod HaTorah*) they will get *Olam Haba*. I know they have no other way of earning it, so I walk this way every day to give them that opportunity!' "

We must not underestimate the small acts we do, nor the seemingly simple acts that others do. But aside from that, is not the *Chidushei HaRim's ahavas Yisrael* (love of fellow Jews) remarkable in that he gave Jews (even non-observant ones) the opportunity to gain *Olam Haba*?

◆§ *Relatively Speaking*

The *Gemara* (*Berachos* 5b) describes the unique manner in which R' Yochanan would console mourners. When he visited mourners during the week of *shivah* (the seven days of mourning) and realized they were overcome with grief, he would show them something that he kept with himself at all times. It was a bone of his son, the tenth to pass away in his lifetime. In essence, he was telling the mourner that he too had suffered greatly, perhaps even more than the mourner himself, having tragically lost ten of his children.

In his compassion for his fellow Jews, R' Yochanan took his personal tragedy and turned it into a lesson of acceptance and understanding.

In this remarkable story retold by Rabbi Hershel Leiner of Monsey, New York, we witness a *Rebbe's* empathy for another person's calamity.

In 1979 Rabbi Shneur Kotler (1918-1982), the *Rosh Yeshivah* of Beth Medrash Govoha in Lakewood, New Jersey, suffered a great personal loss. His beloved son R' Meir passed away after a long and painful illness, leaving behind a wife and a small child. R' Shneur was devastated. R' Meir was known as an exceptional *talmid chacham* (Torah scholar), with a bright future ahead of him.

Now, as R' Shneur sat *shivah* in his home in Lakewood, hundreds of people came daily to console both him and his bereaved family, but he was inconsolable.

One afternoon, the Bluzhover Rebbe, R' Yisrael Spira (1889-1989), came to be *menachem avel* (comfort the mourners). As the *Rebbe* made his way into the room, the thick crowd of people assembled there pressed back like a human wall, making a path for the *Rebbe* to walk up front to where R' Shneur was sitting.

The *Rebbe* sat down and at once recognized R' Shneur's intense anguish. "*Rosh Yeshivah*," he began, "I am jealous of you."

The gathered crowd had been hushed so that they could hear the words of these two great Torah sages. However, what they heard from the *Rebbe* shocked them. R' Shneur didn't reply, and so the *Rebbe* said those same words again, this time wistfully and sadly, "*Rosh Yeshivah*, I am jealous of you."

R' Shneur's head perked up. Surely the *Rebbe* couldn't be serious. How could anyone be envious of a father who had recently buried a grown child? Obviously the Bluzhover *Rebbe* had a message in mind, but no one could imagine what he intended.

The *Rebbe* continued. "*Rosh Yeshivah*, you should know that I once had a beautiful daughter. She herself had a daughter, but both were taken from me during the terrible period of the Holocaust. They were both killed, but I have no idea where or when. I have no *yahrtzeit* for my daughter, I can never visit her grave, nor do I have any living reminder of her. You at least have a *yahrtzeit* to commemorate, you at least will have a gravesite to visit, you have grandchildren from whom you will have *nachas* (pride). I have none of these."

❦   ❦   ❦

A few days later, when the *shivah* was over, R' Shneur made it a point to call the *Rebbe*. "You gave me a perspective to live with," he told the *Rebbe*. "My attitude changed from the moment you uttered those words. I thank you for coming."

And then two anguished yet uplifted hearts bid each other farewell.

ᴥᙢ Support System

The *Gemara* (*Berachos* 6b) extols the virtue of a person having a set and steady place for *tefillah*. R' Huna teaches (ibid.): "Anyone who sets aside a fixed place for prayer [will merit that] the G-d of Avraham [*Avinu*] will be his helper (see p. 146)."

In the following interesting episode we learn of the novel assessment made by the famous *Rav* of Jerusalem, Rabbi Shmuel Salant (1816-1909), regarding the system of priorities in a particular place of prayer.

In Jerusalem there were two individuals who *davened* in the same *shul*, Adas Yerei'im.* One of them, R' Yaakov, *davened* in the Adas Yerei'im *shul* every day of the week but *davened* elsewhere on Shabbos. The second gentleman, R' Binyamin, *davened* in the Adas Yerei'im *shul* only on Shabbos, but *davened* elsewhere throughout the week.

One day both R' Yaakov and R' Binyamin realized that they had *yahrtzeit* coming up on the following Tuesday. Customarily, one who has *yahrtzeit* is given the opportunity to "*daven* before the *amud*" (lead the services) so that the response by the congregants (of "*Amen*" [to all the blessings], and "*Amen*" and "*Yehei Shemei Rabbah*" in *Kaddish*), elicited by the *chazzan*, may be of benefit to the soul of the deceased.

Both R' Yaakov and R' Binyamin wanted to "*daven* before the *amud*" on that Tuesday, and each of them felt strongly that he had

---

* Name of the *shul* has been changed.

precedence over the other. R' Yaakov argued that since he *davened* in the Adas Yerei'im *shul* during the week, he had priority, while R' Binyamin contended that since he *davened* there on Shabbos, it was "his" *shul* and therefore he had priority even during the week.

Wishing to settle this dilemma they went to Rabbi Shmuel Salant for his decision.

Rabbi Shmuel Salant listened to both sides and announced that R' Binyamin, who *davened* in the *shul* every Shabbos, had priority even during midweek.

"My reasoning is as follows," explained the great sage. "Those who support the *shul* have precedence when it comes to 'davening before the *amud*.' "Those who *daven* in a *shul* on Shabbos and *Yom Tov* support it, while those who *daven* there merely on weekdays don't support it financially. Therefore they must give way to those who do."

When I recently told this story to a noted *rav,* he said wistfully, "Today, even those who *daven* in a *shul* on Friday nights don't support it. It is mainly the Shabbos morning people who do."

Is a check of our support system in order?

⪰ Signs of Eminence

The *Gemara* (*Shabbos* 130a) recounts a remarkable incident involving a pious man named Elisha. It seems that Elisha, unlike others who were afraid, defied the Roman authorities who decreed that any Jew caught wearing *tefillin* on his head would be killed. Elisha boldly disregarded this threat and bravely wore his *tefillin* in public.

One day a Roman officer spotted Elisha wearing his *tefillin*. Realizing that he had been seen, Elisha began to run away, but the officer gave chase and caught up with him. Elisha snatched the *tefillin* off his head and covered them with both hands.

"Open your hands," demanded the officer, "and show me what you are carrying!"

"I am carrying a dove," said Elisha.

"Release your grip," the officer ordered.

The *Gemara* relates that miraculously, when Elisha opened his hands, a bird flew from his outstretched fingers.

From then on he was referred to as Elisha *Baal Kenafayim* (Elisha, man of wings), an eternal tribute to his commitment to this sacred *mitzvah*.*

In our era, too, there lived a pious Jew with an extraordinary commitment to the hallowed *mitzvah* of *tefillin*. In life's most dire circumstances, he risked his life so that he and others like him could observe this daily *mitzvah*.

His story was retold by family members who rightfully regard their relative with awe, as should we.

In 1940 R' Binyamin Schachner (see page 178) was hauled from his home in the small town of Susnofsza, Poland to the first of seven concentration camps he was eventually to be in. Among the few possessions that he managed to take along with him were his *tefillin*. R' Binyamin always kept a close watch on his *tefillin*, shielding and safeguarding them as though they were his life's greatest treasure. Every day, when he was sure that none of the Nazi guards were looking, he would remove the *tefillin* from their hiding place, don them on his hand and head and say the *Shema Yisrael*. Others in his barracks, inspired by his actions, would borrow the *tefillin* and do the same.

R' Binyamin was transferred from concentration camp to concentration camp until he was eventually brought to a slave labor camp in Markstadt. Aside from the toil demanded and torture inflicted there daily, this place was an area of such filth and of conditions so inhuman that survival was difficult. Food was scarce and hard to come by and every day Jews perished from disease and starvation.

When he first came to Markstadt, R' Binyamin was confronted by an S.S. guard who demanded to know whether he was a

---

* Indeed, some people are accustomed to wrap the *retzuos* (straps) of their *tefillin shel rosh* over both sides of the *tefillin* (on the *titurah* — the base on which the *tefillin* rests) to resemble the wings of a dove (*Mishnah Berurah Orach Chaim* 28 note 9).

carpenter. Instinctively he replied that he was, although actually he had never built anything in his life except a family. Because he knew that those deemed "useless" were put to death at once, R' Binyamin decided to claim that he was, indeed, handy. In order to survive he would try anything.

It was in the carpenters' woodshed, under a loose floorboard, that R' Binyamin hid his *tefillin* while he was in Markstadt. Throughout the weeks and months of his stay, every day without fail, he and others who dared, would disregard their privation and exhaustion and remove the *tefillin* from under the loose wooden plank. Each man would, in turn, wrap the *tefillin* around his hand and on his head and tearfully say the *Shema Yisrael*, proclaiming, even in this most dire of situations, the uniqueness and Oneness of Hashem and *Klal Yisrael's* devoted loyalty to Him. Then the *tefillin* would be hidden away once again.

One day a particularly vicious S.S. guard walked into the woodshed unexpectedly and saw the *tefillin*. Realizing that this must be a religious item of sorts, he began to scream in bloodcurdling tones, demanding to know what and whose they were. Frozen with terror, no one dared say a word.

The Nazi began to yell again, this time threatening to kill everyone in the room if he didn't get a reply.

R' Binyamin's words somehow made it out of his throat. "This used to belong to a young boy who died recently," he said softly.

"But if he died, and you all kept these things here, then they belong to you now," the guard retorted in anger. And with that he ordered R' Binyamin to come outside with him.

R' Binyamin had no choice but to obey, for if he didn't comply now he would be killed immediately. Outside, and within the hearing of those inside the shed, the guard began to beat R' Binyamin mercilessly. His screams and cries pierced the hearts of everyone inside until they could stand it no longer. They ran to the barracks' *kapo* (Nazi-appointed leader — who in this case was a Jewish informer) and beseeched him to go out to the Nazi guard and beg for mercy. None of the regular inmates would dare ask the Nazi soldier for a favor; only someone who had the confidence of the oppressors could even make an attempt. R'

Binyamin's friends knew that only the *kapo* could intervene on his behalf.

The *kapo* pleaded with the Nazi guard, who finally agreed to stop beating R' Binyamin. The Nazi then ordered R' Binyamin to march back into the barracks. When he walked in, the others were shocked by his appearance. He was bleeding from multiple body wounds and was clutching his ear. (His hearing was impaired for the rest of his life from that beating.)

The guard ordered that the religious articles be burned at once and he announced that he would be coming back to see that it was in flames.

R' Binyamin didn't say a word to anyone but went right over to the shelf where he had his tools and scraps of wood. He brought them to his workbench and, as fast as he could, he began to carve little square boxes to resemble *tefillin*. He glued the sides together as the others around him watched, astonished by his courage and ingenious idea.

A few men built a fire, and soon the boxes were tossed in. Two people removed their leather belts and threw them into the fire as well, to resemble the *retzuos* (straps) of the *tefillin* that had once again been hidden.

The guard came in, saw the fire, inspected it closely and walked out with a satisfied smile on his devious face. But the *tefillin*, now securely hidden, remained intact. R' Binyamin and his friends cried as they thanked Hashem for this miracle amidst their agony.

R' Binyamin guarded and protected his *tefillin* for the remaining time of his incarceration at Markstadt. When he was finally liberated, his treasured *tefillin* were still intact, and he was able to leave the camp clutching them tightly in his hands.

❈   ❈   ❈

Now, decades later, the precious legacy of R' Binyamin's adherence to the *mitzvah* of *tefillin* lives on. The *tefillin* were recently checked by a *sofer* (scribe) who verified that they are perfectly valid. However, he did advise against their being used on a regular basis. Today, every grandson of R' Binyamin's is given the honor of putting on these extraordinary *tefillin* on the day of his *bar mitzvah*.

Tefillin have always symbolized the boy who becomes a man.
Tefillin in this case symbolize how a man became a legend.

✍§ Table Manners

Rabbi David Leibowitz (1890-1941), founder of the Yeshivah Rabbeinu Yisrael Mayer HaKohen (Chofetz Chaim), was molded in the Slabodka tradition of *mussar* (ethical behavior) which stressed *gadlus ha'adam* — seeing and accentuating the greatness in every person.

Rabbi Abba Zalke Gewirtz of Cleveland, a devoted *talmid* (student) of R' David's, recalls that in one of his early *mussar shmuessen* (discourses) R' David depicted a scene that could occur in any Jewish home, on any Friday night.

"Imagine," said the *Rosh Yeshivah*, "a father and his children coming home from *shul* after they have *davened Kabbalas Shabbos* and *Maariv*. They walk into their home where they are greeted by the rest of the family. The table is bedecked with the glowing Shabbos candles and the sparkling wine which will soon be used for *Kiddush*.

"Everyone gathers around the table, ready to sing the 'Shalom Aleichem' (the greeting to the two angels that escort each person home from *shul* on Friday night). However, as the father of the house takes his place beside his chair, he notices that the decorative *challah* cover is lying flat on the table before him. Someone — either his wife or one of the children — had forgotten to put out the *challos*!

"The father gets angry. 'Who was supposed to bring the *challos* to the table?' he snaps. He then goes on to admonish sarcastically, 'Is this the first time we have made Shabbos in this house?' His wife is embarrassed, the children feel humiliated, and any guests present squirm in their places.

"But what the father doesn't realize," continued R' David, "is that the *challah* cover is beckoning to him with a message of great significance. The *Mishnah Berurah* (*Orach Chaim* 271 note 41, written by Rabbi David Leibowitz's uncle, the Chofetz Chaim) notes that we cover the *challos* 'שֶׁלֹּא יִרְאֶה הַפַּת בִּשְׁתוֹ — so that the bread (*challah*) doesn't see its humiliation.' Customarily, when one is about to eat a meal which will include both wine and bread, the *berachah* on the bread is made first. This is because in the Torah's listing of the Seven Species, wheat is mentioned before wine (see *Devarim* 8:8).

"At the Shabbos table, though, because of the significance of making *Kiddush* on wine, the *berachah* on wine takes precedence over the *berachah* on *challah*. The *challah*, therefore, is covered so that 'it doesn't observe its shame' of being bypassed for the moment.

"But in reality," concluded R' David, "Does a *challah* actually have sensitivities? Does it have feelings? Of course not! Yet *Chazal* instructed us to behave in a manner that conveys consideration and sensitivity to the *challos*. How much more important is it for us to show sensitivity to human beings who do have feelings!

"Thus, the inconsiderate man in denigrating his family members in the presence of the *challah* cover is actually blind to what lies right in front of his eyes."

A Shabbos discipline that merits maintaining all week.

⋙ *Covered*

Rabbi David Cohen of Brooklyn recently recalled a poignant short story he heard years ago from his *Rosh Yeshivah*, Rabbi Yitzchak Hutner (1904-1980).

It seems that when Rabbi Yisrael (Lipkin) Salanter (1809-1883), the father of the *Mussar* (ethical behavior) Movement, passed away, he was just about penniless. He left very few, if any, material possessions to his surviving descendants. There was, though, one man in R' Yisrael's neighborhood who managed to get hold of R' Yisrael's hat.

The hat was old, creased and misshapen from years of wear. Yet this man treasured it and wore it every Shabbos. At first the people in his *shul* paid no attention to the hat, but eventually they began to ridicule him about it.

"How can you wear that thing?" they asked in derision. "It is so dirty, worn and tattered. To wear that hat is a lack of *kavod* (respect for) Shabbos."

The man gazed at these people and replied softly. "Would you grant me that there is a certain 'hidur' (extra refinement) in not speaking *lashon hara* on Shabbos?"

"Yes," they agreed reluctantly. "Not speaking *lashon hara* certainly is a measure of *kavod Shabbos*."

"Then you should know," continued the gentleman, "that when I wear R' Yisrael's hat, I find it impossible to speak a word of *lashon hara!*"

We all acknowledge that we behave differently in the presence of *gedolim* (great Torah scholars). But who would have thought that their garments could have a similar effect? Incredible.

◆§ Learning and Yearning

Chazal (*Shabbos* 31a) tell us that when each of us comes before the Heavenly Court on the ultimate Day of Judgment, we will be asked numerous questions about our behavior in this world. One of the questions will be, "צִפִּיתָ לִישׁוּעָה — Did you hope for the Salvation?" This is a reference to one's longing for *Mashiach*.

One must wonder: Doesn't every Jew hope for *Mashiach*? Why is there the need for such a query? The sad fact is that not every Jew awaits *Mashiach*. Rabbi Chazkel Levenstein (1885-1974), the world-renowned *Mashgiach* of the Ponevezher

Yeshivah in Bnei Brak, Israel, points out (see *Ohr Yechezkel*, Vol. 3, p. 288) that one of the reasons that Hashem brought the plague of darkness on the Egyptians (*Shemos* 10:22) was so that the Egyptians should not see how thousands of Jews died and were buried.

These Jews died because they did not want to leave Egypt. They had achieved wealth and glory and saw no value in redemption from Egypt. For this they were punished and were not allowed to leave the land of slavery. (See *Shemos Rabbah* 14:3.) "It will be the same," says R' Chazkel, "at the final Redemption and the coming of *Mashiach*. Only those who really desire it will merit it."

And so the question asked by the Heavenly Court is indeed valid. We will be asked whether we felt so comfortable, and were filled with such a sense of security, that our longing for *Mashiach* was just a passing fancy — if even that.

The following touching episode, which highlights an individual's yearning for *Mashiach*, was told by Rabbi Nisson Wolpin, editor of *The Jewish Observer*. He witnessed it first hand during his tenure as Learning Director in Camp Munk, a summer camp for boys in Ferndale, New York.

Every day of the summer, the boys in Camp Munk attend learning groups. Small clusters of boys are taught by one of the special *rebbeim* (teachers) on staff.

In one particular group there was a young boy who daydreamed through each class and never seemed to pay attention to the subject being studied. After a few weeks the *rebbi* abandoned his efforts to get the boy involved in what was going on. From then on, as long as the child wasn't disruptive he was left alone.

One day the *rebbi* was teaching the section of *Gemara* in *Masechta Sukkah* (41a) that deals with the exact time one may begin eating from the year's new produce (חָדָשׁ). The *rebbi* explained, "*Chazal* say that we must take into account the fact that the third *Beis HaMikdash* could conceivably be built soon."

The *rebbi* expounded, "*Mashiach* could come at any time. The *Beis HaMikdash* would be built, and people might become confused regarding the laws of the year's new produce because they would be accustomed to what they had been doing before the *Beis HaMikdash* was built. Thus, *Chazal* stipulated certain rules and regulations to avoid possible confusion."

"It would be great if *Mashiach* would come!" came a voice from the back of the group. Everyone turned to see who had made that statement, and to their surprise it was the child who the *rebbi* thought never paid attention. The *rebbi* himself was taken aback because he hadn't realized that the boy had been listening.

That afternoon, in a casual conversation with the Learning Director, Rabbi Wolpin, the *rebbi* mentioned that he was quite surprised that the boy responded to something.

"I believe I know why he warmed to the idea of *Mashiach*," Rabbi Wolpin said. "You see, this particular boy no longer has parents. They died when he was small and he is being raised by his grandparents. He probably feels that when *Mashiach* comes he will be able to see his parents once again."

The *rebbi* listened respectfully but remained skeptical of Rabbi Wolpin's reasoning. He decided to conduct a little experiment the next morning.

At the learning group the next day, the *rebbi* once again studied the *Gemara* with the boys and reviewed the details of when the new produce may or may not be eaten. The *rebbi* explained, "We have this *halachah* because, as *Chazal* teach us, one never knows: *Mashiach* could come right away, the *Beis HaMikdash* would then be built and we must know what to do."

"Now," the *rebbi* said, seeming to interrupt his own flow of thought, "wouldn't it be wonderful if *Mashiach* came?"

"Yes!" shouted one boy. "Then we could all *daven* in the *Beis HaMikdash*."

"It would be great," chimed in another child, "because then we could all live in *Eretz Yisrael*."

The *rebbi* looked at the boy in the back and waited for his response. The child paused for a moment and then said softly, almost inaudibly, "It would be good, because then there would be *techias hameisim* (resurrection of the deceased)."

The young boy longed for *Mashiach* because it meant something to him personally. If *Mashiach* would mean that much to every Jew, no doubt he would indeed come quickly.

➔§ *Tabletop Teachings*

There are no guarantees that the wealth a man has today will still be his tomorrow. Quite often wealth changes hands, and those who were once considered affluent must, as their fortunes steadily diminish, step aside and make room at the top for others whose turn it is to ascend to prestige and prosperity.

The *Midrash* in *Bamidbar* (22:8) explains that the Hebrew word for possessions is נְכָסִים because possessions are [eventually] נִכְסִים *hidden* (taken) from one person and revealed (given) to another. Currency is referred to as זוּזִין because legal tender זָזִים (moves), i.e., is transferred (by the will of Hashem) from one person to another. Money is termed מָעוֹת, a conjunction of two words "מַה לָעֵת — What [are you concerning yourself with]? It is only for a [temporary period of] time."

Ideally, all those who attain money should understand that they are merely the temporary guardians of the funds they have procured. They should view their prosperity as a spiritual challenge in which they must prove that they can handle and channel their money in accordance with Torah values.

❧ ❧ ❧

Rabbeinu Bachya in his commentary to *Shemos* (25:23) cites the Talmudic (*Berachos* 55a) teaching that as long as the *Beis HaMikdash* stood, people could get atonement by [offering up a sacrifice on] the *mizbeiach* (altar). Today, in the absence of the *Beis HaMikdash*, a person can receive atonement by [providing for the needy at] his table.

Rabbeinu Bachya then describes the burial arrangements made by the very pious people of France. After a person's death, his dining table would be cut into sections, and these panels would be used to construct the coffin in which to lay the deceased to his eternal rest.

This sobering custom constantly reminded these devout people while they were alive, that what man brings with him to the Next World is not his money, but rather the merit of his *mitzvos* and charitable deeds. This understanding caused them to exercise great caution in how they used their funds.

❦ ❦ ❦

It is interesting, therefore, to note what occurred when the Rogatchover *Gaon*, Rabbi Yosef Rosen (1858-1936), the unparalleled Torah genius from Dvinsk, passed away. The Rogatchover was known both for the phenomenal *bekius* (wide scope) and *amkus* (depth) of his Torah knowledge. At any one time he could have a dozen *sefarim* open on his table as he leafed through them with a legendary diligence and rapidity.

When he passed away, a decision was made by those who were close to him to take the table at which he always learned at and cut it into sections from which to make a coffin for the great *Gaon*.

"Obviously," notes Rabbi David Cohen, of Brooklyn, "only for people of the caliber of the pious people in France or the Rogatchover *Gaon*, who used their tables primarily for charity and holiness, would such measures be taken. For others of a lesser caliber, making a coffin from a table where *lashon hara* or *devarim beteilim* (idle chatter) were spoken could, Heaven forbid, have an opposite, detrimental effect. Though these procedures were highly unconventional, the message they convey is relevant to each of us."

❧ The Mourning After

Rabbi Shoul Dolinger, the *Rosh Yeshivah* of Yeshivah Pri Eitz Chaim in Ashdod, Israel, recently retold how the Ponevezher *Rav*, Rabbi Yosef Kahaneman (1886-1969), was once approached by a gentleman who had just attended a funeral. The man seemed puzzled and asked the *Rav*, "What is the reason for the custom that one does not return from a funeral using the same route that he took to get there?" (See *Taamei HaMinhagim*, no. 1034; *Gesher HaChaim* 14:20.)

The Ponevezher *Rav* pondered for a moment and then, with typical perception, lent a new perspective to the matter. "How can any thinking person go to a cemetery," exclaimed the *Rav*, "and come back the same as he went?"

Rabbi Kahaneman was most likely referring to a concept taught by Shlomo *HaMelech* in *Koheles* (7:2). Shlomo *HaMelech* wrote, "It is better to go to the house of mourning than [to go] to a house of partying, for [death] is the end of all man, and those [that are] living should take it to heart."

When one is confronted with death, be it in a mourner's home or at a funeral, one should ideally reflect on the severity and seriousness of life. The Ponevezher *Rav* felt that this sobering experience should change a man and thus he should leave a funeral differently (both physically and spiritually) from the way he arrived.

Part D:

Torah — Teachers and Talmidim

◆§ *The Bus Stops Here*

Rabbi Yaakov Salomon, a noted *talmid chacham* and psychotherapist in Brooklyn, devotes a segment of his time to leading seminars for the Aish HaTorah Discovery Program. These seminars are held for people with very little religious background who have come to hear what *Yiddishkeit* is all about.

Every lecture is slightly different, for he must always gear the Torah thoughts he is about to explain towards his audience's level of understanding. However, regardless of the level, he always ends with this touching story.

One afternoon as he was walking in Brooklyn, R' Yaakov noticed a sizeable crowd gathered outside a small *shul*. The assembled all seemed very serious and were talking in hushed tones. He realized that a funeral was about to take place. He inquired as to the identity of the deceased, and learned that it was R' Binyamin Schachner (see p. 165), the father-in-law of one of his friends. He had often heard his friend speak highly of Mr. Schachner and so, as a sign of respect, he walked into the *shul* to attend the funeral.

It was then that he heard a particular *Rav* recount this personal incident in his *hesped* (eulogy).

❧ ❧ ❧

The *Rav* described how every morning, when he came out of his *shul*, he noticed R' Binyamin standing at the bus stop across the street. Rain or shine, R' Binyamin was always there, never missing a day. The *Rav* didn't make much of this, simply assuming that R' Binyamin was off to work and was a very organized person, as he never seemed to be late.

One day, however, the *Rav* happened to be watching as the bus drew towards the curb, accepted passengers and then pulled away. Much to the *Rav's* surprise, however, R' Binyamin remained standing at the bus stop. As the bus had not seemed particularly crowded, R' Binyamin's behavior struck the *Rav* as somewhat puzzling.

When a few days later this happened again, the *Rav* decided to find out why the gentleman continued to wait at the bus stop. He approached R' Binyamin and said, "I couldn't help but notice that you are here every day at this bus stop, yet twice I've seen that when the bus came by, you didn't get on. Is everything all right?"

"Yes," smiled R' Binyamin, "everything is wonderful. But let me explain why I'm here.

"You see," he began slowly, "I went through the *Gehinnom* of the concentration camps and suffered losses in the Holocaust. After we were liberated I knew that the future of *Klal Yisrael* rested with the children. So many of the adults had suffered greatly, so many were killed and broken in spirit. I realized that only with the new generation of children could Torah be revitalized. Therefore, when I came to this country and saw that little children were indeed learning Torah, it gave me great pleasure and hope for the future.

"I once figured out," he continued, "that if I stand right here at this bus stop I can watch thirty-two busloads of Jewish children pass by on their way to the various *yeshivos* and *Bais Yaakovs* in the area. I stand and count them as they go by and if, G-d forbid, I count only thirty-one, my day is incomplete. I have to know each morning that every busload of children made it to school. That's why I'm here, just to see this beautiful spectacle every morning. This is my greatest thrill, to know that Jewish children are once again learning Torah. To me it is the most wonderful sight in the world."

After telling this story, Rabbi Yaakov Salomon says to his audience, some of whom are hearing about Torah for the very first time, "Now you know why he stood there. And now you know why I stand here."

৶§ The Living Torah

The Rizhiner *Rebbe*, R' Yisrael (1797-1851), was revered not only by his own *chassidim* (disciples) but by countless Jews from all walks of life. Even in his youth he achieved great acclaim. It happened one day that as R' Yisrael was walking among his *chassidim*, his *gartel* (special belt worn around the waist in preparation for prayer; see *Orach Chaim* 92:2) fell to the floor.

The Apter *Rav*, Rabbi Avraham Yehoshua Heshel (1755-1825), author of the classic *sefer* on *Chassidus*, *Ohev Yisroel*, who was much older than the Rizhiner, was present at the time and noticed that the Rizhiner's *gartel* had fallen to the ground. He quickly rushed over to where the *gartel* lay, bent down, picked it up and girded it around the much younger *Rebbe*. The *talmidim* (students) of the Apter *Rav* were stunned.

"Why did the *Rebbe* stoop to put the Rizhiner's *gartel* back on him?" they asked in amazement. They felt that because the Apter was much older than the Rizhiner it did not seem fitting that he should be of service to the younger Rizhiner, and additionally there were Rizhiner *chassidim* standing by who themselves could have helped their *Rebbe*.

The Apter *Rav* turned to his *talmidim* and said with a smile, "I did it because I wanted to fulfill the *mitzvah* of *gelilah* on a *Sefer Torah!* (wrapping the *gartel* around a Torah scroll)."

The *Gemara* in *Makkos* (22b) states that at times people act quite foolishly. On one hand they make sure to stand whenever a *Sefer Torah* is in their presence, yet they fail to stand and show respect when a "living *Sefer Torah*" (a person who personifies all that Torah teaches) is near them.

Each of us has the potential to be a "*lebedike*" (living) *Sefer Torah*. The Apter *Rav* viewed the Rizhiner, albeit young in years, as a person who had already achieved that lofty status. He thus accorded him appropriate honor.

·◆§ Food for Thought

Rabbi Elya Lopian (1872-1970), the revered *tzaddik* and *Mashgiach* (spiritual advisor) of the *yeshivah* in Kfar Chassidim, Israel, once depicted in a *shmuess* (*mussar* lecture) a tragic scene he had heard about many years earlier.

During World War I, explained R' Elya, poverty was rampant and people in many towns and villages throughout Eastern Europe suffered terribly from malnutrition and hunger. In one particular family in Lithuania there was a young boy who became very ill and exceedingly weak from lack of food.

One day a group of children came to visit him. As they entered the room and walked towards his bed, the little boy looked up at his father and asked "Who are these boys?"

"They are the boys from your class," his father replied sadly.

The father realized that because of the illness his son's mind was beginning to fail him, and therefore he did not recognize his own classmates.

A few days later the boy's brother came into the room. Once again the child asked his father, "Who is this?"

The father bent down and whispered softly into his son's ear, "It is your brother, my child."

Not more than a week later a man stood alongside the bed of the sick child. The youngster looked up and said, with great strain, "Who are you?"

The man looked down at the little boy and with tears welling in his eyes, said, "It is I, my son. Your father."

❈ ❈ ❈

Rabbi Elya Lopian paused for a moment as he pictured that sorrowful scene in his mind's eye, and then he exclaimed, "One of the harsh consequences of famine and hunger is that it can cause a child to fail to recognize even his own father!

"Do you know what I learn from this?" R' Elya cried out to his *talmidim*. "Every Jewish person is created with a *nefesh* [soul], and like the body, the soul must have its nourishment. The *nefesh* must be satiated three times a day with the *tefillos* of *Shacharis, Minchah* and *Maariv.* * The *nefesh* requires a daily diet of Torah, supplemented by the performance of *mitzvos*. If a person does not provide this nourishment to his *nefesh* it will become weak and infirm to the point where the person will no longer even recognize his Father. . .in Heaven."

⋖§ Knot for Purim Only

This story took place decades ago. Yet it etched such an indelible impression on the minds of the individuals to whom it occurred that the passage of time has not dimmed their recollections. Because the story deals with sensitive issues, the names of all people and places have been changed. The lessons to be learned, however, are as relevant today as they were in the years when this took place.

Purim is a time of heightened emotion for all in *Klal Yisrael*. This is especially so in many *yeshivos* throughout the world where fun and frolic are the order of the day. Some of the younger *talmidim* don costumes or wear clothes and outfits they wouldn't even consider wearing during the rest of the year, while others (usually older) write and perform plays in which they satirize world events outside the *yeshivah* or events in the inner world of *yeshivos*, both their own and others.

Often, *rebbeim* and *roshei yeshivah* grapple philosophically with *talmidim* as to what should constitute the limits of sarcasm and ridicule directed at authorities. A prominent *rosh yeshivah* once exclaimed that individuals must know the difference between permissible *Purim* levity, jesting, and impermissible uncivilized rudeness.

> [Interestingly enough, it had been the custom in the great yeshivah in Volozhin for the individual who was the "Purim Rav," the central character who poked fun at the authorities of the yeshivah, to go to the Rosh Yeshivah [or

---

* See *Kuzari, Maamar* 3, and *Daas Chachmah U'Mussar*, Vol. 2, p. 146.

others who were the victims of his barbs] the day after *Purim* and request forgiveness if he had overstepped his bounds. For some unknown reason this custom has fallen by the wayside.]

The following story took place in a world-famous *yeshivah* where the *Rosh Yeshivah* was a very good-natured man who was revered, respected and beloved by his *talmidim*. Aside from being a great *talmid chacham*, the *Rosh Yeshivah* was clever and witty. On *Purim*, when the *talmidim* would recite "*grammen*" (whimsical and humorous poetry), he would stand up and reply with "*grammen*" that he composed right then and there, in response to those he had just heard.

In that particular *yeshivah*, *bachurim* took a certain liberty on *Purim* with this *Rosh Yeshivah*. Every year, after the *Megillah* reading at night, they would enter his private office, remove his *tefillin* from its pouch and change the *kesher* (knot) of the *tefillin shel yad* (*tefillin* of the hand) from *Ashkenaz* to *Sephard*.

[The *kesher* on the *tefillin shel yad* determines how the *retzuos* (straps) of the *tefillin* will be wrapped around the arm. The *Ashkenazic* custom is to wrap them in a motion towards the body, whereas the *Sephardic* custom is to wrap the *retzuos* on the arm away from the body.]

The next morning the *Rosh Yeshivah*, who knew how to fasten and unfasten the various *kesharim* on the *tefillin*, would good-naturedly change the *kesher* from *Sephard* back to *Ashkenaz* before *davening* and come to the *beis hamidrash* with a smile.

One year on *Taanis Esther*, the *Rosh Yeshivah* hid his *tefillin* in an office cabinet to prevent their being found that evening after the *Megillah* reading. However, that did not faze the *bachurim*. Somehow, they were able to open the cabinet and once again they changed the *kesher*.

The next *Purim* the *Rosh Yeshivah's* assistant suggested that he take his *tefillin* home with him, but he just smiled and explained that this year he had a new plan. "I will use a combination lock this *Purim* and the *bachurim* won't be able to get to the *tefillin*."

In order to remember the combination for the lock, the *Rosh*

Yeshivah penciled the numbers lightly on the wall near the cabinet. Sure enough, the *bachurim* found the faint scrawling on the wall, opened the lock, took out the *tefillin* and changed the *kesher*. The *Rosh Yeshivah* was startled the next morning when he saw that they had gotten to his *tefillin*, but once again he retied the *kesher* according to the *Ashkenazic* custom and walked into the *beis hamidrash* in time for *davening*, a broad smile on his face.

The next year, though, was different. This time a new *bachur* joined the regulars involved in this prank, and the *kesher* was tied so tightly that the next morning the *Rosh Yeshivah* had a very difficult time trying to undo it. Slowly he became exasperated as he struggled to open the knot. Try as he might, he could not manage it.

Precious moments were slipping by, and *davening* had already commenced in the *yeshivah*. By the time the *yeshivah minyan* reached the *Shema*, the *Rosh Yeshivah* still had not come into the *beis hamidrash* because he was still occupied with trying to untangle the tightly fastened *kesher*.

Grueling minutes later he realized that he had missed *tefillah b'tzibbur* (reciting *Shemoneh Esrei* with a *minyan*). The *Rosh Yeshivah* was devastated! Now this was no longer a joking matter.

For the rest of *Purim* he was deeply downcast because of what had happened. He did not rebuke or reprimand anyone on *Purim*, but that Friday night when he gave his weekly *shmuess* (lecture) to the entire *yeshivah* in the *beis hamidrash*, he said, "That which occurred on *Purim* was terrible. I cannot and will not forgive the *bachur* who tied the *kesher* on my *tefillin* so tightly that I could not open it, and thereby caused me to miss *tefillah b'tzibur*." He did not even reveal that the *retzuos* eventually had to be cut in order to undo the *kesher*. One can only imagine his personal anguish.

The *Rosh Yeshivah* went on to say that he could not remember the last time he had missed *davening* with a *minyan*. He concluded by saying, "The *bachur* must come to me and ask for *mechilah*." But no one stirred.

For days afterwards the *Rosh Yeshivah* waited for someone to come forward to talk to him about the incident, but no one did. He did not mention this prank again in subsequent *shmuessen*, and over the summer the incident was forgotten.

Months later, on *Shabbos Shuvah* (the Shabbos between *Rosh Hashanah* and *Yom Kippur*), the *Rosh Yeshivah* delivered a *shmuess* to the entire *beis hamidrash* in which he cited the *Rambam* in *Hilchos Teshuvah* (2:9) that states that *Yom Kippur* atones only for those sins that a person has committed against Hashem, but not for those sins that one person has committed against another.

The *Rosh Yeshivah* exclaimed, "*Yom Kippur* cannot and does not atone for that type of sin until the one who sinned asks forgiveness from the one he sinned against."

He continued, "I would therefore like to say publicly that the *bachur* responsible for making the *kesher* on my *tefillin* so tight this past *Purim*, causing me to miss *tefillah b'tzibur*, must come to me and ask for forgiveness. Otherwise I cannot pardon him."

Once again no one, either publicly or privately, came forth.

A few weeks after *Yom Kippur* the *Rosh Yeshivah*, who had been ailing, passed away.

❊ ❊ ❊

By the next *zman* (semester), the young man who had changed the *kesher* in previous years had entered a different *yeshivah*. Several months passed uneventfully until one day, a few days before *Purim*, something unusual happened while he was *davening Shacharis* in a local *shul*. A man he had never seen before approached him and asked if he would do him a favor.

"How can I help you?" the young man asked.

"The *kesher* of my *tefillin shel yad* opened up," the man said, "and I don't know how to fasten it. By any chance, do you know how to fasten it?"

"As a matter of fact I do," the young man replied. Quickly and efficiently he fastened the various segments of the *kesher* together, and the gentleman expressed his supreme gratitude.

The next year, the day after *Purim*, in a different city than the year before, as this same young man was about to begin *davening*, a young boy from the neighborhood who had recently become *bar mitzvah* came over to him. He showed the young man that the *retzuos* of his *tefillin* were slipping and sliding on his arm. "I think there is something wrong with the *kesher* of my *tefillin*. Could you fix it for me?" he asked.

Once again the young man was only too happy to help the boy. He smiled to himself as he remembered the good times he had in the *yeshivah* with his *Rosh Yeshivah's tefillin* around this time of year.

The third year after his *Rosh Yeshivah's* passing, a few days before *Purim*, this young man was in a small *shul* when he realized that an older man seemed to be having a problem with his *tefillin*. The man suddenly turned to the young man and said, "Excuse me, but could you help me here?"

The *bachur* suddenly recalled the similar requests that individuals in different cities had directed to him concerning *tefillin*. It occurred to him that all these incidents had occurred immediately before or after *Purim*. That was strange, he thought. Why did people never ask him about their *tefillin* throughout the year? Why only around *Purim*? Were these incidents merely a coincidence?

After some contemplation he forgot about the latest incident. But the next year as *Purim* approached, he began to wonder whether the same thing would happen again. And then remarkably, on *Purim* itself, a man came over to him and asked for help with the *kesher* of his *tefillin*. The young man's heart trembled as he fastened the *kesher* for the gentleman.

Now, after four consecutive years in which he had fixed people's *tefillin* at essentially the same time of year, he was convinced that a message was being directed to him from Heaven. The more he thought about it the more frightened he became, because now he was sure that he had to make amends.

That evening he called one of his longtime friends who was still in his former *yeshivah* and explained the unusual circumstances that had occurred on or around *Purim* for four years in a row. He pleaded with his friend. "Please, I beg of you, take a *minyan* and go down to the *kever* (gravesite) of the *Rosh Yeshivah* and ask him for *mechilah* (forgiveness) in my name." (See *Rambam Hilchos Teshuvah* 2:11).

A few days later, a *minyan* of young men went to the gravesite and recited numerous chapters of *Tehillim*. Then a representative of the group asked the *Rosh Yeshivah* to forgive their friend, for he was indeed remorseful and sorry for what he had done years earlier.

Since then no one has ever asked him to fix or fasten their *tefillin*!

☙ ☙ ☙

That young man, who today is an older gentleman, says, "I was stubborn in those years, and I realize now that I should have come to the *Rosh Yeshivah* and asked for *mechilah*. But the reason I didn't do it then was that I knew in my heart that the *Rosh Yeshivah* was angry with me because he thought I was the one who had made the *kesher* so tight, since I was the one who had tampered with his *tefillin* every year.

"In reality, though, it was the new boy who joined us that night who tightened the *kesher* with a vengeance, not I. I was the one who merely changed it from *Ashkenaz* to *Sephard* just as I had done for years, and the *Rosh Yeshivah* had never been upset with me in previous years."

Then he added, "But perhaps I should have gone to him anyway."

"What happened to the fellow who actually tightened it?" I asked. "Why didn't he ask for *mechilah*?"

"He died young," came the reply.

And this man who told the story? He is still alive but he has unfortunately encountered a significant share of life's difficulties.

Who are we to know for certain whether the *Purim* prank had a direct relationship to the way these individuals' lives turned out? How can we know for sure which actions are tied in to which results? We can only speculate and wonder.

Warning: *Purim* can be serious business.

Rabbi Yeruchem Olshin, one of the *Roshei Yeshivah* at Beth Medrash Govoha in Lakewood, New Jersey, recently retold this illuminating incident to a group of *bachurim* in the *beis hamidrash*. He heard it originally from Rabbi Leib Bakst, *Rosh Yeshivah* of the Yeshivah Gedolah in Detroit, who was kind enough to give me the particulars of the story.

Rabbi Bakst's cousin, Rabbi Yechezkel Chefetz, used to travel to Dvinsk, Latvia twice a year to study personally with Rav Meir Simchah HaKohen Katz (1843-1927), the *Rav* of Dvinsk and author of the famous *sefarim, Ohr Somayach* and *Meshech Chachmah*. Dvinsk was a small town in which there was no major *yeshivah*, so R' Meir Simchah offered *bachurim* from *yeshivos* in Lithuania the opportunity to stay for months at a time in his own home, where he would be their personal *chavrusa* (study partner).

One year, after R' Yechezkel had spent a considerable amount of time learning with R' Meir Simchah, he traveled to the Bakst home in Dalatitz, a small town near Novorodok and Vilna, for *Sukkos*. It was then that he related, with awe, an incident that had happened just a few months earlier.

R' Meir Simchah and R' Yechezkel had been learning together when they came upon a very difficult *Tosafos*. They spent a great deal of time trying to comprehend what that particular *Tosafos* was trying to say, but their efforts were in vain. The *pshat* (proper meaning) seemed to escape them.

After a while, R' Meir Simchah turned to R' Yechezkel and said, "Let us take a moment and *daven* that we merit to have *ahavas haTorah* (love for Torah)."

R' Yechezkel was surprised. "Why *daven* for *ahavas haTorah?*" he asked. "Would it not be better that we *daven* for understanding of Torah and say the words 'וְהָאֵר עֵינֵינוּ בְּתוֹרָתֶךָ — Enlighten our eyes in your Torah'?"

R' Meir Simchah smiled and said, "Let me explain this to you with a parable. Did you ever notice what happens sometimes when a mother leaves a child with a baby-sitter? After a short time the baby may begin to cry. The baby-sitter gives the child a toy, but it doesn't help. The child is still unhappy and continues to wail.

"A second person walks into the room and, trying to help, gives the child its milk bottle. But that doesn't help either. Finally the child's mother comes back, sees her child crying, picks him up and hugs him. In a moment the child is calm and content.

"How is it," asked R' Meir Simchah, "that the mother is able to calm the child and make him content? How did she know immediately what to do?

"The answer is that a mother has such an exceptional and intense love for her child that she is able to detect, by the child's slightest hint, what the child needs. The child's movements, his particular whimper, his specific cry — all these mean distinctive things to a loving mother. Her understanding of her child's desires stem from her great affinity and love for him.

"So it is with us too. If we would truly have an unbounded love for Torah, then we would be able to decipher even the slightest nuance and understand what the Torah (and in this case the *Tosafos*) wants from us."

◄§ Confrontation in Haifa

The most renowned *Maggid* in our generation is Rabbi Sholom Mordechai Schwadron, who is known throughout the world as the *Maggid* of Jerusalem. For more than five decades, R' Sholom has delivered *drashos* (lectures) throughout Israel, America and Europe, and wherever and whenever he speaks, he attracts a large and attentive audience. (See Introduction to *The Maggid Speaks* and *Around The Maggid's Table*.)

At one of R' Sholom's public *drashos* early in his speaking career, an incident occurred which led him to gain an insight from a *gadol hador* (one of a generation's most eminent Torah scholars), as to the proper function and objective of a public speaker. He has never forgotten that advice and he repeats it often, because the wisdom inherent in the advice is applicable beyond the realm of speakers and lecturers.

It is remarkable that R' Sholom even tells this story, because in reality the lesson came at his own expense. However, this in itself is a measure of the man. He views his role as *Maggid* as one who should teach, inspire and guide people regarding how to act and react as Torah Jews. To R' Sholom the message is significant, not his personal glory.

In the early 1950's, Haifa was the only city in all of Israel where public buses operated on Shabbos. In all other cities throughout the country, public buses remained in their garages from just before sundown Friday evening until some time after sunset Saturday night.

This blatant desecration of the Shabbos, sanctioned by the local government of Haifa, had an adverse effect on the general public's concern for the honor of Shabbos in that city. For this reason, the observant Jews of Haifa initiated an annual seminar which was open to the public and dedicated to the furtherance of Shabbos observance. Speakers from all over Israel would be invited to participate in the seminar, and over a particular weekend speeches would be held in various synagogues in which the splendor, significance and importance of Shabbos were discussed. Every year R' Sholom was invited to be one of the principal speakers.

In 1951 the Shabbos seminar took place immediately after *Yom HaAtzma'ut* (Israeli Independence Day). As part of the *Yom HaAtzma'ut* celebration there had been an Israeli Army parade in which the air force, navy, paratroopers and foot soldiers were represented.

Leading the parade was the mayor of Haifa, sitting in an open car alongside a number of female army personnel, who waved and smiled to the cheering crowds.

R' Sholom has a great love for *Eretz Yisrael*, but when he heard about the parade in which women participated in the public marching and fanfare he became incensed. He felt this was totally inappropriate. He had already spoken out numerous times against women being inducted into the Israeli army, and this public spectacle, in which they had participated, he found utterly distasteful. He considered it an open affront to authentic Torah Judaism.

That Friday night R' Sholom took his place in front of an anxious audience. Although the people were expecting to hear about the laws and sanctity of Shabbos, he felt it his duty to speak out against what he considered immodesty. He began by sharply criticizing the citizens of Haifa for having allowed this indecency, and castigated the Israeli army for what he considered improper behavior. It was only after he finished his strong diatribe that he began to talk about Shabbos.

However, by then his listeners were very disturbed, even angered. R' Sholom had roundly rebuked them, their mayor and their army. They felt that he had abused the privilege they had given him to address the public. They had come to be inspired, but instead they were disheartened. They hardly absorbed a word he said about Shabbos.

On Shabbos morning and Shabbos afternoon when he spoke in other *shuls*, R' Sholom again began by criticizing Friday's events. In every instance the people he addressed became enraged by his comments.

If R' Sholom's speech was a storm, the reaction to it was a tornado. On Sunday morning a meeting was held in the town's municipal building and its result was that the local government officials decided to ban R' Sholom from speaking publicly in Haifa for one full year.

When R' Sholom returned to Jerusalem he was notified of the governmental edict, which disturbed him. Being a very sensitive person, R' Sholom gave the matter a great deal of thought. Had his actions been correct? On the one hand he felt that it was his duty to speak out against what he perceived as improper behavior, but on the other hand, in so doing he had offended and alienated many people. Perhaps, he thought, his approach to the problem had been wrong. He decided to seek the counsel of one of the *gedolei hador* of the time, the Brisker *Rav*, Rabbi Velvel Soloveitchik (1887-1959).

R' Sholom presented the facts to the Brisker *Rav* as he perceived them. The parade, the participation of female army personnel and his obligation to speak out at the Shmiras Shabbos Seminar were all mentioned in detail.

The Brisker *Rav* listened attentively to the whole story, and then asked R' Sholom, "Did you ever wonder why the blessing that we recite every morning on learning Torah is worded the way it is? We say, 'אֲשֶׁר קִדְּשָׁנוּ בְּמִצְוֹתָיו וְצִוָּנוּ לַעֲסוֹק בְּדִבְרֵי תוֹרָה — *Who has sanctified us with His commandments and has commanded us to engage ourselves in the words of Torah.'* Why do we use the words לַעֲסוֹק בְּדִבְרֵי תוֹרָה (to engage ourselves with the words of Torah)? We should really use the words לִלְמוֹד תוֹרָה (to study Torah), for is not studying Torah the essence of the *mitzvah?*

"The answer is," continued the *Rav*, "that the word עֵסֶק also means 'business.' In order for one to have *hatzlachah* (success) in Torah, one must treat it as he would a business — with a sense of purpose, with diligence and with primary goals always in mind.

"Your purpose in Haifa was to inspire people about *shmiras Shabbos.* Had you been in Haifa to raise money for a business, would you have spoken against the parade? Certainly not. You were diverted from your goal and talked about something else. As a result, your objective of getting people to adhere to the laws of Shabbos failed. You didn't accomplish anything for Shabbos, nor did you accomplish for *tznius.*"

❀ ❀ ❀

"The Brisker *Rav* made me realize," says R' Sholom, "that it was the *Yetzer Hara* (Evil Inclination), not the *Yetzer Tov* (Virtuous Inclination), that caused me to speak out the way I did. And all this was to prevent me from furthering the cause of *shmiras Shabbos.*"

When a person says, "I mean business!" it indicates his seriousness. The Brisker *Rav* taught that Torah demands no less of a commitment.

No Kidding!

The obligation of every Jewish parent and *mechanech* (Torah educator) is to maintain and strengthen the bond that links every Jewish child to our forefathers who accepted the Torah at Sinai, and to our heritage that began with Avraham *Avinu*. This is our greatest investment for the days and years ahead, because every Jewish child is not only a link to the past, but a link to the future as well.

The following story, told by Rabbi Alter Metzger of Brooklyn, illustrates this point in a delightfully unusual manner. The episode may seem whimsical, but the lessons to be learned are serious.

A number of years ago Rabbi Metzger received a call from a family in Israel, the Kesslers.* Mr. Kessler explained that he, his wife and their daughter, who was about to get married to an American boy, were coming to the United States for the wedding. They needed a place to stay for a short time both before and after the wedding, and they wondered whether Rabbi Metzger had an apartment available in his house. Rabbi Metzger offered them a few unused rooms on the first floor of his home, and several weeks later the three visitors from Israel moved in.

The Metzgers and the Kesslers became quite friendly and grew to enjoy each other's company. The wedding took place and was followed by a week of *Sheva Berachos* (lit., seven blessings, a reference to the blessings recited at meals during the first week of marriage), and shortly afterwards the Kesslers and the newly married couple began to prepare for their return trip to Israel.

A day before they were to leave, the Metzgers hosted a family dinner in honor of their new Israeli friends and the *simchah* in which they had all taken part. The mood that night in Rabbi Metzger's home was festive, a culmination of the joy of the past few weeks.

---

* Name has been changed for personal reasons.

The conversation centered around marriage and building a home, and each of the family members peppered the talk with their own perspectives and thoughts. Suddenly Rabbi Metzger remembered a story that he had heard years ago. It had been told to him by his longtime friend, Rabbi Hershel Fogelman from Worcester, Massachusetts. Rabbi Metzger hadn't told the story very often because he was a bit skeptical about the ending. However, now that everyone was talking about "the future" he thought he would retell it, for he considered the message in the story invaluable.

❈   ❈   ❈

In a small town in Russia, before the revolution in 1917, there was a *cheder* (elementary school) for neighborhood children which met every day in a local *shul*. The *rebbi* in charge was very diligent and tried to imbue his students with a love of Torah and *mitzvos*. There was one boy in the class, however, who was wild and disruptive. Every day he came up with a new way to disturb the class.

One day the boy left his home very early in the morning and went to a local farm. There he took a baby goat and brought it into the little *shul*. None of the *cheder* boys had arrived yet, so he led the goat to the *Aron Kodesh* (Holy Ark), picked up the animal and somehow managed to squeeze it into the *Aron Kodesh*. He then closed the doors tightly.

A short time later, when the *rebbi* and the boys were assembled, the *rebbi* began to *daven* fervently with the children. Their loud and resonant voices frightened the little goat in the *Aron Kodesh*, and soon wild bleating was heard coming from the front of the room. At first no one could imagine where the noise originated. Some children became frightened and began to cry, while others howled with laughter. The *rebbi* walked hesitantly up to the *Aron Kodesh*. The noise seemed to be coming from inside it! Slowly he opened the doors — and the little goat jumped out, almost toppling him! The *rebbi* nearly fainted from fright. By then the class was in an uproar and in turmoil as children were scampering around uncontrollably.

It did not take too long to figure out who the culprit was and the *rebbi*, now in a genuine rage, grabbed the young troublemaker and took him down the road to the local *Rav*. The *Rav* scolded the boy and told him that because he had disrupted the class and troubled the *rebbi* countless times before, this incident with the goat was simply too much to tolerate. He told the child that he was going to be expelled from the *cheder*.

As a matter of *cheder* policy, the proposed expulsion was referred to the person in charge of all the *chadarim* in the area, the fifth Lubavitcher *Rebbe*, Rabbi Shalom Dov Ber Schneerson (known as the RaSHaB) (1860-1920). The child was brought before the *Rebbe*. The *Rebbe* explained to the child that the child's past history and this latest episode gave him no choice but to order him to leave the *cheder* and never come back.

The boy listened intently and then, looking up at the *Rebbe*, he exclaimed with a seriousness beyond his years, "*Rebbe*, if you throw me out, you are throwing out my children, my grandchildren and my great-grandchildren for eternity!"

The *Rebbe* was stunned by the remark. The viewpoint expressed by this seemingly reckless child bespoke thoughtfulness and maturity. His comment displayed a perception beyond his age. The *Rebbe* thought for a moment and decided that this child deserved at least one more chance. The boy was taken back to the *cheder*, and after consultation with the *Rav* and the child's *rebbi*, the child was reinstated.

❀   ❀   ❀

Rabbi Metzger paused as he ended the story and then added somewhat hesitantly, "I am told that this *bachur* (young student) eventually became a fine, upstanding fellow, but I really have no idea."

There was a hush in the room. At first no one spoke, but soon the father of the *kallah* (bride) turned to Rabbi Metzger and stated, in a questioning voice, "You know, of course, that the story is true, don't you?"

"I don't really know that it's true," said Rabbi Metzger. "It was told to me and I repeated it because I think it teaches a valuable lesson. But do *you* know for sure that it's true?"

"Yes, of course," the father replied. "My wife, the mother of the *kallah,* is the granddaughter of that young boy in the story! We always thought it was a family secret in Israel. We never realized that the story was known in America as well!"

This anecdote had been told and retold within the Kessler family as a lesson regarding the importance of recognizing the sometimes hidden potential and holiness of every Jewish *neshamah* (soul). The message though is universal.

Every child deserves a chance — and sometimes more than one — because a Jewish soul which is lost not only terminates all that previous generations have striven and struggled for, but suppresses, possibly forever, the progression of our great heritage and legacy.

◆§ Something Missing

A number of years ago, during the *Asseres Yemei Teshuvah* (Ten Days of Repentance between *Rosh Hashanah* and *Yom Kippur*), I had the opportunity to address a Jewish community outside the New York area on the topic of "Children, *Chinuch* and Communication." The audience that evening consisted of members of the various local *shuls,* teachers and parents from the area's day school, *kollel* men with their wives, and staff and students from the community *yeshivah* high school.

In the lecture I shared a particular thought that I felt had a strong message. It wasn't the first time I had related this idea to an audience; what happened there afterwards, however, was startling.

Focusing on the role of parents and teachers I noted the following:

Shlomo *HaMelech* advised: "חֲנֹךְ לַנַּעַר עַל פִּי דַרְכּוֹ — Educate a child according to his level" (*Mishlei* 22:6). A parent at home or a teacher in class must recognize that every child is different. Each child possesses distinct qualities, talents and capabilities. Shlomo *HaMelech* instructed that every child should be viewed as an individual and not merely as an insignificant cog in the wheel of humanity.

Interestingly, the word חֲנֹךְ (lit., educate) is written here with the letter *vav* missing. Normally this word is spelled חֲנוֹךְ, with the letter *vav* in place.

Perhaps *Shlomo HaMelech* was trying to teach us a lesson. It is not an overwhelming accomplishment to be able to educate an intuitively bright child who is highly motivated. Just about any qualified teacher or parent can teach a child of such caliber. Real accomplishment in education is achieved when one is able to reach a child who may be missing some of the qualities found in other children.

When a child lacks the power of concentration or lacks the capability to comprehend matters as quickly as others do, and a teacher or parent takes the time with the child to help him or her understand, that is education in the truest sense. Thus *Shlomo HaMelech* was saying חֲנֹךְ: Educate your child, even when there are qualities in him or her that are missing. Spend the time (even if it means coming late to a wedding); have the patience (even if you have to explain the *passuk* three times); realize that every child is unique, different and distinct.

That is why I thought the letter *vav* is missing.

I then told a story about a father who once went into a toy store in the Williamsburg section of Brooklyn to purchase toys for each of his seven children. The toys were hanging over each other from all shelves, dangling like yo-yos suspended in mid-air. The choices seemed endless and that made his quest all the more confusing. The father was on a strict budget, and his search for just the right toy seemed hopeless.

As he walked around the crowded little store, he said to himself, "I just don't know what to give my children." The proprietor, an older gentleman who had probably seen thousands of fathers like this in his lifetime, put his hand warmly on the shoulder of the younger man and said, "I'll tell you the best thing to give your children."

"What is that?" asked the father.

The proprietor smiled and said, "Time. That's what children need from their parents more than anything else. Just time."

❦ ❦ ❦

After the lecture, I was driven to a nearby *yeshivah* to *daven Maariv*. Sitting in the back seat of the car was a *yeshivah* high school student who had heard the speech. He leaned forward and said in a voice that was barely audible, "I want to thank you for that wonderful talk."

"It's kind of you to say that," I replied. And then, just to make conversation I asked, "Was there any particular thing that struck you?"

"Yes," came the immediate response. "I loved what you said about the word חֲנֹךְ."

I was surprised. I had told numerous stories, related personal incidents and explained several *maamarei Chazal* (Talmudic teachings). Why, of all things, would he appreciate the thought about חֲנֹךְ?

"Of all the things I discussed," I asked, "why was that the most significant?"

His answer shocked me. "Because I am that child," he replied. "You see, when I was a youngster, I hardly understood anything. I had such a hard time in school, but my parents had a great deal of patience with me. They explained things over and over again and always took their time with me. That's why eventually I was able to be accepted and mainstreamed into this wonderful *yeshivah*."

I was too astonished to say anything, but he continued speaking and said something even more touching. "In a few days it will be *erev Yom Kippur*. I am going to call my parents and tell them what you said about חֲנֹךְ, and then I will thank them again for all that they did for me."

I fought to hold back tears.

> Fortunate is the family in which children appreciate all that their parents do. Fortunate is the family in which parents recognize all that their children can't do.

◆§ A Blessing Abridged

The *Tosefos Yom Tov*, in his commentary on a *mishnah* in *Bava Metzia* (2:11), suggests an interesting interpretation of the well-known phrase רַבּוֹ מוּבְהָק. This term is usually understood to mean the primary teacher of a particular student. However, the *Tiferes Yisrael* suggests that the root of the word מוּבְהָק is בהק, which means to shine or glow. Thus he understands the term רַבּוֹ מוּבְהָק as meaning a teacher whose prodigious input causes the radiance and brilliance of his student's knowledge to glow (lit., his teacher who generates [the student's] brilliance).

Rabbi Chaim Volozhiner (1749-1821) was one such *talmid*. Everything he did and wrote in his life, particularly his classic *sefer, Nefesh HaChaim*, was a reflection of what he reaped from his *rebbi,* the Vilna Gaon (1720-1797).

In this light we can better appreciate the following story which appears both in the biography of Rabbi Chaim Volozhiner, *Avi HaYeshivos*, by Rabbi Dov Eliach, and in Rabbi Betzalel Landau's biography, *HaGaon HeChassid M'Vilna*.

R abbi Chaim Volozhiner was once walking with a group of *talmidim* (students) near a bridge in the town of Slutzk. As he approached the bridge he recited the blessing, "בָּרוּךְ . . . שֶׁעָשָׂה לִי נֵס בַּמָּקוֹם הַזֶּה — Blessed [are You, Hashem . . .] Who performed a miracle for me at this place."

The *talmidim* were quite surprised because they were not aware of anything miraculous ever having happened to their *rebbi* at this location. They inquired as to why he had made that blessing, and R' Chaim replied by telling them the following story.

Many years earlier, on a freezing winter day, a young mother was walking across the bridge wheeling a baby carriage in which her infant daughter, Traina, lay sleeping. Suddenly a tremendous gale-force wind came roaring across the bridge, sweeping the carriage out of the mother's grasp. It caromed off the side wall of the bridge and the impact hurled the baby out of the carriage, into the air, over the side of the bridge and into the freezing water below. Some people who were standing nearby and had seen what happened jumped into the water to rescue the little girl.

After a few desperate moments they plucked the child out of the icy water. One of the bystanders whipped off his coat and wrapped the baby snugly in the warm, dry garment. She was rushed to a house near the bridge and placed close to an oven to warm her shivering little body and ward off the effects of exposure.

In their flustered haste they positioned the child's feet too close to the fire in the oven and, much to everyone's dismay, her feet were accidentally singed! Thus, the poor infant was simultaneously suffering from heat and frost. After a while the little girl's complexion resumed its usual color as her temperature returned to normal. For the rest of her life, people talked about the miracle that had occurred to her as a child.

Traina grew up, eventually married a noted *talmid chacham* named R' Shlomo Zalman, and on the first day of *Pesach* she gave birth to a child who was given the name Eliyahu. He eventually became the great Vilna *Gaon*.

After detailing the incident, R' Chaim explained, "If not for the miracle that happened to the *Gaon's* mother, the *Gaon* would not have been born and I would not have had the great fortune of having such a *rebbi*. It is for this reason that I recited the blessing."

☙ ☙ ☙

A question regarding the text of the blessing still remains. The *Shulchan Aruch* (*Orach Chaim* 218:6) mentions that one is required to make a blessing when he passes a place where a miracle happened to his *rebbi*. The text of that blessing is "בָּרוּךְ ... שֶׁעָשָׂה נֵס לְרַבִּי בַּמָּקוֹם הַזֶּה — Blessed [is Hashem . . .] Who made a miracle happen to my *rebbi* in this place." Rabbi Chaim Volozhiner, though, recited the blessing that would apply if the miracle was a personal one (בָּרוּךְ שֶׁעָשָׂה לִי נֵס בַּמָּקוֹם הַזֶּה" — Blessed [is Hashem ...] Who performed a miracle for me at this place") In reality, though, nothing actually occurred to R' Chaim himself at this bridge?

HaGaon Rabbi Shlomo Zalman Auerbach, the *Rosh Yeshivah* of Yeshivas Kol Torah in Jerusalem, explains that R' Chaim was so close to, and learned so much from his *rebbi*, the Vilna *Gaon*, that he felt that had he not had the opportunity to be the *Gaon's talmid*, he would not have been the same person; he would have been a different [R'] Chaim Volozhiner. Thus, the miracle that saved the girl, which, years later, allowed the *Gaon* to be brought into this world, had a direct effect on the essence of R' Chaim. He therefore recited, "בָּרוּךְ ... שֶׁעָשָׂה לִי נֵס בַּמָּקוֹם הַזֶּה" — Blessed ... [are you Hashem] for having performed a miracle for me at this place."

✑ The Teacher's Teacher

The influence that people have on each other is immeasurable. Parents, teachers and friends all have an effect on the way their children, students and acquaintances think and act. However, no person can ever be sure about what it is within themselves that inspires others to a course of action. It is thus imperative that we always be totally consistent in what we do, for in our roles as parents, teachers or friends, the effect of our actions can at times change another person's life, whether we realize it or not.

In this touching story told by Mrs. Leah Trenk of Adelphia, New Jersey, we witness an incredible exchange of influence.

From the time he entered first grade, Jeffrey Levinson* attended Akiva Academy,* a day school in a small town in New Jersey. A large percentage of the children at Akiva Academy came from

---

* Names have been changed by personal request.

homes in which Shabbos observance was limited to the ceremonial, and only minor adherence to the laws of *kashrus* was the norm. Jeffrey, the only child of the Levinsons, came from a family that believed in studying the culture and heritage of Judaism, but not in the practical side of things. Shabbos observance in their home was practically non-existent, and Jeffrey, an only child, was expected to help his parents tend their store on Saturdays.

As Jeffrey's *bar mitzvah* drew near, the boy was torn between his parents' "traditional" way of life and the way of life that his education had convinced him was that of authentic *Yiddishkeit*.

The Levinsons lived miles away from the small *shul* in a town along the Jersey coast where the *bar mitzvah* was to be held. Actually, there were large synagogues situated near the Levinson home, but over the years the Levinsons had never seen fit to become members of these institutions; therefore, these synagogues would not host Jeffrey's *bar mitzvah*. Only this little *shul*, that barely had a *minyan* on Shabbos, agreed to host Jeffrey's affair.

The *shul* was located more than ten miles from his home and Jeffrey realized that his parents, grandparents, out-of-town guests and friends would all be driving to *shul* that Shabbos morning. He understood that somehow he would have to show up as well, but he simply could not see himself getting into a car to be driven on the Shabbos of his *bar mitzvah*, thereby beginning his initiation into Jewish manhood by violating one of the basic *mitzvos* of *Yiddishkeit*.

A month before the big event, Jeffrey decided to break the news to his parents. "I really don't want to be driven to *shul* for my *bar mitzvah*," he announced one evening.

"And so how do you expect to get there?" his mother asked sarcastically. "Walk?"

"No," he replied. "It's much too far. I'll sleep there Friday night."

His parents were furious, and they tried to dissuade him. But it was useless. Jeffrey's mind was made up and if there was going to be a *bar mitzvah*, he was going to have it on his own terms. He explained to his incredulous parents that he would prefer to be driven to the *shul* on Friday afternoon before candle-lighting time (approximately eighteen minutes before sundown), and that he would greet the family cordially as they arrived on Shabbos morning.

The Levinsons were beside themselves with concern. How would they explain this "lunacy" to their relatives? Was it safe to leave their only child alone in a building at night? Was there at least a phone he could use in case of emergency? Finally, realizing that there was simply no way they could convince Jeffrey to ride with them on Shabbos morning, Mr. Levinson reluctantly called the *shammash* (attendant) of the *shul* to inquire if Jeffrey could stay at his home Friday night.

The *shammash* laughed and said, "So you got yourselves a little rabbi!"

"No, not a rabbi," Mr. Levinson replied. "A rebel."

The *shammash* told Jefferey's father that he and his wife, who lived only twenty minutes' walking distance from the *shul*, would be honored to accommodate the *bar mitzvah* boy. It was finally agreed that Jeffrey would indeed stay there.

❦ ❦ ❦

Although he felt a bit lonely and frightened that Friday night in the *shammash's* home, Jeffrey was comforted and fortified by the fact that his determination that weekend was a statement: He would begin his life as a Jewish man by being a *shomer Shabbos*, and he would never deviate from its observance. Jeffrey regarded this decision as the cornerstone of a commitment, a foundation on which he would build from that day on.

That Shabbos, the *bar mitzvah* was celebrated by friends and family. To Jeffrey's surprise the Levinsons, in deference to their son, did not travel back home after the morning's festivities, but remained in the area with him until after nightfall.

❦ ❦ ❦

A number of weeks after the *bar mitzvah*, Jeffrey's *rebbi* (teacher) at Akiva Academy inaugurated a night learning session for the eighth graders of the school. Jeffrey lived too far from the school to be able to participate in this program, and so the *rebbi* sought other means to augment Jeffrey's daytime learning.

The Levinsons lived reasonably close to a *yeshivah* high school in Adelphia, and so the *rebbi* called the *menahel* (principal) of the *yeshivah*, Rabbi David Trenk, whom he knew to be a warm and inspiring individual. The *rebbi's* intention was to see whether he could arrange for someone to learn with Jeffrey. When Rabbi Trenk heard about the boy's commitment and sincerity, he undertook to learn with the boy himself. Thus, for the remainder of the year, R' David and Jeffrey studied together two evenings every week.

One evening, after Jeffrey had finished learning with R' David and the two of them were talking, the subject of Jeffrey's sleeping away from home the Friday night before his *bar mitzvah* came up. Jeffrey, who was soft spoken and a bit shy, made nothing of his determination to become a *shomer Shabbos*. But Mrs. Trenk, who happened to overhear the conversation, was curious. "What made you want to become religious?" she asked. "After all, your parents are not religious and neither are many of your classmates."

Jeffrey looked up wistfully and said, "My fourth-grade teacher. When I was in her class, I was so inspired by her that I decided that some day I would like to be as religious as she is."

Interested to know the identity of that teacher, for she personally was acquainted with quite a few of the teachers at Akiva Academy, Mrs. Trenk asked, "Do you remember her name?"

"Mrs. Melamud,"* Jeffrey replied simply.

"Did you ever tell her that she inspired you this way?" Mrs. Trenk asked.

"No," the boy replied. "I would be too embarrassed to mention it to her."

Mrs. Trenk knew Mrs. Melamud casually and so she made a mental note to call her the next morning to let her know about the influence she had had on one of her former students. But the morning came and went and she never got around to making the call. For weeks Mrs. Trenk meant to make that call, but projects always kept her busy and the call became further delayed. Soon summer came, schools closed, everyone became involved with their summer vacations — and still the call had not been made.

One day in early September, Mrs. Trenk was shopping in a local mall when she noticed Mrs. Melamud in the distance. She immediately remembered that she had meant to talk to Mrs. Melamud months ago and still hadn't done so. She went over to her and said, "Mrs. Melamud, I'm so glad to see you. I should have called you months ago! I simply must tell you what happened."

Mrs. Melamud listened intently as Mrs. Trenk exuberantly filled her in.

"Do you recall that you once had a student named Jeffrey Levinson?" Mrs. Trenk began.

"Yes," said Mrs. Melamud. "I remember him from a few years ago."

"Well," said Mrs. Trenk, her eyes shining, "he is an exceptional boy and was chosen as valedictorian of his class. But that is not everything," Mrs. Trenk continued. "A few months ago he celebrated his *bar mitzvah*."

"Oh, *mazal tov*," Mrs. Melamud interupted.

Mrs. Trenk went on. "His family, you may recall, is not *shomer Shabbos*, nor did they want Jeffrey to be *shomer Shabbos*. Yet on the Shabbos of his *bar mitzvah* he refused to be driven to *shul* and actually slept over in the *shammash*'s house Friday night in order to be able to walk to *shul*. Regardless of what anyone said, he would not ride in a car on Shabbos!"

Mrs. Melamud was amazed. She remembered the boy's intelligence and recalled that when she had him as a student in fourth grade he had already shown strong leanings towards authentic *Yiddishkeit*.

[Mrs. Melamud relates that during the year she had him as a student, she noticed that he *davened* with a seriousness beyond his years.]

Mrs. Trenk explained that since his *bar mitzvah* Jeffrey had refused to violate the Shabbos and had grown immensely in his practice of Torah and *mitzvos*. She described how her husband had recently begun to learn with Jeffrey, and went on to describe how one night they had asked him what made him turn religious.

"Do you know what he said?" Mrs. Trenk asked. "He said it was you, his fourth-grade teacher, that inspired him. He said he wanted to be just like you. But he has never been able to get himself to tell this to you."

By now Mrs. Trenk was smiling broadly, but Mrs. Melamud wasn't. Tears were rolling down her face. Mrs. Trenk's demeanor changed at once. "What's wrong?" she asked.

"I just can't believe what you're telling me," Mrs. Melamud said slowly. "I have been grappling for days with making a decision about teaching. For years school started at 9:00 in the morning, but now they've changed it to 8:30. I realized that because of the new schedule it would be so much more difficult for me because not only would I have to get up half an hour earlier, but I would have to leave the children earlier with the baby-sitter as well. Just today," Mrs. Melamud continued, "I told my husband that I would call the school and tell them I can't teach there this year. But now you've changed that. You made it all worth it. It is *hashgachah pratis* (Divine Providence) that we met just today, because now I intend to call and tell them that I plan to remain there as a teacher. It's obviously worth the effort."

And indeed, Mrs. Melamud did go back to teaching.

At times, influence is not a narrow, one-way path, but a two-way road of reciprocal reaction.

◆§ A Heightened Awareness

In 1958 a stately, dignified gentleman from Detroit, Mr. Alexander Roberg, went to Israel to visit his sister in the town of Petach Tikvah. Mr. Roberg, who was a teacher in both the Chachmei Lublin and the United Hebrew School in Detroit, had come to America with his wife after escaping the Nazi persecution in his home town of Stuttgart, Germany. He hadn't seen his sister in more than two decades, and their reunion in Israel was the fulfillment of a dream they never thought would come true.

On Shabbos, Mr. Roberg and his brother-in-law, Mr. Avraham Glueckstein, went to *daven* in the M'kor Chaim *shul* in Petach Tikvah. As is the custom in most *shuls*, Mr. Roberg, being a guest, was given an *aliyah* (the honor of being called to the Torah).

When the *baal korei* finished *leining* the *parshah*, the *gabbai* approached Mr. Roberg and honored him once again, this time with *hagbah* (the *mitzvah* of lifting the Torah so that it could be rolled together by the *gollel*).

Mr. Roberg was surprised at having been given two honors. "Why did you honor me with *hagbaah* when you had just given me an *aliyah?*" he asked the *gabbai*.

"A prominent person here in *shul* insisted that you get *hagbaah*," replied the *gabbai*, "and so I did as he asked me."

"May I know who that was?" Mr. Roberg asked courteously.

"Yes, certainly. It was that man over there," the *gabbai* replied, pointing to an elderly person.

Mr. Roberg approached the gentleman and politely inquired as to why he had requested that he (Mr. Roberg) be given *hagbaah*.

The man smiled and said, "You don't remember me, but I remember you."

And then Mr. Felix Beifuss went on to detail this beautiful episode.

"Twenty-five years ago, in 1933, my family was living in a little town, Bad Mergentheim," Mr. Beifuss explained, referring to a town in Germany. "We were very well-to-do and our family business was prospering. At that time the Germans were beginning to harass Jews, and my brother-in-law, who was a young man at the time, was taken to jail for no apparent reason.

"The family feared that we would never see him again. My mother-in-law [Mrs. Bertha Froelich] made a promise that if she lived to see her son released safely from prison, she would donate a *Sefer Torah* to our *shul*.

"A few months later her son was indeed released. She immediately engaged a *sofer* (Torah scribe) from Frankfurt to write a *Sefer Torah*.

"When it was completed our family tendered a *Hachnasas Sefer Torah* (a ceremony in which the Torah is usually carried through the streets under a *chuppah*, accompanied by song and dance as it is brought into the *shul* for the very first time. Because of the situation in Germany, the procession began in the *shul* itself).

"When the Torah was placed on the *amud* (lectern from where it is read), and the *sofer* wrote in the last letters, our family decided that you should be the one honored with *hagbaah*. At the time you were a teacher of little children, and we felt that because you raised their level of Torah understanding you deserved this distinction.

"Mr. Roberg," Mr. Beifuss continued, "our family was fortunate in being able to save this Torah, and we brought it with us to Israel. The Torah we read from today is the same Torah you lifted twenty-five years ago. When I saw you, I remembered that, and I wanted you to have the opportunity of lifting this same Torah once again!"

How beautiful it is when recognition is given to the unsung heroes in *Klal Yisrael* — the *rebbeim* (and *moros)* of our children.

◆§ To Outwit and Out Wait

In the early 1900s, waves of Jewish immigrants came from Europe to settle in the United States, particularly in the Lower East Side of New York City. This flow of humanity consisted by and large of impoverished people, and finding a job became a desperate imperative for the breadwinner of the family.

Employers realized that because competition for jobs was fierce, they could afford to pay minimal wages and still have no shortage of applicants. Thus, even those immigrants who managed to land jobs still lived meagerly. Many heads of families would come from Europe by themselves, leaving their wives and children behind. They would work for a few years and save all the money they earned until they had enough to bring their families to America.

Rabbi Avraham Yitzchak Gold was one such individual. Shortly after his son Yankel was born in 1913, he left Europe for America with the hope of eventually bringing over his wife and children. He found a job repairing sewing machines. Not long after his arrival, World War I broke out and R' Avraham Yitzchak remained in New York, separated from his family for nine years. Finally, in 1922 he was able to reunite his family. His wife, Rachel, arrived with their children, to settle in this Jewishly hostile environment.

While yet in Galicia, Rachel Gold had heard about the problems and pitfalls of "*treife* America." From the beginning she decided that she would not let her children join the hordes who had succumbed to what they considered the necessities and practicalities of American life, including *chillul* (desecration of) Shabbos, eating *tarfus* (non-kosher food) and educating Jewish children in public schools. The day after her arrival in America she began to work on her main priority — finding a *yeshivah* for her nine-year-old son, Yankel.

Mrs. Gold found out that there was one *yeshivah* in the Lower East Side — Yeshivas Rabbeinu Yaakov Yosef, otherwise known as RJJ (Rabbi Jacob Joseph), on Henry Street. That morning she walked with her son into the office of the principal at RJJ.

"My name is Mrs. Gold and we just came from Europe," she began politely. "I would like my son Yankel to attend your *yeshivah*. When can he begin?"

The principal smiled apologetically and replied, "We are overcrowded, Mrs. Gold. There is no room for your son here in the *yeshivah*. I am very sorry."

"But that is impossible!" Mrs. Gold cried. "My son has to be in a *yeshivah*. How else will he remain a religious Jew?"

"There are so many immigrant children here with the same problem," the principal replied. "We simply can't handle everyone."

"But my son is even willing to sit together with another boy on the same seat!" Mrs. Gold protested. "Two boys sharing the same seat — that's not so bad."

"Yes, Mrs. Gold," the principal replied patiently as he had already said to dozens of parents before. "You are so right, but we are doing that already. Come see for yourself. Walk into any classroom and you will see boys doubled up — using the same desks, the same seats, the same *chumash* and the same *siddur*. I am truly sorry, but we can't take your son right now."

Mrs. Gold was exasperated. "How long must I wait to get him into your *yeshivah*?" she pleaded.

The answer shocked her. "Two years!"

It was as though someone had punched her in the heart. But she was resolute so she announced with pride, "If we have to wait, then we will wait."

Mrs. Gold went home and about fifteen minutes later she came back with Yankel. Mother and son sat down on one of the steps on the front stoop of the *yeshivah*. "Let him hear the children *davening*," Mrs. Gold thought. "Let him hear the voice of a *rebbi* instructing a child. Let him see *yeshivah bachurim*. We'll wait right here."

Mrs. Gold and Yankel sat there for hours, she sewing, he counting cars and passersby. Soon it was time for recess. Droves of children flocked out of the classrooms, spilling over onto the sidewalk and playground nearby. Mrs. Gold watched the playing children enviously as others inadvertently bumped and pushed both her and Yankel who remained seated on the steps.

One of the *rebbeim* noticed her sitting there and asked if he could be of assistance. She answered simply, "I am waiting." He didn't make anything of it, assuming that she was waiting for one of the students. But when he noticed her a few hours later in the very same spot, he approached her and said, "Excuse me, but whom are you waiting for?"

"I am waiting for my son to be accepted into the *yeshivah*," she replied matter-of-factly. "Can you help?"

The *rebbi* went to the principal and told him about the lady on the front steps. The principal came to the door to see for himself. He didn't say anything to the woman because he knew he couldn't help her.

For three days she sat there with her son, sewing, talking, praying and waiting. She explained to anyone who would listen that all she was doing was waiting.

By the fourth day her wait was over. Somehow, room had been made for Yankel.

Yankel attended RJJ, as did his children after him. All of Rachel Gold's children, grandchildren and great-grandchildren have remained *frum*. Many have made contributions to Jewish life in the various neighborhoods in which they reside. One of her grandchildren, named after her husband, is Rabbi Avie Gold who, through his many published Torah works, has taught Torah to thousands of Jews throughout the world.

It is he who told me this story with justifiable pride.

✑ Business Ethics

Rabbi Yaakov Kamenetzky's (1891-1986) perception and original style of analysis were extraordinary (see p. 39). Consequently, when he experienced an event or became aware of a specific occurrence, his interpretation of the matter was uniquely distinctive.

The following episode, related to me by Rabbi Yoni Levinson of Brooklyn, was first told by Rabbi Pinchas Teitz, the famous *Rav* of Elizabeth, New Jersey. The episode is a beautiful example of R' Yaakov's ingenuity.

When R' Yaakov came to New York from Toronto in 1945 to become the *Rosh Yeshivah* of Yeshiva Torah Vodaath in the Williamsburg section of Brooklyn, he was faced with a personal quandary.

He remembered that when he was learning in the *yeshivah* in Slabodka, Lithuania, he had difficulty with a particular section of *Gemara* in *Masechta* (Tractate) *Gittin*, a difficulty which remained unresolved. His question on the *Gemara* at that time was so strong that it was debated and discussed throughout the *beis hamidrash* and *kollel* (study center for married fellows) and no one could explain the *Gemara* satisfactorily.

One who is sophisticated in learning understands that not every question can or must be answered. There are numerous Talmudic commentators who pose a particular problem and then, after considerable discussion, remain with the dilemma and write simply, "This requires further intensive study." At times the Talmud itself remains in a quandary, and after a lengthy debate of an issue the *Gemara* may end with the statement, "תֵּיקוּ" (lit., let it stand).*

---

* Some explain the word תֵּיקוּ as an acronym for the words תִּשְׁבִּי יְתָרֵץ קוּשְׁיוֹת וְאִיבָּעִיוֹת (Tishbi [Eliyahu *HaNavi*] will [eventually come and] resolve the difficulties and problems).

When R' Yaakov came to Torah Vodaath he understood that the level of learning reached by students in America at the time was considerably lower than the European standards of learning to which he was accustomed. He therefore was worried that when the yeshivah would learn *Masechta Gittin* and he would have to give a *shiur* on that baffling section of *Gemara*, he would have no choice but to tell his *talmidim* that he didn't understand it. He felt, however, that to tell young and impressionable *bachurim* in America that their *Rosh Yeshivah*, who theoretically embodied the epitome of Torah comprehension, did not understand elementary *pshat* (meaning) in the *Gemara* could be detrimental. Such a confession might possibly lead to a disregard for Torah, he feared, and a disrespect for those who study it.

When the *zman* (semester) for learning *Gittin* eventually arrived, and R' Yaakov approached that particular *daf* (page), he wondered what he would tell his class.

R' Yaakov was always noted for his unstinting honesty. He once said that even as a child, from the time he reached maturity, he never knowingly told a lie. Therefore, it was inconceivable for him to mislead his *talmidim* by merely "getting by" on a *pshat* that he didn't think was accurate and factual.

The night before R' Yaakov was to deliver the *shiur* on that enigmatic *daf*, he spent hours trying to find an answer to his perplexing question, but nothing satisfied him. True *pshat* eluded him.

However, the next morning, as he was giving the *shiur*, the true meaning suddenly came to him. Like a lightning bolt that abruptly brightens the horizon and makes it crystal clear, the *Gemara* was now perfectly plausible. The correct understanding of the *Gemara* that had eluded him for years now seemed plainly obvious.

R' Yaakov smiled and explained to the *bachurim* that by the grace of Hashem he had just thought of the accurate *pshat* for the *Gemara*, and a problem that had been bothering him for years had just been resolved. Content, he then went on with the *shiur*.

That afternoon, and for days afterwards, R' Yaakov discussed the matter with numerous *Roshei Yeshivah* in Torah Vodaath and with other *talmidei chachamim* in Williamsburg, seeking their opinion on his *pshat* in the *sugya* (topic). Unanimously they agreed that what he said was correct and that it was the appropriate resolution to his problem.

A while later R' Yaakov met his friend Rabbi Pinchas Teitz to whom he related the whole episode. R' Yaakov, in his distinctive manner, then said smilingly, "Let me explain to you what I believe happened here.

"The *Gemara* says in *Megillah* (6b), 'אִם יֹאמַר לְךָ אָדָם יָגַעְתִּי וְלֹא מָצָאתִי אַל תַּאֲמֵן — If someone tells you, "I labored [in the study of Torah], but did not succeed," do not believe him. לֹא יָגַעְתִּי וּמָצָאתִי אַל תַּאֲמֵן — [If he tells you,] "I have not labored [in the study of Torah] yet I have succeeded," do not believe [him]." יָגַעְתִּי וּמָצָאתִי תַּאֲמֵן — [If, however, he tells you,] "I have labored [in the study of Torah], and I have succeeded," you may believe [him].

"However," continued R' Yaakov, "the *Gemara* has a qualification. הֲנֵי מִילֵּי בְּדִבְרֵי תוֹרָה אֲבָל בְּמַשָּׂא וּמַתָּן סִיַּיעְתָּא הוּא מִן שְׁמַיָּא' — This is true of Torah study — but with [regard to] business, [one's success is dependent on] assistance from Heaven [not on one's personal efforts].'

"You see," said R' Yaakov, "when I was learning in Slabodka I was learning Torah *lishmah* (solely for the sake of the *mitzvah*), and thus I was confined within certain parameters. Obviously the *Ribono Shel Olam* felt that I had not labored enough in learning and thus I did not merit to attain the proper *pshat*. However, now that I am giving a *shiur* and I am getting paid for it, my success in learning is no longer dependent solely on my struggling. Torah is now my livelihood so I receive special Heavenly assistance. In His mercy He granted me His assistance that I should now know the correct *pshat*."

R' Yaakov, now smiling, said to Rabbi Teitz, "From this we learn that if a person wants to be successful in his Torah study he should make תוֹרָתוֹ אוּמָנָתוֹ (lit., make Torah his occupation), and then he will be granted great achievement and accomplishment."

When I told this story with its astute insight to my brother R' Kolman, he told me that a certain *Rosh Yeshivah* once came to R' Yaakov and told him that he was concerned because he had a problem preparing *shiurim* (lectures) for his class.

R' Yaakov counseled the *Rosh Yeshivah*, telling him, "You have to *daven* and have the proper intent in the section of *Shemoneh Esrei* 'וְתֵן בְּרָכָה — Give blessing' — the section that deals with livelihood and prosperity!"

⋘ Rabbinical Rewards

In 1890, the *Rosh Yeshivah* of the great *yeshivah* in Volozhin, the *Netziv* (Rabbi Naftali Tzvi Yehudah Berlin — 1817-1893), brought his son, Rabbi Chaim Berlin (1832-1913), then a prominent *Rav* in Moscow, to Volozhin, so that he could give *shiurim* in the eminent *yeshivah* of Volozhin.

The *yeshivah* was going through a very difficult period as edicts being issued by the hostile Russian government interfered more and more with the running of the *yeshivah*. The government demanded, among other things, that no learning of Talmud take place at night, that secular studies (especially the Russian language) become a major part of the curriculum and that all faculty members become recognized by virtue of diplomas received from Russian educational institutions.

Sadly, in 1892 the *Netziv* was forced to close the doors of the prominent *yeshivah* for the final time. R' Chaim Berlin took a position as *Rav* in the town of Kobrin, where he remained for three years. At the end of that time he shocked his contemporaries by announcing that he had accepted a rabbinical position in a town that was not nearly of the same spiritual level as his previous positions. The town located in southern Russia was called Yelisavetgrad.

Very few people could understand why a Rabbi of his stature would go to an area where there were so few Jews with an appreciation of, or commitment to, Torah and *mitzvos*.

On his way to Yelisavetgrad he stopped in Brisk, where the great *gaon*, Rabbi Chaim Soloveitchik (1853-1918), tended a *seudas preidah* (farewell gathering) in his honor.

At the *seudah*, R' Chaim Berlin overheard some of the guests questioning the wisdom of his taking a position where there was "no Shabbos, no *kashrus*, and little semblance of *Yiddishkeit*."

"You are right, what you are saying is all true," called out R' Chaim Berlin. "There is very little *Yiddishkeit* where I am going. However, if you deem the rabbinate as a means for compensation in *Olam Hazeh* (this world), then of course it makes sense to be a *Rav* in a place like Volozhin, Brisk or Ponevezh where you can give *shiurim*, learn Torah and be involved with fully observant people. There are spiritual pleasures to be had, but they are nonetheless primarily for the here and now.

"However, if you deem the rabbinate as a vehicle toward achieving merit in *Olam Haba* (the World to Come), then a *Rav* in Yelisavetgrad who closes one store on Shabbos, or who influences one butcher not to sell *treife* (non-kosher) meat, or who gets one family to become *shomer Shabbos*, or gets one child to go to a *yeshivah* — such a *Rav* can merit more reward in *Olam Haba* than any *Rav* in a big city, saturated with many religious Jews, can ever hope to attain!"

ᴇᴥᴄᴦ Stop That Thief!

Rabbi Elya Lopian (1872-1970) would often relate an incident that occurred in the *beis hamidrash* of Kelm, Lithuania that made a lasting impression on him.

One day, when he and the other *bachurim* (young students) of the *yeshivah* were studying *mussar* (ethical behavior), Rabbi Simchah Zisel Ziv (1824-1898), their renowned *Mashgiach* (spiritual mentor), walked into the *beis hamidrash*, slapped his hand down on the *bimah* (central podium) to get everyone's attention, then called out, "Is that how you talk to a *ganav* (robber)?"

The *bachurim* in the *beis hamidrash* were stunned! What was their *Mashgiach* talking about?

Seeing the surprised expressions on the faces of the *bachurim*, R' Simchah Zisel explained. "The *Yetzer Hara* (Evil Inclination) is a *ganav!* He is trying to rob you of your time and your potential to be great, by lulling you into laziness and enticing you to become occupied with matters other than the study of Torah and the observance of *mitzvos*.

"Tell me," R' Simchah Zisel continued, "if, G-d forbid, you saw a thief in your home, would you gently tell him to leave or politely ask him not to steal anything? Of course not! You would yell at the top of your voice, 'Stop! Robber! Get out!'

"It is the same with learning *mussar*. The study of *mussar* is directed at the *Yetzer Hara* within man and therefore must be learned *b'hispeilus* — with tremendous passion and fervor."

Whenever Rabbi Elya Lopian retold this story, he would indicate what this meant by chanting, in a powerful, haunting melody, the first thirteen words of the classic *sefer Mesilas Yesharim*: "יְסוֹד הַחֲסִידוּת וְשׁוֹרֶשׁ הָעֲבוֹדָה הַתְּמִימָה הוּא שֶׁיִּתְבָּרֵר וְיִתְאַמֵּת אֵצֶל הָאָדָם מַה חוֹבָתוֹ בְּעוֹלָמוֹ — The essence of piety and the basis for perfect worship [of Hashem] is [dependent] on one's ability to define with precision his obligation in his world." Inevitably, whenever he recited those words in that cadence, it brought tears to the eyes of everyone present.

❦   ❦   ❦

Rabbi Sholom Schwadron, the *Maggid* of Jerusalem, was very close to R' Elya and heard R' Elya retell this story many times. Once R' Sholom himself related the aforementioned episode in a *shmuess* (*mussar* lecture) to a group of *bachurim* as he encouraged them to learn *mussar* with passion and fervor.

After the *shmuess*, a *bachur* came over to R' Sholom and said, "R' Sholom, I know in my heart that you are right. But I am too embarrassed to learn *mussar* that way."

R' Sholom smiled gently at the young man and replied, "Picture in your mind, for a moment, a sophisticated young man walking in the street, dressed immaculately, who walks with his head high and his shoulders back and makes a favorable impression on all who see him. Suddenly he slips and falls and severely injures his ankle. He is rushed to the hospital where he is x-rayed and diagnosed as having fractured an ankle.

"His foot is fitted with an unsightly cast, over which he can put neither shoe nor sock. Now I ask you," exclaimed R' Sholom, "would a young man like that be ashamed to walk in the street even though he is not wearing a shoe and sock on one foot? Of course not. Why? Because since he is in pain and this condition is part of the healing process, embarrassment is not an issue.

"And you, too, my dear one," continued R' Sholom, "if you really feel pain at what the *Yetzer Hara* is doing to you, then you will feel no shame in talking to him sternly when you learn *mussar*. In that manner your *neshamah* (soul) will come to be healed."

◆§ A Spark in a Snowdrift

At a recent Torah Umesorah convention, Rabbi Shlomo Braunstein, *Rosh Yeshiva* of Yeshivah Darkei Noam in Brooklyn, told the following story to a group of *mechanchim* (Torah educators) in order to illustrate the attitude one must have when teaching Torah. Rabbi Braunstein heard the story from Rabbi Moshe Samuels (1923-1985), who was a *rebbi* in Mesivta Torah Vodaath for thirty-six years.

R abbi Shlomo Heiman (1893-1944) was a world-renowned *talmid chacham*, a *talmid* of Rabbi Baruch Ber Leibowitz. He eventually became a *Rosh Yeshivah* first in Baranovich and then later in Vilna. In 1936 he came to America to become the *Rosh Yeshivah* of Mesivta Torah Vodaath. R' Shlomo and his wife, Feige, unfortunately had no children of their own. Therefore, R' Shlomo's *talmidim* became their beloved children.

R' Shlomo always delivered his *shiurim* with great enthusiasm. He would stand and excitedly explain every nuance of the *Gemara*, expounding with almost breathless rapture the *chiddushim* (innovative thoughts) he wished to convey. He encouraged the many *talmidim* in the class to interrupt the *shiur* with their questions, and at times the give-and-take with his *talmidim* left him perspiring and breathless.

One winter morning, when Rabbi Moshe Samuels was in R' Shlomo's *shiur*, New York was hit by a major snowstorm. Trolleys and buses could hardly get through the streets, and cars were stranded in awkward positions sandwiched in between snowdrifts that were three feet high.

Very few *bachurim* made it to the *yeshivah* that day. The four boys who did show up that morning, including Moshe Samuels, wondered among themselves if R' Shlomo would give his regular *shiur*.

He did. Not only did he give his *shiur*, he gave it with the same gusto and fervor as usual. The four *bachurim* in the classroom could not believe their eyes. Here was the great *Rosh Yeshivah* standing in front of them, waving his hands to make a point, talking at a rapid pace, straining at the top of his vocal range as he reached the crux of a particular *chiddush* — just as he did every day in the *shiur*. Suddenly he paused for a moment to catch his breath.

"*Rebbe*," one of the boys ventured politely, wishing to allow his *Rosh Yeshivah* the liberty of relaxing a bit. "You are only talking to the four of us."

Rabbi Shlomo Heiman turned to the *bachur* and with great seriousness said, "You are wrong. I am not merely talking to you. I am talking to you and to all your *talmidim* and to all your *talmidim's talmidim!*"

> Considering that at least one of the four in the class (Moshe Samuels) eventually became a *rebbi* and taught in Yeshiva Torah Vodaath for over three decades, R' Shlomo was actually talking to more than seven hundred people that morning — certainly a good enough reason to be enthusiastic.
>
> Torah is eternal, and if those who teach it keep that in mind, its message is penetrating. Thus it was the fire in Rabbi Shlomo Heiman's voice that helped ignite in young Moshe Samuels the burning desire to become a *rebbi* and teach Torah to the next generation of children in *Klal Yisrael*.

*A Voice to Remember

The wife of the late Ponevezher *Rav*, *Rebbetzin* Hinda Kahaneman, was a sensitive, caring woman who took a personal interest in the *talmidim* of her husband's *yeshivah* in Bnei Brak, Israel. It was her custom to tender a *kiddush* in her apartment for any foreign *talmid* in the *yeshivah* on the occasion of his *aufruf* when he was called to the Torah on the Shabbos before he was to be married.

One of the boys so honored was Raphael Wolpin, the son of the noted editor of *The Jewish Observer*, Rabbi Nisson Wolpin of Brooklyn, New York. As father of the *chassan*, Rabbi Wolpin attended the *kiddush* in the *Rebbetzin's* home along with the *kallah's* father, Rabbi Moshe Yehuda Schlesinger of Jerusalem. It was then that the *Rebbetzin* told this touching story.

🦋 🦋 🦋

Many years earlier her husband, the Ponevezher *Rav*, Rabbi Yosef Kahaneman (1886-1969), studied in Poland together with the grandfather of the *kallah*, Rabbi Yechiel Mechel Schlesinger (1898-1949). Late one evening, the Ponevezher *Rav* left the *beis hamidrash* (study hall) and went outside the building. As he began walking, he noticed R' Yechiel Mechel's wife pacing slowly back and forth alongside the *yeshivah*.

Rabbi Kahaneman knew, as did most others in the *yeshivah*, that *Rebbetzin* Maita Schlesinger came from an aristocratic family in Hamburg, Germany, where full-time Torah study was not the conventional mode of life. Yet to *Rebbetzin* Schlesinger there was nothing in the world as important as her husband's growth in learning. This gave her the fortitude and the will to forego a life of luxury and convenience in Germany and accept, instead, the simple and materially frugal way of life in the *yeshivah* community. Everyone recognized her self-sacrifice and acknowledged that she was a woman who deserved honor and recognition.

"Can I help you in any way?" Rabbi Kahaneman asked *Rebbetzin* Schlesinger as she passed him in front of the *beis hamidrash*.

"No, thank you," the woman replied. "I was to meet my husband outside the *yeshivah*, but I will just wait here until he comes out."

"I can go in to get him for you," offered the *Rav*. "He is sitting in the back by the window."

"No, please don't disturb him," *Rebbetzin* Schlesinger replied. "You see, as I walked by the *beis hamidrash*, I happened to hear his voice raised in study, and so for now 'Ich shpatzir mit zein Kol Torah' (I am [happy to be] strolling with his voice of Torah study)."

The *Rav* was overwhelmed. He paused for a moment and then said to her reflectively, "Your husband is a great man. His devotion to Torah is total and your recognition of his learning is remarkable. Perhaps one day he will be fortunate enough to build a *yeshivah* and if he does, I will encourage him to call it 'Kol Torah.'

❦   ❦   ❦

And that is how the great *yeshivah* Kol Torah in Bayit Vegan, Jerusalem. got its name. It was indeed founded by *Rebbetzin* Schlesinger's husband, R' Yechiel Mechel, in 1939 and is headed today by the *gaon*, Rabbi Shlomo Zalman Auerbach.

⌘§ Propheteering

Chazal (*Horayos* 14a) debate which style of Torah learning is more valuable: *Sinai* — the sparkling breadth of knowledge spanning the wide horizon of Torah, often referred to as *bekius*, or *oker harim* — profundity of comprehending a *sugya* (Torah topic) to its very depth, often referred to as *lamdus* or *amkus*.

Although *gedolei Torah* customarily come to be associated with a particular specialty and approach to learning, they usually contain a blend of *Sinai* (*bekius*) and *oker harim* (*amkus*) in their arsenal of Torah knowledge.

The following story told by Rabbi Yosef Scheinberger, the secretary of the Beis Din Tzedek in Jerusalem, who witnessed it first-hand, is dazzling in its portrayal of two *gedolei Torah* with their unusual insight and scope of Torah knowledge.

In the late 1950s Rabbi Scheinberger completed writing his *sefer*, *Amudei Aish*, on the life of Rabbi Yehoshua Leib Diskin (1817-1898), the renowned *Rav* of Brisk. Prior to having the *sefer* published, he took the manuscript to Rabbi Velvel Soloveitchik (1887-1959), the Brisker *Rav*, in Jerusalem to get his opinion on what he had written.

Rabbi Scheinberger waited anxiously for the review of the great Torah sage. After a few days he was summoned to see R' Velvel.

"There is an expression in your manuscript that must be deleted," said R' Velvel.

"Which one is that?" asked the surprised Rabbi Scheinberger.

"You write that my father, Rabbi Chaim Soloveitchik (1853-1918), once remarked that the depth of Torah knowledge possessed by R' Yehoshua Leib was of such authenticity that it was worthy of the accolade 'אֵלָיו תִּשְׁמָעוּן (To him you shall listen).' That expression is taken from the Torah (*Devarim* 18:15) where Moshe *Rabbeinu* tells *Klal Yisrael* that they must listen to the prophet that Hashem will send them. The phrase אֵלָיו תִּשְׁמָעוּן is applicable only to a prophet, not to an ordinary human being no matter how great his stature. It should therefore be removed."

"But," protested Rabbi Scheinberger, "this is a direct quote from R' Chaim about R' Yehoshua Leib, and if R' Chaim said it, why should I not be able to quote him?"

"Still," insisted R' Velvel, "the Torah uses it only for a prophet, a messenger from Hashem, and so it should not be used regarding human beings."

Rabbi Scheinberger omitted the quote from the manuscript and was left with an indelible impression of R' Velvel's exactness. It was the typical Brisk approach, with emphasis on the integrity of every nuance in the Torah.

❧ ❧ ❧

Many years later, Rabbi Scheinberger was in the Williamsburg section of Brooklyn and was visiting with the Satmar *Rav*, Rabbi Yoel Teitelbaum (1887-1979). The Satmar *Rav* was known for his tremendous *bekius*, and for his extremely sharp and attentive mind.

During their conversation, Rabbi Scheinberger told the *Rav* about the *sefer* he had written, and then relayed the incident with Rabbi Velvel Soloveitchik. The Satmar *Rav* listened without saying anything, and when Rabbi Scheinberger finished, the *Rebbe* smiled.

"Does the *Rebbe* see anything amusing here?" asked Rabbi Scheinberger.

"It's nothing," said the *Rebbe*. "It's nothing really signifigant."

Rabbi Scheinberger, though, pursued the matter. "I see there is something on the *Rebbe's* mind. Please share it with me."

The *Rebbe* then asked someone who was in the room with them to bring him a *Shulchan Aruch, Orach Chaim*. The *Rebbe* then turned to the laws of *Kedushah* (*Orach Chaim* 125:1), specifically the section regarding the proper way for the *chazzan* and the *tzibbur* (congregation) to recite it.

The *Beis Yosef* writes (ibid.) that the *tzibbur* should not begin their recitation of *kedushah* with the word "*nakdishach*." Rather, the *chazzan* alone begins with the word "*nakdishach*" and the *tzibbur* merely concentrates and listens attentively as the *chazzan* recites the first sentence of the *Kedushah*. When the *chazzan* reaches the words *kadosh*, the members of the congregation respond, saying the words *kadosh* following the *chazzan's* recitation.

"Take a look at the comments of Rabbi Akiva Eiger," said the Satmar *Rav*.

What Rabbi Scheinberger saw in the tiny letters of the *Hagaos Rabbi Akiva Eiger*, as he held the *Shulchan Aruch* close to his eyes for a better view, astounded him. Citing the *Neziros Shimshon* (Rabbi Shimshon Bloch), Rabbi Akiva Eiger notes, "In the writings of the *Arizal* it is brought that the congregation should indeed say the entire *Kedushah* [beginning with the words נַקְדִּישָׁךְ]." And then the *Neziros Shimshon* adds two words: "וְאֵלָיו תִּשְׁמָעוּן" (To him you shall listen)."

The *Neziros Shimshon* had cited the view of the *Arizal*, and to show that he agreed with the *Arizal's* view, he had added two words for emphasis — the same two words that R' Chaim had used about R' Yehoshua Leib, the same words Moshe *Rabbeinu* had used for a prophet, a messenger of Hashem.

Rabbi Scheinberger's face registered amazement at the *bekius* of the Satmar *Rav*. At the same time, though, he couldn't help but wonder about R' Velvel's comment. Wasn't the expression אֵלָיו תִּשְׁמָעוּן reserved only for a messenger of Hashem?

The Satmar *Rav*, anticipating his question, smiled and said, "The *Arizal* was different. He was like an angel of Hashem."

⊷§ A Light in the Darkness

During *Shacharis* on Mondays and Thursdays, after the Torah reading, a moving prayer is recited for the sake of Jews who are either in captivity or are oppressed by foreign governments. The prayer begins with "אַחֵינוּ כָּל בֵּית יִשְׂרָאֵל" — All our Jewish brethren" and concludes with "הַמָּקוֹם יְרַחֵם עֲלֵיהֶם וְיוֹצִיאֵם מִצָּרָה" לְרְוָחָה, וּמֵאֲפֵלָה לְאוֹרָה, וּמִשִּׁעְבּוּד לִגְאֻלָּה — May G-d have mercy on them and remove them from distress to relief, and from darkness to light, and from subjugation to redemption. . ."

Avrohom (Abie) Rotenberg of Toronto composed a beautiful haunting melody for this prayer. Sung communally, the melody is exceptionally uplifting. It captures in music the pain and anguish so eloquently expressed in the words of this supplication. Sung hundreds of times by thousands of people, this song recently became the catalyst for a touching insight by a child in Russia.

Shortly after *Sukkos*, 1991, Rabbi Aaron Brustowsky of Lakewood, New Jersey went with his wife and family to Moldavia, formerly of the Soviet Union, to help start a *yeshivah* and to encourage the Jews of the surrounding areas to become more aware of their heritage and become involved in Torah study and *mitzvah* performance.

R' Aaron found that many Jews there, both adults and children were hungry for authentic *Yiddishkeit*. A *yeshivah* was started in a small apartment almost immediately, and every day parents brought their children to register.

R' Aaron is known, not only for his teaching talents, but also for his voice and musical talents. One evening, after being in Moldavia for a few months, he taught a group of boys the beautiful melody and the meaning of the prayer "אַחֵינוּ כָּל בֵּית יִשְׂרָאֵל — All our Jewish brethren."

As the boys sang the melody over and over again, tears streamed from R' Aaron's eyes. He knew that he would be returning to the freedom and comforts of America, while these children would remain in Moldavia, with little hope of ever leaving.

Suddenly, Rabbi Aaron stopped the singing and said to his students, "When we sang this song back in America, we felt that the words were intended for you — that you should be able to escape to freedom. Now all of you are singing the song. About whom are you singing?"

For a few moments they were all quiet, and then sixteen-year-old Maxim (now Menachem) spoke up. "I have come to understand that every person needs to communicate with Hashem. Every person must find the language in which to converse with the Supreme Being. If one has found that language, one has found light. If not, then one remains in darkness, regardless of where that person lives — be it Israel, America or England. I sing and pray that my brethren in the darkness, wherever they may be, become as fortunate as I, to find this light."

מִצָּרָה לִרְוָחָה, וּמֵאֲפֵלָה לְאוֹרָה, וּמִשִׁעְבּוּד לִגְאֻלָּה" — . . .from distress to relief, and from darkness to light, and from subjugation to redemption. . ."

> Within the first six months of learning Maxim found that light — in the darkness of Moldavia. What progress have each of us made in the last six months?

◆§ High Time

R abbi Yitzchak Hutner, *Rosh Yeshivah* of Yeshiva Chaim Berlin in Brooklyn, once wrote a letter (see *Pachad Yitzchak* no. 132) to an out-of-town community for the installation dinner for their new *rav*. In the letter he taught an interesting perspective on the rabbinate.

"Actually," he wrote, "I should be standing up for all of you, for *Chazal* (Sages of the Talmud) teach us (*Kiddushin* 33a) that one is required to stand up when he witnesses people performing a *mitzvah*. All of you, involved in bestowing honor upon your *rav*, now perform the sacred *mitzvah* of *kavod haTorah* (giving honor to those who study Torah). Therefore, please consider that even from a distance, I have accorded all of you your due respect.

"However," continued Rabbi Hutner, "you should remember this: In the old cities of yesteryear there was always a very high tower or building situated in the center of town on which there was a huge clock. This was for the benefit of all the townsmen so that they would always know the correct time.

"People suggested two reasons as to why the clock tower was so high. The simpletons were convinced that the reason was that everyone throughout the town should be able to see the correct time regardless of where they might be. The intelligent people, however, understood that there was another purpose altogether, for the clock being so high. It was so that no one could tamper with or change it! For if the clock were within everyone's reach, an individual might be inclined to move the hands on the clock to synchronize it with his personal timepiece. Soon every man would be fiddling with the clock, and eventually no one would know what the true and correct time really was.

"The same is true of a *rav* in a community," continued Rabbi Hutner. "He must be regarded with such high esteem that when he guides and teaches he is able to do so unhindered. A *rav* who the community feels they can change according to their own whims and desires is not a leader but a follower."

And in most cases it is only a matter of time until they replace him.

Shlomo *HaMelech* wrote in *Mishlei* (28:14): "אַשְׁרֵי אָדָם מְפַחֵד תָּמִיד — Praiseworthy is the person who is always afraid." *Tosafos* (*Gittin* 55b ד"ה אשרי) point out that it is sinful to always be fearful, and therefore the fear that Shlomo *HaMelech* referred to was the apprehension one should have with regard to his Torah study. One should continually be concerned and fearful that he might forget a segment of Torah he had once learned. Thus, say *Tosafos,* it is imperative that one constantly review that which he has already studied. (See *Berachos* 60a.)

Rabbi Yosef Buchsbaum, director of the Machon Yerushalayim Institute in Israel, had the good fortune to live in the same apartment building in Shaarei Chessed, Jerusalem as did the Tshebiner *Rav*, Rabbi Dov Berish Weidenfeld (1879-1965), for more than two decades. He recently retold a story that depicted the expanded dimension of the *Rav's* understanding of Shlomo *HaMelech's* teaching.

The Tshebiner *Rav* went out of his way not to trouble others. If, however, he did need someone's assistance, he would beseech the person in his pleasant, soft voice by starting his request with, "*Zeitz mir moichel* (Please forgive me), but can you please get me. . .?" Or "*Zeitz mir moichel,* but can you please find out for me. . .?" He carried on in this gentle and humble manner until his last days.

During the final stage of his life, when he was already very ill, the Tshebiner *Rav* had a *hoiz bachur*, a young student who resided in his home and tended to his needs. As the days and nights seemed to trudge along slowly, the *Rav* would lose consciousness every once in a while. One night he dozed off, into what the *bachur* thought was a very deep sleep.

Suddenly, in the middle of the night, the *Rav* called out to the young man. The *bachur* hurried into the room, thinking that something must be very wrong. "*Zeitz mir moichel* (Please forgive me)," began the *Rav* in a hoarse voice, "but could you please bring me the *Noda B'Yehudah, Mahadura Tinyana* (the *sefer* of responsa written by Rabbi Yechezkel Landau (1713-1793)?"

The *bachur* hurried to get the *sefer*. The *Rav* sought out a certain *teshuvah* (responsa) dealing with *Hilchos Treifos* (*kashrus* laws), then returned the *sefer* to the *bachur*. The remainder of the night passed uneventfully.

The next morning, the Tshebiner *Rav's* son-in-law, Rabbi Baruch Shimon Schneerson, came to visit. As he walked into the *Rav's* home he asked the *bachur*, "How was the night?"

"Everything was quite all right," replied the *bachur*, "except that in the middle of the night, the *Rav* wanted a *Noda B'Yehudah*. I had been sure that he was asleep," the *bachur* continued, "but he woke up and asked for that particular *sefer*."

When Rabbi Schneerson entered the room of his father-in-law, he first inquired about his health and then asked, "Why did you need the *Noda B'Yehudah* in the middle of the night?"

The Tshebiner *Rav* said softly. "Every man has to know where he is headed, and I realize what stage of life I am now in. The Talmud (*Kesubos* 77b) teaches us: אַשְׁרֵי מִי שֶׁבָּא לְכַאן וְתַלְמוּדוֹ בְּיָדוֹ — Praiseworthy is the person who comes here [to the World to Come] knowledgeable of his Talmud (Torah studies).' It is for this reason," continued the *Rav*, "that I am reviewing all the Torah I learned in my lifetime: so that I will be ready when I appear in the Heavenly Court. At night I was reviewing the responsa of the *Noda B'Yehudah* and the exact language of that particular responsa eluded me. That's why I wanted to check it one more time!"

If the Tshebiner *Rav*, who had a photographic memory, felt compelled to review what he had learned, how much more so do we, with our limited capacities, need to review what we have learned?

⋙ A Lesson in Not Giving One

The following story was told to Rabbi David Sanders, a *Rosh Yeshivah* in Johannesburg, South Africa, by the Ponevezher *Rav*,

Rabbi Yosef Kahaneman. Rabbi Kahaneman himself had been a participant in this incident many years earlier.

When he was the *Rav* and *Rosh Yeshivah* in Ponevezh, Lithuania, Rabbi Kahaneman made numerous trips throughout Europe and overseas to raise funds for the *yeshivah*. He never left the country, though, without first saying good-bye to his *Rebbi*, the Chofetz Chaim.

This story occurred before one particular trip, when the Ponevezher *Rav* traveled to the small town of Radin to say good-bye to the Chofetz Chaim and get his blessings for the journey. He came to Radin early one morning, and when the Chofetz Chaim saw his beloved *talmid* (student), he greeted him with great joy.

"Rav Yoshu," the Chofetz Chaim exclaimed, "I am thrilled to see you! Just today I received the galleys of one of the sections of the *Mishnah Berurah* from the printer. I must go over them and compare them to the original manuscript to make sure there are no errors. I need someone reliable to review this with, and who better than you, my beloved *talmid*? Would you kindly do it with me?"

The Ponevezher *Rav* was honored that his *rebbi* would entrust him with such an important task. "Of course," the Ponevezher *Rav* replied. "It would be a great pleasure for me to work with the *rebbi* on his *sefer*."

For several hours, the Chofetz Chaim and the Ponevezher *Rav* compared the printed galleys to the original manuscript, searching for mistakes, looking for omissions, verifying sources and all the while discussing the various *halachos* which this particular section of the *Mishnah Berurah* dealt with.

As the afternoon drew to a close their concentration was disrupted by a knock on the door. A group of *bachurim* had come to tell the Chofetz Chaim that the time to daven *Minchah* (afternoon service) had arrived. The Chofetz Chaim and the Ponevezher *Rav* closed their *sefarim* and made their way to the *beis hamidrash* (study hall) to join the *talmidim* for *Minchah*.

After *Minchah* the Chofetz Chaim called for attention as he struck his hand atop his *shtender* with a thud. "Today" he announced, "I will be not be giving *mussar*." [It was the custom of the Chofetz Chaim to periodically give a *mussar shmuess* (talk) after *Minchah*.] And then, in the manner of the ultimate pedagogue that he was, he explained himself. "The reason that I can't deliver a *shmuess* is that I did not learn [Torah] today."

The Ponevezher *Rav* was astonished! He personally had just spent many consecutive hours with the Chofetz Chaim learning and discussing the *halachos* and related topics that were relevant to the section of the *Mishnah Berurah* they were proofreading. Wasn't that considered learning Torah?

"It is obvious," said the Ponevezher *Rav* years later on his visit to South Africa, "that the Chofetz Chaim felt that before one can give *mussar* one must be spiritually elevated by his own learning of Torah. And that learning should be *lishmah* (solely for the fulfillment of the *mitzvah*), and not for any ulterior motive. To give *mussar* otherwise would be presumptuous."

❀ ❀ ❀

In this light, perhaps, we can glean an additional meaning of the Talmudic teaching (*Pirkei Avos* 2:5): "אַל תָּדִין אֶת חֲבֵרְךָ עַד שֶׁתַּגִּיעַ לִמְקוֹמוֹ — Do not judge your friend until you have reached his place."

Conventionally, this is understood to mean that a person should not judge the actions of others until he or she has been in a similar situation. For example, people should not criticize others' intense sadness and remorse until they themselves have suffered a similar loss. Similarly, one should not condemn another person who may have succumbed to temptation unless they, too, have successfully overcome a similar challenge.

However, bearing the Chofetz Chaim's concept in mind, the aforementioned teaching may be seen in a different light. "Do not admonish others [through *mussar*] עַד שֶׁתַּגִּיעַ לִמְקוֹמוֹ, until you have reached their [spiritual] level [of piety]."

The *Hakafos* on this *Simchas Torah* night at Yeshiva Torah Vodaath were marked by lively and beautiful dancing. *Yeshivah bachurim, rebbeim, baalei battim* and neighborhood children mingled in crowded circles, singing, clapping, and stomping their feet to the rhythm of the latest *yeshivishe niggunim.*

That evening in Brooklyn it was damp and rainy outside, but inside, the huge *beis hamidrash* was permeated by the warm radiance of camaraderie inspired by the unity that engulfs every *shul* and *yeshivah* in the world on *Simchas Torah.*

During a lull in the dancing, Rabbi Yisroel Reisman, who was then a *talmid* of the *yeshivah*, approached his *Rosh Yeshivah*, Rav Avrohom Pam, with a *halachic she'eilah* regarding the *Krias HaTorah* (Torah reading) of the next day.

On *Simchas Torah*, during the morning *leining*, it is customary in most *shuls* to give *aliyos* to all males present (even boys under the age of *bar mitzvah*). In order that everyone may be called to the Torah, a segment of the *parshah* of *V'zos Haberachah* is read over and over again until everyone has had an *aliyah.*

Each time the *sidrah* is started, a *Kohen* who has not yet been called to the Torah is called for the first *aliyah*. A *Levi* is then called for the second *aliyah*. Rabbi Reisman, who is a *Levi*, wondered what should be done if a *Kohen* receives an *aliyah*, and all the *Levi'im* in the *shul* had already been given *aliyos*. Should a *Levi* who already had an *aliyah* be called again, or is the *Kohen* who had just had an *aliyah* given another one?

Rabbi Reisman approached Rav Pam and asked the *she'eilah*. The *Rosh Yeshivah* said, "I believe that the *Meishiv Davar* (authored by the *Netziv*, Rabbi Naftali Tzvi Yehudah Berlin [1817-1893]) discusses this *she'eilah*, but I don't recall the precise ruling. I have the *sefer* at home and I will check to be sure what he says." (At that time the *Meishiv Davar* was out of print and therefore not available in the *yeshivah*.)

Rav Pam thought for a few more moments and then said something halachically remarkable. "I believe the *Netziv* rules that in this situation a *Yisrael* receives an *aliyah bimkom* (in place of the) *Levi*."

This was astonishing, because throughout the year a *Yisrael* is never given an *aliyah* in place of a *Levi*, once a *Kohen* has been called for the first *aliyah*.

Rabbi Reisman thanked his *Rosh Yeshivah* and returned to the dancing. Shortly thereafter, he noticed that Rav Pam was motioning to him. "Do you have a raincoat?" the *Rosh Yeshivah* asked his *talmid*.

When Rabbi Reisman said that he did, Rav Pam said, "Then let's go to my home now and look up the *Meishiv Davar*."

As they were about to leave the *yeshivah*, another *talmid* approached Rav Pam and said, "I overheard the *she'eilah* that was raised, so I asked Rabbi [Avraham] Talansky (a faculty member and *gabbai* of the Torah Vodaath *minyan* for decades) if he had ever encountered that situation. He told me that this exact *she'eilah* was posed years ago to Rabbi Yaakov Kamenetzky (1892-1986) during his tenure as *Rosh Yeshivah* of Torah Vodaath. R' Yaakov ruled that on *Simchas Torah*, when the *Levi'im* have already had their *aliyos*, a *Yisrael* may be called up for the second *aliyah*, even after a *Kohen*."

Rav Pam thanked the boy for the information and said, "I believe that is exactly how the *Netziv* rules as well, but I would still like to check it."

Rav Pam and Rabbi Reisman walked the two blocks to Rabbi Pam's home. Once there, Rabbi Pam took out the *Meishiv Davar* and indeed, in the second volume at the end of responsa 48, the *Netziv* rules that on *Simchas Torah* only, once the obligatory reading has been done, a *Yisrael* may be called in the place of the *Levi* if all the *Levi'im* in *shul* have already had their *aliyos*. (For the ruling throughout the year, see *Mishnah Berurah*, *Orach Chaim* 135, note 28.)

Rav Pam then showed Rabbi Reisman other interesting responsa that the *Netziv* had written and discussed them briefly. They then headed back to the *yeshivah*. On the way back, Rabbi Reisman couldn't help but wonder what had compelled the *Rosh Yeshivah* to go home and check the *she'eilah* in the middle of *Hakafos*, particularly since he had actually remembered the *psak* (*halachic* ruling). He worked up the courage to ask.

Rav Pam smiled and said, "Let me tell you a story." He then related the following episode.

> It happened one night that Rabbi Zalman Volozhiner (1756-1788; the younger brother of Rabbi Chaim Volozhiner and one of the most prominent *talmidim* of the Vilna Gaon) was missing. He had left his home to spend a night in the local *beis hamidrash*, but in the middle of the night he could not be found. Early the next morning he was seen coming down the road, returning from a nearby town.
>
> Those who saw him asked R' Zalman, "What were you doing there? There is a *beis hamidrash* in our own town. You could have learned just as well here!"
>
> R' Zalman replied, "I needed a certain *sefer* which we didn't have in our *beis hamidrash*, so I went for it to the next town. You see," R' Zalman explained with interesting insight, "Moshe *Rabbeinu* told *Klal Yisrael*: לֹא בַשָּׁמַיִם הִוא — The Torah is not in Heaven [it is attainable by all]' (*Devarim* 30:12). *Rashi* there (citing *Eruvin* 55a) comments that if indeed the Torah were so far away, we would be obligated to seek it out.
>
> "This," said R' Zalman, "is a clear indication that if we need something related to Torah and for the moment it is out of our reach, it is our responsibility to pursue it. It is for this reason that I traveled to the next town — to get the *sefer* I needed."

Rav Pam paused for a moment and continued. "Just this afternoon, on *Shemini Atzeres*, numerous *bachurim* from the *yeshivah* came over for a *Simchas Yom Tov*. I told them this story regarding the correct approach to Torah. Earlier tonight, when you asked the *she'eilah*, I was reluctant to go home right away to look up the answer. However, I remembered that I had told the *bachurim* this story just this afternoon, and it's only right that I abide by what I myself said."

R abbi Eliyahu Mayer Bloch (1894-1955), *Rosh Yeshivah* and founder of the Telshe Yeshiva in Cleveland, was a meticulous man whose every act and every spoken word was accounted for. His *talmidim* remember to this day the delicate preciseness in all that he did.

In 1949 a *talmid*, R' Rafael Altman* of Brooklyn, accompanied R' Elya Mayer to Detroit to collect funds for the *yeshivah*. The two were caught in a drenching downpour which showed no sign of letting up. As they still had many people to visit, and the notion of entering people's homes and tracking mud on their floors was unthinkable to the *Rosh Yeshivah*, he had no choice but to buy rubbers.

As the *Rebbi* and *talmid* were walking in the rain, R' Elya Mayer asked, "Who should pay for these rubbers?"

The rubbers cost only a dollar and twenty-five cents, but in 1949, not only was that a considerable amount of money, but Rabbi Bloch was so poverty stricken he could not afford even that amount.

The question was whether R' Elya Mayer or the Telshe Yeshiva should pay. On one hand, R' Elya Mayer reasoned, he alone would benefit from the rubbers (and even if he were to bring them back to Cleveland, no other boys in the *yeshivah* would use them, since they probably all had their own), therefore it might be proper that the money come from his pocket. On the other hand, he too had rubbers in Cleveland; he was in Detroit only for the sake of the *yeshivah* and therefore, perhaps, it was proper for the *yeshivah* to view this as part of its expenses.

[R' Elya Mayer ended up absorbing the cost of the rubbers.]

❦ ❦ ❦

R' Elya Mayer's meticulousness also manifested itself in the way he felt a *yeshivah's* property should be maintained. If there was a discarded piece of paper on the floor of the *beis hamidrash* (study hall) or in the corridors of the *yeshivah*, he would motion to a

---

* Name has been changed upon personal request.

bachur standing nearby to pick it up. It was his way of imparting a lesson regarding cleanliness and dignity in a *makom kadosh* (holy place).

On one of his first days in Telshe, the young Rafael Altman went out to the hallway to get a drink of water. As he approached the water fountain he noticed, to his amazement, a *bachur* scraping a hard piece of dried gum off the floor. No one had instructed the *bachur* to do this, but he himself understood that his *Rosh Yeshivah* would want it removed. That *bachur* eventually became one of R' Elya Mayer's most renowned *talmidim* and is today one of the *Roshei Yeshivah* of Telshe in Chicago, Rabbi Avrohom Chaim Levin.

It is the following story, though, that R' Rafael Altman claims is most remarkable.

Rabbi Bloch tragically lost his wife and four of his children to the cruelties of the Nazis in World War II. After he had been in Cleveland for a while he remarried and had two other children. Understandably, they were greatly loved by their father. On his son Yosef Zalman's third birthday, two *bachurim* in the *yeshivah*, from well-to-do families, decided to buy the child a special gift. They knew that their *Rosh Yeshivah* could not afford "a luxury item," and even if he could, he would not allow himself the indulgence. Therefore, out of love and admiration for their *rebbi*, they bought his son a tricycle. The child treasured it.

A short time later R' Elya Mayer was scheduled to give the *bechinah* (examination) on *Yoreh Deah* (a section of the *Code of Jewish Law*) for *semichah* (Rabbinic ordination). These two *bachurim* were among those who were to be tested.

When they came in for their *bechinah*, Rabbi Elya Mayer smiled warmly and said, "The other night I sat down to write both of you a letter of thanks. I am so grateful for your beautiful gesture to Yosef Zalman and I wanted to express my thoughts to you in writing. However, because I feel so grateful I realize now that I view both of you differently than before, and thus I cannot possibly give you the *bechinah!* I would not be objective. I might favor you in some way and treat you in a manner different from the way I treated the others who have taken the *bechinah*. This would be both unfair and incorrect. I will arrange for the other *Rosh Yeshivah,* [Rabbi Chaim Mordechai Katz (1894-1964)] to give you the *bechinah!"*

He wished them well, thanked them again and made the necessary arrangements.

> The Torah (*Devarim* 16:19) warns that a gift of blatant bribery will cause even the wise and the righteous to pervert justice. The Talmud (*Kesubos* 105b) further cautions that even accepting seemingly innocent favors (such as receiving a helping hand when crossing a bridge) will color one's judgment.
>
> R' Elya Mayer, in his meticulous honesty, broadened this precept to include even a gift to his son. R' Elya Mayer understood that although the gift was actually a gesture of kindness to his child, it was an act of affection to him as well, and his appreciation of it could therefore possibly taint his thinking.

⮥ Belated Remorse

In 1938, Rabbi Yaakov Galinsky, now the well-known orator from Bnei Brak, Israel, was a *bachur* (young student) learning in the Beis Yosef Yeshivah in Bialystok, Poland. The *Rosh Yeshivah* at the time was Rabbi Avraham Yoffen (1887-1970), who headed a network of seventy *yeshivos* throughout Poland which inculcated their students with the unique Novorodok approach to *mussar*.

Nighttime came early during the winter in Bialystok, and by three o'clock on Friday afternoon, Shabbos had already begun. By five o'clock the Shabbos *seudah* (meal) was over, and the *bachurim* returned to the *beis hamidrash* to continue their Torah studies. Much later in the evening, at ten o'clock, the *bachurim* would go to the home of Rabbi Yoffen where he would deliver a *mussar shmuess* (lecture on ethical behavior) based on the weekly *sidrah*.

One particular Friday night the *shmuess* continued past eleven o'clock. The *seudah* had been over for hours, and many of the *bachurim* were hungry. They approached Rabbi Yaakov Galinsky who had the reputation of getting things done, and asked him if he could arrange for food to be served to the *bachurim*. A few minutes later he was back with a substantial amount of *challah* and a large jar of honey, enough for all the *bachurim* who had assembled in the *Rosh Yeshivah's* home.

A few days later R' Yaakov found out that the jar of honey had been bought by *Rebbetzin* Sarah Yoffen (1885-1985) for the upcoming *Yom Tov* of *Pesach*. Although he felt bad that the honey was gone, he was too embarrassed to express his remorse to the *Rosh Yeshivah*. For years afterwards, though, it bothered him that he hadn't asked permission before obtaining the food for the *bachurim*.

❧   ❧   ❧

Decades later, in 1964, R' Avraham Yoffen came to *Eretz Yisrael* and settled there. He called together all his former Novorodok *talmidim* then living in Israel, and invited them to his home for a *seudah* and a *shmuess*.

The *Rosh Yeshivah* spoke warmly to the assembled, recalling their days together in Bialystok, reminiscing with them about the perils they had lived through together during World War II. He then gave eloquent *chizuk* (encouragement) to all who had come.

When Rabbi Yoffen finished his *shmuess*, R' Yaakov Galinsky requested permission to say a few words. Everyone turned to R' Yaakov to hear what he had in mind.

"אֶת חֲטָאַי אֲנִי מַזְכִּיר הַיּוֹם" — I recall my sins today," R' Yaakov began, quoting the famous words of Pharaoh's chief wine steward (*Bereishis* 41:9). "Many years ago, on a Friday night in the *Rosh Yeshivah's* home, I went to the kitchen and took *challah* and honey for the *bachurim*, who after spending many hours in the *beis hamidrash*, were hungry. I did not realize until afterwards that the jar of honey I took was being saved by the *Rebbetzin* for *Yom Tov*. I would therefore publicly like to ask the *Rosh Yeshivah* and the *Rebbetzin* for *mechilah* (forgiveness)."

Rebbetzin Yoffen — the daughter of the *Alter* of Novorodok,

Rabbi Yosef Yoizel Hurvitz (1848-1920) — who had been standing on the side listening to the words of her husband, now entered the room where all the *talmidim* had gathered and exclaimed, "R' Yaakov, how can you be asking for *mechilah*? It is obvious that you don't understand the approach of Novorodok. "It is we, the *Rosh Yeshivah* and I, who should be asking all of you, the *talmidim*, for *mechilah* for letting you reach such a degree of hunger. In Novorodok, everything in the *Rebbe's* house is there for the *talmidim*. A *Rebbe* must feel the pain of the *talmidim*. We should have known that the *bachurim* needed food. It is therefore we who now ask all of you for *mechilah*!"

This was classic Novorodok behavior — bold, spontaneous, outwardly emotional and self-negating — by both the *talmid* and the *Rebbetzin*.

◄§ Words of a Pressing Nature

The Midrash (*Bereishis Rabbah* 67:3) tells us that when Yitzchak *Avinu* became terror stricken with the realization that he had inadvertently given his heartfelt blessings to Yaakov rather than Eisav, he wanted to curse Yaakov. Hashem, though, said to Yitzchak, "If you curse him, you will in essence be cursing yourself, for you stated [in your blessing to Yaakov (*Bereishis* 27:29), 'אֹרְרֶיךָ אָרוּר — Those who curse him, will be cursed' " Yitzchak then exclaimed, "גַּם בָּרוּךְ יִהְיֶה — The blessing will remain his [Yaakov's]" (ibid. 27:33).

The Midrash then warns that man has six servants: three beyond his control, and three within his control. Man's eyes, ears and nose are beyond his control, for at times man sees things he would rather not see, hears things he would rather not hear and smells things he would rather not smell. However, man's mouth, hands and legs are within his control. He can choose whether to speak words of Torah or speak words of *lashon hara*. Similarly, man may choose to perform a *mitzvah* by taking a *lulav* and *esrog*, or perform a sin by stealing something or writing on Shabbos. Additionally, man can choose to go to a *beis hamidrash* or to a tavern. Thus, because the choice is always his, man is always responsible for the words he utters, the things he touches and the places he visits.

In this remarkable story within a story, we become sensitive to the responsibility of words, both spoken and unspoken.

I am indebted to Rabbi Yisroel Belsky, Rabbi David Frankel, Dr. David Kranzler and Mr. Marvin Heller for the information they supplied regarding these episodes.

In June of 1968 Rabbi Yehudah Leib Lewin (1894-1971), the chief *Rav* of Moscow, visited the United States. At that time the phrase "iron curtain" was an apt description of the chasm dividing the people of the Soviet Union from those of the West. People in the Soviet Union, especially Jews, were permitted very little, if any, contact with the outside world. Jews were jailed and tortured indiscriminately and were constant victims of oppression and cruelty. Additionally, thousands of Jews were deprived of decent jobs and for many of them abject poverty was a standard way of life.

In a cruel bit of sensationalism, the Soviet government under Leonid Brezhnev allowed the tall, imposing *Rav* to visit America as a supposed gesture of good will. However, wherever Rabbi Lewin went he was accompanied by the "*chazzan* from Leningrad" who people suspected was either an informer or a member of the KGB (the brutal Soviet secret police). Because of the *chazzan's* constant presence, Rabbi Lewin could not speak openly during his various public *drashos* (lectures) for fear of what harm might be done to his family or to the tens of thousands of Jews he left behind in Russia. The deeply etched lines in his face, his furrowed brow cresting his sad eyes, and his long, streaked, gray-white beard conveyed his unspoken sorrow and melancholy. When he broke down and wept in public, that in itself revealed the pain, anguish and torment of Russian Jews.

One evening, in the Sefardishe Shul in the Boro Park section of Brooklyn, a large crowd gathered to hear Rabbi Lewin speak. Introducing him that night was one of the *gedolei hador* Rabbi Yaakov Kamenetzky.

R' Yaakov first cited the Talmudic teaching (*Menachos* 99a) לוחות וְשִׁבְרֵי לוחות מוּנָחִין בָּאָרוֹן" — Both the complete Tablets [which Moshe *Rabbeinu* brought down from Heaven the second time] and the [first] Tablets that he had broken, rested in the Holy Ark."

"The *Luchos* that Moshe broke (see *Shemos* 32:19) were treated with respect and dignity which equaled that accorded to the whole *Luchos*," said R' Yaakov.

"I remember Rabbi Lewin as a Torah scholar from the days in the *yeshivah* in Slabodka, long before he became like the broken Tablets by being confined in Russia," continued R' Yaakov. "And just as Hashem ordained (*Devarim* 10:2 and *Menachos* ibid.) that *Klal Yisrael* give equal honor to the broken Tablets, it is similarly our duty to give Rabbi Lewin honor and respect."

R' Yaakov told the assembled that they must learn to understand the chosen words they were about to hear from Rabbi Lewin. "At some point his words might merely be a parable or allegory, at another point he could be saying things that are meant to intentionally camouflage the truth. Therefore, intelligence and insight are required to understand all that he says."

To illustrate his message, R' Yaakov related the following story* which was not only fascinating historically but significant as well, because of the lessons inherent in the events that occurred.

❧   ❧   ❧

In the early 1800s there were very few editions of *Shas* (the entire *Talmud Bavli*) available. Numerous burnings of entire editions of *Shas*, both by anti-Semites and Jewish heretics, in previous decades and centuries had greatly reduced the availability of volumes of the Talmud. Additionally the cost of printing was prohibitive as separate plates had to be made for each page.

In 1810, Rabbi Moshe Shapiro of Slavita, Russia, the son of Rabbi Pinchas Koritzer (1728-1790) (one of the noted *talmidim* of the *Baal Shem Tov*), sought the exclusive right to print an entire *Shas*. In

---

* For more specific details of this episode, see the essay "*Hadfasas HaTalmud*" in Volume One of *Sefer Dikdukei Sofrim* by Rabbi Rafael Rabinowitz, Vol. II of *M'ohran Shel Yisrael*, a biography on Rabbi Akiva Eiger by Rabbi Shimon Hirschler, and the essay "*D'fus Romm*" by Shmuel Shraga Figenson in the book *Yahadus Lita*.

order to protect his astronomical financial commitment, he wanted a guarantee by the Torah scholars of his generation that no other printer would be given permission to print a *Shas*. He was granted this exclusive right for twenty years, and between the years of 1817 and 1822 the *Shas* was published with letters of approbation from such notable *tzaddikim* as Rabbi Shneur Zalman of Liady, the *Baal HaTanya* (1745-1813), and R' Levi Yitzchak from Berditchev (1740-1810).

By 1834, nearly all of the sets of *Shas* had been sold and only thirty-seven of the original sets remained. At that time, the two sons of Rabbi Shapiro, R' Shmuel Avraham Abba and R' Pinchas, who were now running the business, wanted to print another edition of the *Shas*. By this time, though, Rabbi Menachem Mann Romm of Vilna, Lithuania, along with his partner, Rabbi Simchah Zimel of Horodna, began making preparations for an edition of *Shas* that they wished to print. The publishers in Slavita were angered because they felt that the years of their exclusive right were not up yet, and they alone had the authority to reprint. The Vilna printers argued, however, that the exclusive right had been granted to the Slavita printers only to allow them to sell their books so they would not lose money. Now that most of the editions had been sold and the Vilna printers had offered to buy the remaining thirty-seven editions, they felt that the Slavita printers were no longer entitled to retain their exclusive right.

Both the Slavita printers and the Vilna printers went to many *talmidei chachamim* to buttress their case. Each side had prominent Torah scholars who agreed with and defended their point of view. Many *talmidei chachamim* — notably Rabbi Yaakov Ornstein (1775-1839), author of the *Yeshuos Yaakov*, and the Rizhiner *Rebbe*, R' Yisrael (1797-1851) — sided with the Slavita people, whereas many others, including Rabbi Akiva Eiger (1761-1837), the undisputed *gadol* of his era, ruled in favor of the Romm family. In 1836 both printing presses published their respective editions of *Shas*.

Though both the Slavita and Vilna publishers were administered by G-d-fearing, Torah-observant Jews, their argument unfortunately degenerated into a bitter conflict of words and accusations that enveloped towns and communities throughout eastern Europe. The flames of contention seemed to ignite Jews everywhere.

The people of Slavita accused Rabbi Shlomo Eiger (1786-1852), the son of Rabbi Akiva Eiger, of accepting a bribe from the printers in Vilna and then going on to convince his aged father of the righteousness of the Vilna printers. It was said in Slavita that just as in an earlier time Bar Kochba had misled R' Akiva into believing that he, Bar Kochba. was *Mashiach* [see *Rambam*, *Hilchos Melachim* 11:3], today, too, a R' Akiva was being led astray by an individual in whom he had confidence, namely his son, R' Shlomo.

When Rabbi Akiva Eiger heard this slander, he was shocked and humiliated. That anyone would question his integrity was shameful. That anyone would charge him with distorting *halachah* was devastating. But that anyone would claim that his son, a well-known *talmid chacham* and *tzaddik*, would accept a bribe was appalling.

Rabbi Akiva Eiger wrote a powerful letter in which he stated unequivocally that although he forgives the people in Slavita who insulted him personally, under no circumstances does he forgive those who ridiculed his son or those who denigrated the Torah's *halachah* and caused a *chilul Hashem* (the desecration of Hashem's name).

Many *rabbanim* were sharply critical of the audacity shown by the Slavita people to the *gadol hador*, and they protested with speeches and public letters.

A short while afterwards, one of the bookbinders in the Slavita printing company was found dead in his workplace. It became obvious almost immediately that the disgruntled man had taken his own life because he had recently been fired for his penchant for drunkenness, and so his funeral and burial were carried out very quietly, without any fanfare.

Much to the consternation of the religious Jews in Slavita, a priest in town managed to hear about the suicide. He maliciously went to the local government with the outrageous claim that the Shapiro brothers had actually killed one of their own workers because he had threatened to inform government sources that the Slavita press was about to print numerous forbidden *sefarim* without the consent of the government censor. (Some say that it was the members of the bookbinder's family who were the informers.)

This accusation caused a tremendous commotion, and the local judges in Kiev, who harbored a long-standing hatred of all Jews, gave their predetermined ruling at the trial and ordered that the Shapiros be jailed at once and eventually be taken to a slave-labor camp in Siberia.

The Shapiros and their relatives realized that their only chance for freedom would be realized by winning a plea in a higher court, so a formal letter of appeal was composed.

Procedure dictated that the letter of appeal be stamped with an official seal. The case was then handled in accordance with the level of the seal affixed to the letter. If payment of one ruble accompanied the plea letter, the case was given to the municipal court and tried on a designated calendar date. If five rubles were paid, the case would be deemed an emergency and with priority status it would be heard immediately by the municipal court. If ten rubles were paid, the case would be classified as one of extreme importance and be taken to Czar Nikolai I who resided in St. Petersburg, the capital city of Russia. The Czar would give the matter his *personal* attention. If, however, twenty-five rubles accompanied the letter of appeal, the case would be deemed of such extreme urgency that even if the Czar were asleep he would be awakened to attend to the matter at once.

The Shapiros paid the exorbitant fee of twenty-five rubles, and the case was dispatched at once to the Czar. It was brought to his attention in mid-afternoon while he was in his courtyard. After a while the truth became known and the Czar announced that the employee at the Slavita Press had indeed taken his own life, and the Shapiros were innocent.

However, Czar Nikolai I was infuriated that the Jews had deemed this relatively simple case to be so vital that they were even willing to wake him if necessary. This, he said, was an insult to his honor, and he proclaimed, "Though they may be innocent, they have shamed the Majesty by their actions, and for this they deserve severe punishment."

Tragically, the brothers were then given a dreadful penalty. On *Rosh Chodesh Elul* in 1839 they were ordered to "run the gauntlet," between two rows of over a hundred Cossacks each, who stood with clubs poised, ready to beat them. No one imagined that the brothers could survive the inhumane torture of such beatings and so, before they were to run the gauntlet they were allowed a final request. The younger brother, R' Pinchas, who insisted on going first, requested that if he died from the beatings, he be buried in a Jewish cemetery. The beating of R' Pinchas was horrifying, but somehow, although terribly battered and bloodied, he survived.

When the older brother, R' Shmuel Avraham Abba, had to run (some say that his hands were tied) between the cruel Cossacks, he, too, was beaten mercilessly. He was running as fast as he could to avoid the clubs when his *yarmulke* fell off, and although the vicious beating continued without stop, he would not take another step until his *yarmulke* was put back on! Remarkably, even in his agonizing torment he was willing to risk his life for the sake of portraying his acknowledgement of Hashem above him.*

❧ ❧ ❧

As R' Yaakov came to the end of this story, he told the audience that when the Rizhiner *Rebbe*, R' Yisrael, heard the quote from Czar Nikolai, he commented that at times people use certain phrases and don't even realize the significance of what they have said. One may mean to say something in particular, but Hashem puts specific words in his mouth so that he says it in a way that can encapsulate a totally different message.

The Czar had said that though the brothers may have been innocent in the case of the dead bookbinder, they deserved punishment anyway because they had shamed "the Majesty." "The majesty," said the Rizhiner, "was not that of the Czar, but the majesty of Rabbi Akiva Eiger [מַאן מַלְכֵי רַבָּנָן, *"Who are the Kings? The Torah Scholars* (see *Gittin* 62a)]. They had shamed the splendor of Torah, with their criticism of the *gadol hador*, and it was that which led these *tzaddikim* to their unfortunate punishment."

Having heard R' Yaakov's words, the assembled were now ready to listen attentively to what the chief *Rav* of Moscow, in the

---

* Some say that the word *yarmulke* is actually a conjugation of two Hebrew words, יְרָאָה (*yirah*) and מֵאֱלוֹק (*m'Elokah*), lit., fear of Hashem. (See *Shabbos* 156b: "כַּסֵּי רֵישָׁךְ כִּי הֵיכִי דִּתְהֱוֵי עֲלָךְ אֵימָתָא דִּשְׁמַיָּא — Cover your head so that the fear of Heaven will be upon you.")

presence of the KGB, intended to convey with the carefully chosen words he could safely articulate.

Hashem had warned Yitzchak *Avinu* about the responsibility of one's words. Those with caution in their hearts and discretion in their minds — even if they have *mitzvos* in their hands — must heed that warning well.

✑§ *Paws and Reflect*

In this famous story about Rabbi Shmuel Salant, there is wisdom applicable to many spheres of life. What happened at his table could happen almost anywhere, and often does.

Rabbi Shmuel Salant (1816-1909), *Rav* of Jerusalem for close to seventy years, was known for his brilliant insights and innovative approach to deciding *she'eilos* (religious questions). People constantly came to his door, seeking his counsel, advice and wisdom.

One day a simple-minded woman came to ask a *she'eilah*. She was very disturbed by a careless thing she had done, and was worried about the possibility of a serious consequence.

As she began to relate her problem, some of Rabbi Shmuel Salant's *talmidim* (students) moved a bit closer to their *Rebbe* so as to gain an insight into how to "*paskin*" (rule) in the future.

"I had some meat that was not yet ritually salted [and therefore not yet kosher] out on a counter," the woman began. "And before I could remove it, my cat came and ate the non-koshered meat. *Rebbe*," she inquired, "what is the status of my cat?"

The students who were listening could hardly control themselves from laughing. A cat is *treif* even if it eats kosher meat and a kosher animal remains kosher even if it eats meat that is *treif*. What an animal eats does not change its status, and besides, who would eat a cat anyway? The question was ludicrous.

However, out of respect to their *Rebbe*, the students controlled themselves from bursting out in laughter and just smiled knowingly at each other and waited for the *Rav's* reply.

Rabbi Shmuel Salant opened one of the *sefarim* on his desk and began to look through it as the woman waited anxiously. After leafing through some pages, R' Shmuel said to the woman, "You must remember never to do this again. What you did, could at some time in the future, lead to a serious problem. If you leave meat like that on the counter, a Jew could eat that meat in error! But for now, you can keep your cat. Its status remains as it was before. You are free from worry and concern."

The woman thanked the *Rav* profusely and left. When she was out the door, R' Shmuel turned to the *talmidim* who were now giggling. "Let me tell you something about *piskei halachah* (judgments on religious rulings)," he said. "One day you may be *poskim*," he said, "and it is imperative for you to remember that whenever a person comes to ask a *she'eilah* you must always treat the question and the questioner with dignity and respect. For if you laugh at or scorn the question, even though such a reaction may be well deserved, the person will refrain from coming back in the future, when the *she'eilah* may really be a serious one. Your answer [and demeanor] today will affect the bringing of questions tomorrow."

A thought worth remembering by (impatient) teachers and parents as well.

⋅§ A Piece of Wisdom

The *Gemara* says in *Tamid* (32a): "אֵיזֶה חָכָם הָרוֹאֶה אֶת הַנּוֹלָד — Who is a wise man? He who anticipates eventualities." Most people have little choice but to react to events after they have already occurred. Only those with the intelligence of foresight, though, can prepare appropriately to resolve a problem.

In this story-within-a-story, recounted in Rabbi Shimon Hirschler's biography of the great *gaon* Rabbi Akiva Eiger (1761-1837), M'ohran Shel Yisrael, we witness clever anticipation by two different noted Torah personalities.

Rabbi Akiva Eiger's son, R' Shlomo, a noted *talmid chacham* in his own right, lived in Warsaw, Poland. Rabbi Shlomo's father-in-law was a very wealthy individual who made a provision in his will stating that the first member of the family to name a son after him would be entitled to a fortune of money from his estate.

After the wealthy man passed away, R' Shlomo Eiger and his wife were the first couple in the family to have a boy. They named the child after the deceased grandfather. Unfortunately, the child became very ill and before he was a month old, he passed away.

A while later a second daughter of the wealthy man also gave birth to a boy, and he, too, was named after his deceased grandfather. Soon afterwards the child's father claimed the bequest in the will. R' Shlomo Eiger, however, felt that he too had a right to a share of the money because, after all, he had also named his child after his father-in-law. A discussion ensued between the two brothers-in-law and they decided to go to the *beis din* of Warsaw, headed by the *Chemdas Shlomo*, Rabbi Shlomo Zalman Lipshutz (1765-1839), for a ruling.

The two brothers-in-law presented their case and the *Chemdas Shlomo* said that he needed thirty days to think about it. He instructed them to return a month later.

When the two brothers-in-law came back in thirty days, the *Chemdas Shlomo* issued his ruling: The money belonged to the second brother-in-law and not to Rabbi Shlomo Eiger.

Understandably, R' Shlomo was disappointed. "Perhaps you can discuss the matter with my father," R' Shlomo suggested respectfully. "I know that you are very fond of him and that you highly respect him. Perhaps his view would give you a different insight on the matter."

[The esteem and reverence with which the *Chemdas Shlomo* regarded Rabbi Akiva Eiger, the father of Rabbi Shlomo Eiger, was well known. When R' Akiva Eiger once came from his home town in Posen, Poland to Warsaw (see p. 60), the *Chemdas Shlomo*, as *av beis din* (head of the religious court), ordered candles to be lit in Jewish homes and synagogues, and all Jewish shops to close for the day so that all Jews in Warsaw, numbering in the thousands, would come out to greet the great *tzaddik.*]

The *Chemdas Shlomo* did not take offense at the suggestion and said to R' Shlomo Eiger, "I would like to tell you a little story":

When the *Rebbe* R' Heshel (*rebbi* of the Shach) was a young child in Cracow, Poland he was sitting at the *Seder* with his parents and siblings. As the *Seder* drew to a close, R' Heshel's father began to look for the *afikoman.* He couldn't find it, so he asked each of his children in turn whether he or she had it. Each one denied having taken it until only Heshel was left. The father asked his young son, "Do you have the *afikoman?*"

"Yes, Father," Heshel admitted.

"May I have it, please?" the father requested.

"Yes," the son said, "but I would like you to promise me something in return."

"And what might that be?" the father inquired.

"A silk jacket," came the reply.

The father had no choice but to agree and the son turned over the *afikoman* with great joy. The father broke up that piece of *matzah* and began to parcel it out to all sitting at the *Seder* table. That is, to all except Heshel.

"And what about me?" he asked his father. "Am I not entitled to a piece of the *afikoman?*"

"Certainly, my son, you are entitled, but only after you release me from the promise I just made. Release me and I will gladly give you a piece."

Heshel said nothing. Instead, with a smile, he removed from his pocket a little piece of the *afikoman* which he had broken off before returning the *afikoman* to his father. Having anticipated his father's reaction, he had taken steps to resolve the problem in advance. Now he ate his portion with delight.

After the *Chemdas Shlomo* told this engaging episode to R' Shlomo Eiger, he reached into his pocket and produced a letter from

R' Akiva Eiger. In it, the great *gaon* issued the exact ruling which the *Chemdas Shlomo* had delivered.

"I thought you would ask me to consult with your father," said the *Chemdas Shlomo* to R' Shlomo Eiger. "That's why I wanted the thirty days. During that period I contacted him and received this letter which concurred with my ruling."

Part E:

Who and What We Are

The *bar mitzvah seudah* (festive meal) in Chicago was over and now, after most of the guests had already left and only close friends and family members remained, Rabbi Abish Greenbaum,* the father of the *bar mitzvah* boy, sat for a moment alone at an empty table, reflecting on the evening's events.

"I have so much to be grateful for," he thought to himself, as recollections of his son Sruli's medical history flitted through his mind. There were times in the past when R' Abish and his wife weren't sure their son would make it to this day. His difficult birth ... his illnesses ... the hospital stays ... the doctors ...

The boy's *rebbi*, Rabbi Tzvi Gross,* saw R' Abish sitting alone. He approached the *baal simchah*, sat down next to him and remarked, "What a wonderful *simchah* this was tonight. I'm glad that I could be here."

Rabbi Gross, who was new in town, did not know the family that well. However, in the few months that he had been teaching the *bar mitzvah* boy's class, Rabbi Gross had realized that Sruli was a special child, and had become very fond of him.

"Yes, the evening was wonderful, *baruch Hashem*," sighed the father. "It truly is a great *simchah*, but for reasons that most people here cannot truly appreciate."

"Really?" asked Rabbi Gross.

Obviously there was a story behind R' Abish's comment, but Rabbi Gross wasn't sure whether or not to pursue the matter. He sat quietly, courteously giving Rabbi Greenbaum the option of continuing to talk if he so desired, or to simply let the subject drop.

"You probably don't know this..." R' Abish began, and with that comment he started to detail segments of Sruli's history that had preceded this momentous occasion.

❧ ❧ ❧

---

* All names and places in this story have been changed by personal request.

Thirteen years earlier, when the Greenbaums were living in Pittsburgh,* Sruli was born prematurely. He weighed just a few ounces over two pounds, and the doctors gave him little chance of survival. For weeks he was in the neo-natal unit of the Cedar Sinai Hospital,* and every day his parents would come to stand by his bassinet, praying quietly, as they worried over their child who was hooked up to tubes and monitors bigger than he was. Each day they waited anxiously for news of even modest progress. Sruli was close to four months old by the time he left Cedar Sinai and it wasn't until he was five months old that the doctors allowed his *bris* to be performed.

Aside from the early complications arising from their child's premature birth, the Greenbaums were told that Sruli would always be short. Just how short no one could know, but as the boy began to grow, the Greenbaums realized that he was noticeably smaller than other toddlers his age.

Throughout his school years Sruli was always the smallest in his class, always seated in the bottom row of his class picture, and constantly being called such inconsiderate names as Shorty, Shrimp, Peanut or Pee Wee. His parents, on the other hand, kept telling and retelling him that Torah "giants" such as Rabbi Moshe Feinstein and Rabbi Yaakov Kamenetzky were short, that diamonds are small and that "good things come in small packages."

Although Sruli developed a strong personality and considerable poise, the fact that his younger brothers and sisters were taller than him did not make his lot in life easy to bear. Besides this, he was a sickly child and his parents always seemed to be taking him to the office of one doctor or another. However, uppermost in their minds was their quest to learn about any new drug or hormone that could possibly stimulate growth or strengthen a young, weak and frail body.

In 1985, a growth hormone became available. Proponents of this drug were convinced that this hormone would spur growth and that a child taking this medicine would no longer be small in frame. Those advising against the use of the growth hormone, however, were concerned about the possible side effects it might have in future years. Actually, no one was even sure whether there would be side effects. Debate raged for months, and the Greenbaums became increasingly perplexed, wondering what would be best for their son.

R' Abish and his wife, who were now living with their children in Chicago, decided that Sruli should travel to Mount Sinai Hospital* in New York, where he would be seen by one of the country's top endocrinologists. It took weeks to get an appointment, but finally R' Abish and Sruli flew to New York and made their way to the Manhattan office of Dr. Maria Kelso.*

R' Abish and the doctor, a non-Jew, spoke at length about Sruli's background and condition. Sruli underwent a battery of tests, and then Rabbi Greenbaum met with Dr. Kelso to discuss her findings. The conversation naturally turned towards the possibility of administering the new growth hormone to Sruli. After a lengthy discussion, during which the pros and cons of this treatment were addressed, the concerned father decided to be very candid with the doctor. "Dr. Kelso," he said, "you see that I am torn about what is best for my son. Tell me as a mother of a child, not as a doctor: If this were your son, what would you do?"

Dr. Kelso, her elbows resting on the table, covered her eyes with her hands and remained in deep thought for a few moments and when she uncovered her eyes, to the utter surprise of R' Abish, they were filled with tears. "Rabbi," she said softly, "there is a great difference between your people and my people. I live in a 'Scarsdale society' with a 'Scarsdale mentality.' [Scarsdale is a wealthy suburban town in Westchester, north of New York City.] I would have no choice," Dr. Kelso continued, "but to have my son try this hormone, because so much of our way of life is based on superficial appearance. How one looks, how one dresses, what first impression one makes are all of paramount importance. But you, Rabbi, you and your people are different. You are internal people, among whom wisdom, character and intelligence count for everything.

"Your son is a well-adjusted boy. He is astute and has a healthy attitude towards his situation. If I were you, because of what you are, I would not take the chance."

Somewhat embarrassed about having allowed her inner emotions to spill forth, Dr. Kelso dabbed gently at her eyes. She wished R'

Abish well and told him to feel free to call whenever he deemed it necessary.

R' Abish walked out of the doctor's office deeply moved. He had just received an unexpected *mussar shmuess* (ethical lecture) from an unexpected source, and his spirits were uplifted. He felt as though the weight of the problem had been lifted from his shoulders, at least for now. He would never forget this moment.

❀ ❀ ❀

As R' Abish finished telling this story, the boy's *rebbi*, Rabbi Gross, continued to sit spellbound, shaking his head. After lingering a few moments longer, Rabbi Gross thanked Rabbi Greenbaum for telling him about Sruli's history and background, and wished him *mazal tov* once again. As Rabbi Gross drove home that evening he thought to himself, *I know just who to call and tell what I heard tonight.*

He made that call and I am deeply grateful that he did so.

❀ ❀ ❀

Shlomo *HaMelech* wrote in *Mishlei* (27:2), "יְהַלֶּלְךָ זָר וְלֹא פִיךָ — *Let a stranger praise you, not your own mouth.*" According to *Metzudas David* (ibid.), the second part of that verse merely reiterates the same thought in different words, "נָכְרִי וְאַל שְׂפָתֶיךָ — *[Let praise come from] another but not from your own lips.*" This story indicates, however, that the word נָכְרִי can also be understood to mean "gentile."

How encouraging it is when even people from the nations of the world recognize the inherent greatness of *Klal Yisrael*.

> A noted *mechanech* (Torah educator) once pointed out that the word "facade," taken from the word "face," refers to an exterior view, whereas the Hebrew word for "face", פָּנִים, is closely related to another Hebrew word, פְּנִים, meaning internal.
>
> The secular "face," it would seem, reflects superficiality, while the Jewish face (ideally) reflects inner values. Indeed, it is the internal composition of a person that is primary in *Yahadus*, not the exterior veneer..

⇜§ Old City Apartment — Good View

The following classic story told by Rabbi Yosef Scheinberger,
the secretary of the Beis Din Tzedek in Jerusalem, depicts the
intimate bond that Jerusalem shares with its holy inhabitants.

In 1920, shortly after England gained control of Palestine from the
Turks, Sir Herbert Samuel, an assimilated Jew, was appointed by
the English government as High Commissioner of Palestine. One of
his first official functions was to pay his respects to the prominent
rabbanim in the country. His itinerary therefore included a visit to
Rabbi Yosef Chaim Sonnenfeld, the chief *Rav* of Jerusalem, who
lived in the Old City.

R' Yosef Chaim lived in a very simple basement apartment which
was not only devoid of luxuries, but even devoid of electricity.
Rabbi Moshe Blau, the administrator of Agudas Yisrael, who was
handling the arrangements for the meeting, approached R' Yosef
Chaim and asked if he would be willing to meet the High
Commissioner in a home other than his own. Rabbi Blau felt that R'
Yosef Chaim's home was not distinguished enough to receive the
High Commissioner with the honor due his office.

R' Yosef Chaim refused, saying that it would be deceptive to let
it appear as though he lived somewhere else. R' Blau backed off
slightly, then came up with another suggestion. Perhaps a new table
and chairs could be purchased for R' Yosef Chaim's home to replace
the rickety furniture that was currently in the apartment? R' Yosef
Chaim refused again, claiming that this, too, would be deceitful.
Seeing that R' Yosef Chaim could not be persuaded to make any
changes at all, the appointment was made for a Wednesday
afternoon, at midday, at the *Rav's* residence in the Old City.

On the appointed day a squad of police accompanied the
entourage of the High Commissioner, who was personally escorted
by Dr. Moshe Wallach, founder of the Shaare Tzedek Hospital in
Jerusalem. Dozens of people followed behind them.

The group wound their way through the Old City to the Battei
Machseh neighborhood, and stopped at R' Yosef Chaim's home.

When they arrived, R' Yosef Chaim, wearing his *Yom Tov* clothes as a sign of respect, came forward to greet the High Commissioner, the representative of the King of England.

Sir Herbert Samuel then descended the many steps to R' Yosef Chaim's apartment. As he walked into the little abode and glanced around, he asked R' Yosef Chaim half-jokingly, "You couldn't find a lower apartment?"

R' Yosef Chaim turned to the sophisticated gentleman and said, "Please come to the window. I would like to show you something."

The two men walked to the window from which the *Kosel HaMaaravi* was clearly visible in the distance. The courtyard of the *mekom HaMikdash* (place of the Holy Temple) lay in ruins with weeds, grass and moss growing rampant everywhere.

R' Yosef Chaim pointed to Heaven and said, "If He [Hashem] can live like that, I can live like this."

ᴇᴈ Generally Speaking

In the city of Ashdod, Israel, in Aizor Gimmel (the Third District), stands a *yeshivah* elemetary school for boys. It is housed in a beautiful building which in large part was donated by a *baal tzedakah* (philanthropist) from Mexico, R' Henoch Abramczyk.*

It took quite a while to complete this building, and when it was finally finished a *chanukas habayis* (dedication ceremony) was held on a grand scale as *rabbanim* and *askanim* from all over Israel participated in the ceremonies.

At the *chanukas habayis*, numerous speeches were given by prominent *Roshei Yeshivah*, *mechanchim* (Torah educators) and local political figures. However, it was the words of R' Henoch, the Mexican *baal tzedakah*, that everyone was eager to hear. People wondered why did he donate such an astronomical sum? What event in his life inspired him to sponsor the building for this *yeshivah*?

What R' Henoch said not only conveyed his humility and love

---

* Actual name has been changed.

for *Klal Yisrael*, but also portrayed his ingenuity in the way he understood a *maamar Chazal*, a Talmudic teaching.

After delivering some introductory remarks, R' Henoch related how he, along with his parents, brothers and sisters, were taken by the Nazis from their home in Poland to concentration camps. Over the next few years, under the ruthless and bestial rule of the Nazis, everyone in his family was murdered — except him.

After the war he came to the United States and then went on to Mexico to rebuild his shattered life.

R' Henoch explained that it always plagued him that he, of all his family members, was the sole survivor. The faces of his parents and siblings were always in his mind. They were gone and he was alive. He had been spared — but why?

R' Henoch revealed that gradually a thought dawned on him and then crystallized in his mind, inspired by a Talmudic phrase that we recite every day at the conclusion of *Korbanos* during the *Shacharis* service.

The eighth rule in the *baraisa* of R' Yishmael is: "כָּל דָּבָר שֶׁהָיָה בִּכְלָל וְיָצָא מִן הַכְּלָל לְלַמֵּד, לֹא לְלַמֵּד עַל עַצְמוֹ יָצָא אֶלָּא לְלַמֵּד עַל הַכְּלָל כֻּלּוֹ יָצָא — Anything that was included in a general statement, but was then singled out from the general statement in order to teach something, was not singled out to teach only about itself, but rather to apply its teaching to the entire generality."*

"If I was a member of the group," said R' Henoch, "but then the *Ribono Shel Olam* singled me out from among the group, He didn't do it only for my benefit. He did it for the sake of a larger entity. That entity is the entire *Klal Yisrael*, and there can be no more beneficial institution for *Klal Yisrael* than a *yeshivah* for children, because teaching the children ensures our continuity. It is for this reason that I sponsored the building of this *yeshivah* in the Holy Land of Israel."

---

* The following is an example of this teaching as R' Yishmael meant it. The Torah (*Vayikra* 7:19) forbids the eating of sacrificial meat by anyone who is טָמֵא, ritually contaminated. The very next verse singles out the שְׁלָמִים, peace offering, and states that a contaminated person who eats of it is liable to כָּרֵת, spiritual excision. The principle [of R' Yishmael] teaches that the peace offering is not an exception to the general rule; rather, the punishment specified for the peace offering applies to all offerings eaten by people who are טָמֵא.

Each of us is a part of the unit that is *Klal Yisrael*. Yet, many individuals are singled out by Hashem and blessed with certain talents. These talents have been granted not merely for personal gain, but rather for the benefit and welfare of *Klal Yisrael*. Those who are so blessed should act accordingly.

◆§ Words of Nobility

The devoted *talmidim* (students) of Rabbi Yitzchak Hutner, *Rosh Yeshivah* of Yeshivah Rabbi Chaim Berlin, regarded him with the kind of reverence usually reserved for royalty. The esteem and respect they accorded him was nothing short of imperial.

One can well imagine, therefore, what it must have been like to be at the *Pesach Seder* with Rav Hutner and his *talmidim*. The *Rosh Yeshivah* sat at the head of the table, majestically leading the *Seder*, peppering the evening with his penetrating insights, as attentive *talmidim* absorbed his words with an almost unquenchable thirst.

At these *Sedarim* there was always one *talmid* who had the duty of filling the wine cups that stood elegantly alongside each setting. One year, as the *talmid* began to fill the *Rosh Yeshivah's* cup with the gleaming red wine, he nervously spilled some of it on the table and onto the *Rosh Yeshivah's* sparkling *kittel* (white robe worn on both the High Holidays and at the *Pesach Seder*).

The assembled *talmidim* were aghast. A sudden silence enveloped the room as everyone waited with bated breath for the *Rosh Yeshivah's* comment. They knew a comment would surely be forthcoming, the only question was whether it would be cordial or caustic.

Rav Hutner looked down at his wine-spattered *kittel* and then, smiling, he proclaimed in his inimitable manner, "A *kittel* without wine is like a Yom Kippur *machzor* without tears!"

In one pithy phrase, he elevated the event — as only he knew how.

In his classic *hesped* (eulogy) for Rabbi Yaakov Yisrael Kanievsky (1899-1985), known as the Steipler *Gaon*, Rabbi Yaakov Galinsky, a noted orator from Bnei Brak, related the following:

When the Chofetz Chaim (Rabbi Yisrael Mayer HaKohen Kagan) passed away in 1933 at the age of ninety-five, the Jewish world mourned. In his eulogy on the great Jewish leader, Rabbi Elchanan Wasserman (1875-1941), *Rosh Yeshivah* of Yeshivah Ohel Torah in Baranovich, Poland, first described and detailed the Chofetz Chaim's numerous accomplishments in his very productive life. Then he asked the assembled to consider a certain scenario.

"Imagine," he said, "if after Moshe *Rabbeinu* passed away, an individual would have wanted to eulogize him. There would have been no end to what that person could and would have had to say, and no time would be long enough for one to do justice in explaining all that Moshe *Rabbeinu* meant for *Klal Yisrael*. Yet the Torah does eulogize Moshe *Rabbeinu*, and does so in two words! The Torah (*Devarim* 34:5) writes: וַיָּמָת שָׁם מֹשֶׁה עֶבֶד ה׳ — And Moshe "the servant of G-d" died there.'

"How," asked R' Elchanan, "do those two words aptly describe all that Moshe did during his lifetime?"

R' Elchanan went on to tell the following story based on the *Midrash Tanchuma* (*Lech Lecha* 8).

> A very wealthy businessman once had to go on a business trip to a foreign country and it was necessary for him to take along an extraordinary amount of money and possessions. He was accompanied by his devoted servant, who went along to serve his master wherever he went. During the course of his business transactions, the gentleman suddenly became seriously ill and realized that he was about to die. He became frantic, for he knew that the servant, loyal though he was, would surely keep the money and possessions that had been taken on the trip for himself, and not give anything to the businessman's one and only son back home.

The businessman also realized that if he wrote a will leaving everything to his son, the servant would not deliver it, but would tear it up en route home. What could he do?

After giving the matter a great deal of thought, the man called his servant to his bedside and told him, "You have been most loyal to me all these years. Therefore, in gratitude, I am giving you all my possessions. However, I ask you please to tell my son that I have not forgotten him. He may have one thing which belongs to me, whatever he chooses for himself, but the rest is yours."

The servant was ecstatic and assured his master that he would deliver the message. The gentleman died and was brought back to his hometown, where he was laid to eternal rest by his family and the faithful servant. After the period of mourning, the servant went to tell the son about his father's deathbed wish. The son was shocked! How could his father, who had loved him so much, been so cruel and thoughtless as to bequeath him only one possession?

He immediately ran to his *Rav* and told him the whole story. The *Rav* thought for a moment and then told the bewildered young man, "Your father was a genius! He knew very well that the servant would not bring back the money he had taken along with him, so your father had to devise a way to make sure that you would get it all. The one thing you are to choose for yourself is the servant himself, for by owning the servant you will own everything your father did, as the *Gemara* (*Pesachim* 88b) says: 'מַה שֶּׁקָּנָה עֶבֶד קָנָה רַבּוֹ — All that a servant acquires, his owner [actually] acquires.' "

"This," said R' Elchanan, "is the significance of the words 'עֶבֶד ה — Servant of Hashem.' Every skill, talent and capability that Moshe *Rabbeinu* had, he used in the service of Hashem. Everything he 'acquired' in life was actually an acquisition for Hashem his Master, for he utilized all his faculties to spread Hashem's glory to *Klal Yisrael*." (See *Radak, Yehoshua* 1:1, ד"ה עבד ה'.)

R' Elchanan concluded, "I feel that during his life, the Chofetz

Chaim earned the accolade of being an עֶבֶד ה', a servant of Hashem, for with every fiber of his being and with every talent he possessed, he was constantly sanctifying the Name of Hashem."

> In almost any field which one may dream to participate, there
> is potential for *k'vod Shamayim* — honoring [Hashem in]
> Heaven. Whether one can sing, write, teach, speak, paint,
> design, cure, cultivate, orchestrate, mediate, or negotiate, if it is
> done for the benefit of the members of *Klal Yisrael* it is an
> elevated way of life. The more one devotes his time in this
> manner, the closer one gets to the exalted level of being an עֶבֶד
> ה', servant of Hashem.

ᴥᕲ The Right Address

A number of *chassidim* (disciples) of the *Imrei Emes* (1866-1948), [Rabbi Avrohom Mordechai Alter, the third Gerrer *Rebbe*], once came to him with a complaint.

"We had been told," they said, "that your father, the *Sfas Emes* (1847-1903) [Rabbi Yehudah Aryeh Leib Alter, the second Gerrer *Rebbe*], once assured his *chassidim* that if they would have the proper *kavanos* (intentions) when they recite the phrase in *Hallel*, אָנָּא ה' — *Please, Hashem*,' their prayers would be answered. We have concentrated and been diligent in our recitation of those verses, yet we find that our prayers have not been answered. How can that be?"

The *Imrei Emes* thought for a moment before replying. "You misunderstood the *Rebbe's* intent," he retorted. "The *Rebbe* was not referring to the recitation of the verse, 'אָנָּא ה' הוֹשִׁיעָה נָּא אָנָּא ה' הַצְלִיחָה נָּא — *Please, Hashem, kindly save us; please, Hashem, kindly make us prosper*' (*Tehillim* 118:25). He was referring to people having the proper intentions when reciting 'אָנָּה ה' כִּי אֲנִי עַבְדֶּךָ — *Please, Hashem, for I am Your servant.*' (*Tehillim* 116:16)."

The *Rebbe* then explained. "Everyone has *kavanah* when reciting 'אָנָּא ה' הוֹשִׁיעָה נָּא — *Please, Hashem, kindly save us*' — for everyone wants to be helped and assisted. However, if one has the proper thoughts and intentions when he recites the words אָנָּה ה' כִּי אֲנִי עַבְדֶּךָ — Please, Hashem, for I am Your servant,' and asks Hashem that he be helped because he is ready and willing to serve Him in any way he is able, such prayers will be answered."

The *Imrei Emes* was telling his *chassidim*, "Ask not merely what Hashem can do for you (by reciting 'Please, Hashem, save me'), but rather ask what you, with your talents and abilities, can do for Hashem ('Please, Hashem, for I am Your servant')."

◄§ A Burdensome Issue

In 1951, the government of Israel announced a policy requiring the mandatory drafting of women into the armed forces. The storm that raged following that proclamation threatened to rip asunder the fabric of cohesiveness that bound Jews together in that tiny country. The argument between religious Jews who opposed the policy and secular Jews who backed it spilled from the political chambers of the Knesset (Israeli Parliament) onto the streets, and found its way into the home of every Jew in Israel.

The *gedolei hador* (great Torah scholars of the generation) opposed the declaration with vehemence. Venerable Torah leaders such as the *Chazon Ish*, Rabbi Avraham Yeshayah Karelitz (1878-1953), decreed that every Jewish girl was obligated to defy the mandate. He maintained this position for he believed that the army life-style, especially for women, would unquestionably wreak havoc on everything traditional Judaism stood for.

The *Chazon Ish*, therefore, ruled that young women (and their families) had to be willing to give up their very lives (יֵהָרֵג וְאַל יַעֲבוֹר) rather than be inducted into the army.

The Israeli Prime Minister of the time, David Ben-Gurion, realized that regardless of the arguments put forth by rabbinic leaders, lay people, politicians, pundits or statesmen, the opposition's opinion was largely being formulated and motivated by a small frail man who lived in a modest home in Bnei Brak. The Prime Minister decided to visit that individual — the *Chazon Ish.*

He first sent a government representative to arrange the meeting, and a few days later the Prime Minister himself arrived. The classic conversation was an outlook on priorities in Jewish life.

After some preliminary discussion Mr. Ben-Gurion said very earnestly, "Such a bitter war is raging between the religious Jews and the secular Jews. Certainly, neither of us wants a civil war in this country. One of us has to accommodate the other. Who will it be?"

The *Chazon Ish* listened to all that Mr. Ben-Gurion said, and then replied. "I am neither a statesman nor a politician," he said, "but I can tell you a *Gemara* that I believe sheds light on the topic.

"The *Gemara* in *Sanhedrin* (32b) poses a question about two camels approaching the top of a mountain from opposite sides. As both approach the top it becomes obvious that the pathway at the highest point is so narrow that only one camel at a time will be able to pass through. The question is: Which camel has priority?

"The *Gemara* answers that the one carrying the heavier burden has the right of way.

"We," continued the *Chazon Ish*, "are carrying the load of Torah and *mitzvos* that *Klal Yisrael* accepted upon itself thousands of years ago. You and your people have, for whatever reason, abandoned that freight. You felt that the burden was too heavy and forsook it. But we continue to shoulder it and therefore it is your people who must accommodate our people."

Delicately but firmly the *Chazon Ish* made his point, and the exemption to religious girls was eventually granted.

✑§ Sustenance

There is always "another side to the story." That is true for almost any situation. But it takes a brilliant man to be able, on a moment's notice, to view an incident and see the other side so that it totally changes the complexion of the episode.

A side from being a world-renowned Torah scholar and author of the *sefer Anfei Erez*, Rabbi Eliezer Silver (1881-1968) was a flamboyant, colorful personality with a keen mind and a sharp sense of humor. Originally from Lithuania, he came to America to serve as a *Rav* first in Harrisburg, Pennsylvania (1907-1925), then in Springfield, Massachusetts (1925-1931), and finally in Cincinnati, Ohio (1931-1968). He was very active in Agudath Israel, and was a founder of the Vaad Hatzolah during World War II. In 1946, he donned a military uniform and went to visit the D.P. (Displaced Persons) camps where Holocaust survivors were taken after the war.

As he made his way among the survivors, giving encouragement to some and exchanging stories of personal experiences with others, a young man approached him and defiantly announced, "Rabbi, I want you to know that I will never be a religious Jew."

Rabbi Silver, never one to walk away from a challenge, turned to the man and asked, "Why would you make a statement like that?"

The young man replied, "Because I saw something in the concentration camp that I will never forget."

Rabbi Silver and the crowd of people that had quickly gathered waited for the embittered man to continue.

"There was a man in our camp — he called himself religious — who had smuggled in a *siddur* (prayer book). As a matter of fact, he was the only one in our group who had a *siddur*. A few people wanted to borrow the *siddur* in order to pray, but he would lend it out on one condition: if whoever wished to borrow it would give him, as payment, half a day's ration of bread!"

"And what happened?" asked Rabbi Silver curiously.

"Many gave him their bread so that they could use the *siddur*," came the nasty reply. "If a person could take advantage of his religion to rob starving people of their bread, then I don't want any part of such a religion!"

Everyone listening was stunned, both by the incident and by the vehemence with which it was recounted. But then Rabbi Silver smiled and said to the young man, loudly, so that all within earshot would be sure to hear. "I ask you, why do you so foolishly concentrate on that one isolated individual who had the *siddur* and made such a demand? Why don't you instead look to all those devoted people who gave up their bread just to pray in that *siddur?"*

The young man and those around him gasped at the reply, for in a flash, Rabbi Silver, with his brilliant perspective, had turned an incident which at first seemed inflammatory and distasteful into an episode that was inspiring and remarkable.

⋑ Know Life or No Life

One of the most noted disciples of Rabbi Yisrael (Lipkin) Salanter (1809-1883) was Rabbi Yitzchak Blazer (1837-1907). Rabbi Blazer was lovingly referred to as Rabbi Itzele Peterburger because he served for sixteen years as the chief *Rav* of the Czarist capital in Russia, St. Petersburg (later renamed Leningrad).

Known as one of the great leaders of the *Mussar* Movement, R' Itzele's every word was uttered and every act in life conducted in preparation for his eventual afterlife in *Olam Haba*. The following two episodes, referred to in a biographical sketch in the *Yated Ne'eman*, reveal R' Itzele's perspective on life.

One day R' Itzele met Rabbi Yosef Yoizel Hurvitz rushing through the street. R' Yosef Yoizel was a well-known and promising young Torah scholar, but because of family tragedies (before his wedding his prospective father-in-law passed away) he entered the business world and became a prosperous merchant who supported his family and widowed mother-in-law.

"Where are you running?" Reb Itzele asked R' Yosef Yoizel.

"I'm going to my place of business," R' Yosef Yoizel replied. "A person must have a source of livelihood. A person must have from where to live."

"I realize that," R' Itzele answered firmly. "But a person must also have from where to die'!"

The words of R' Itzele stunned R' Yosef Yoizel, for R' Itzele, in one terse statement, had crystallized the precise Jewish outlook on life. It struck R' Yosef Yoizel as it never had before that indeed this world is merely an entrance hall for the huge palace (*Olam Haba* — World To Come) that lies ahead (see *Pirkei Avos* 4:21).

That comment became the catalyst for the redirection of R' Yosef Yoizel's life. He began to concentrate in earnest on achieving spiritual heights and ultimately isolated himself and became involved in intensive study and introspection. In the two years of 1894 and 1895 he founded nine *yeshivos* (all under the general supervision of R' Itzele). Eventually R' Yosef Yoizel became known as the Alter of Novorodok, the father of the entire network of Novorodok *yeshivos*.

And all this began because of the impetus of R' Itzele's pithy comment.

❦   ❦   ❦

In 1904, on the last *Yom Kippur* that he spent in Slabodka before emigrating to *Eretz Yisrael*, R' Itzele delivered a powerful *drashah* in the Slabodka Yeshivah. He had been asked to speak just before the assembled were to recite *Shema Koleinu*. Wearing his *kittel* and *tallis*, the great *tzaddik*, whose every step exuded *kedushah*, began by exclaiming aloud, "אַל תַּשְׁלִיכֵנוּ לְעֵת זִקְנָה" (Don't cast us away to [the infirmities of] old age!)."

R' Itzele then told the following parable.

A group of young deserters left their country during a time of crisis. They stayed away from their homeland for numerous years, and when a new king was crowned in their motherland they sought permission to return to their homes. The benevolent king heard of their entreaties and agreed to let them return on the condition that they complete their tour of army duty.

There was one old man among them who had also deserted his country, and now he, too, sought to return to his homeland. He told the king's emissaries that he would also be willing to serve his tour of military duty.

The emissaries flatly rejected his offer. "You are too old," they told him. "You are useless. There is nothing that we can gain from you. You cannot come back!"

When R' Itzele came to this part of the parable, he suddenly burst into uncontrollable tears. "My dear ones," he cried, "you are all so fortunate. You are young and have so many years of strength ahead of you. If only you become determined to serve properly, Hashem the King will accept you back. But look at me: I am a decrepit old man who has spent his years wastefully. My future is bleak. Please have mercy on me and join me as I pray to Hashem: אַל תַּשְׁלִיכֵנוּ לְעֵת זִקְנָה — Don't cast us away to [the infirmities of] old age'!"

Those gathered in the *yeshivah* that *Yom Kippur* were awed by R' Itzele's trepidation. If he who lived a life of saintliness and holiness was worried about his accounting with Hashem, what should the rest of them say about their own accounting?

> The Talmud (*Kiddushin* 38a) states that "Hashem completes the life span of the righteous from day to day." It was for this reason that Moshe *Rabbeinu* passed away on his birthday, the seventh of *Adar,* thereby concluding the last year of his life in perfect totality and symbolizing his having lived an enriched and accomplished life. (See *Torah Temimah* on *Devarim* 32:2.)
>
> R' Itzele's life as well was complete and consummate. He was born on the eleventh of *Av* in 5607 and, as though to symbolize the perfection of his life, he passed away on his birthday seventy years later, on the eleventh of *Av*, 5677.

✦§ The Flicker of the Flame

David *HaMelech* exhorts us (*Tehillim* 100:2): "עִבְדוּ אֶת ה' בְּשִׂמְחָה — Serve Hashem with happiness." Rabbi Shimon Schwab, the *Rav* of K'hal Adath Jeshurun in Washington Heights, New York, explains that we are obligated to serve Hashem with happiness at all times, even in times of sorrow.

"*Simchah* is like the flame on a stove," says Rabbi Schwab. "At times we raise the flame in order to cook, other times we lower the flame and cooking is all but impossible, but the pilot light must always remain lit. That small simmering flame must constantly flicker.

"In the month of *Adar* we are directed by *Chazal* (Talmudic scholars) to increase our *simchah*: 'מִשֶּׁנִּכְנָס אֲדָר מַרְבִּין בְּשִׂמְחָה' (*Taanis* 29a), whereas in the month of *Av* we are instructed to minimize our *simchah*: 'מִשֶּׁנִּכְנָס אָב מְמַעֲטִין בְּשִׂמְחָה' (*Taanis* 26b). *Chazal* say that we must minimize our *simchah*," stresses Rabbi Schwab, "but we must never extinguish it."

But how can there be even a remnant of happiness on *Tishah B'Av* (the ninth day of *Av*) when we commemorate the destruction of both Temples in Jerusalem?

Rabbi Schwab declares, "The fact that we mourn because Hashem wants us to mourn is reason enough for us to feel *simchah*. Fulfilling Hashem's directive is in itself a cause for a Jew's elation."

> Perhaps the following thought can cast some light as well on the elation [albeit subdued] one must feel during the mourning over the Temples.

Rabbi David Cohen, cites an interesting insight by the Kotzker *Rebbe*, Rabbi Menachem Mendel Morgenstern (1787-1859).

"Why," asks the Kotzker, "is the month of *Av* often referred to as *Menachem Av* (lit., the consoling [month of] *Av*)?"

The Kotzker *Rebbe* answers with a parable: Imagine a person walking in the street who sees a young child doing something wrong. Suddenly a man standing nearby rebukes and spanks the child. It is obvious that the gentleman is the child's father, for only a caring father, not an indifferent stranger, would strike a child when he does something inappropriate.

"There is consolation (*nechamah*) in the pain of the destruction of the Temples," said the Kotzker, "because it was inflicted by a Loving Father (*Av*) and not by an uncaring stranger. Hence the term 'Menachem Av'."

❧ ❧ ❧

It is perhaps this aspect of Hashem's concern for us as His

children that allows Jews to retain a flicker of *simchah* even on *Tishah B'Av*, the saddest day of the Jewish calendar.

৵ৄ *A Taste of Unity*

In the second part of the Blessing for the New Month, we recite two phrases that seemingly have no connection to each other. First we say, "הוּא יִגְאַל אוֹתָנוּ בְּקָרוֹב וִיקַבֵּץ נִדָּחֵינוּ מֵאַרְבַּע כַּנְפוֹת הָאָרֶץ — May He redeem us soon and gather in our dispersed from the four corners of the earth." Then we exclaim, "חֲבֵרִים כָּל יִשְׂרָאֵל" — All in [the nation of] Israel are friends." How are these two thoughts related?

Perhaps the answer lies in the *Midrash Tanchuma* (*Nitzavim* 1) which states that: "אֵין יִשְׂרָאֵל נִגְאָלִין עַד שֶׁיִּהְיוּ כּוּלָן אֲגוּדָה אַחַת — [The nation of] Israel will not be redeemed until they will be one united group." Thus, only when all Jews are in harmony, concerned about and caring for each other, will Hashem redeem His nation by gathering His dispersed ones from around the world.

A number of years ago, in a town in the southeastern part of Switzerland, I unexpectedly had a memorable taste of such unity.

It was the summer of 1990 and I was a guest in Mr. L. Bermann's Edelweiss Hotel in St. Moritz, Switzerland. On a Thursday night, as the men began to gather in the hotel's *shul* to daven *Maariv*, we noticed that the Kaliver *Rebbe*, Rabbi Menachem Mendel Taub, from Bnei Brak, was addressing a group of Russian boys who seemed somewhat bewildered and perplexed in their unfamiliar surroundings.

The twenty youngsters, who were there with one of their leaders, Temuri Jakobashvili from Tbilisi, Georgia, were gazing in wonder at the *Rebbe* as they listened respectfully, trying to understand the Hebrew words he was saying. The Kaliver *Rebbe*, smiling constantly, encouraged the boys to observe as many *mitzvos* as they could. At the very least, he enjoined them, they should make sure to recite the *Krias Shema* every day. When the *Rebbe* finished what he had to say, Temuri translated the *Rebbe's* words into Russian and then he instructed each of the boys to come up to the *Rebbe* and kiss his hand.

The contrast of the *Rebbe*, with his thick ivory-white flowing *pei'os*, bright yellow kaftan and wide-brimmed black felt hat, and the boys in their outlandishly colorful jackets and polo shirts, some of them portraying Mikhail Gorbachev exhorting *perestroika* (restructuring), was a kaleidoscope of color that represented shades from every tint in the color spectrum.

In the lobby, meanwhile, a group of Russian girls were milling around aimlessly, bewildered by people the likes of which they had never seen who were speaking languages they did not understand. All this was taking place in an environment with which they were totally unacquainted.

This group of children had been brought to Switzerland by a Jewish organization in order to meet groups of European Jewish children. The purpose of the trip was to give these youngsters, members of the Georgian Jewish Youth Union, an opportunity to spend a month with Jewish friends their own age, traveling together and sharing experiences in beautiful Switzerland.

The summer was to have been a time of solidarity and fellowship, but the plan had soured. The French, Italian, Dutch and English teenagers the Soviet youngsters met and lived with for a week did not live up to the expectations of the Georgian group. These European teens were hardly religious, knew very little of Torah, *mitzvos* and Jewish tradition, and were not helping the Russians at all in their quest for authentic *Yiddishkeit*. The Russian youths became disenchanted and grew homesick. They began complaining bitterly to Temuri and the other leaders, insisting that they wished to go home. After a few days Temuri knew that he could not convince them to stay any longer.

Temuri agreed to travel with them by train to Zurich, where they would board a plane back home to the Soviet Union. It was late Thursday afternoon when the train carrying Temuri and his group pulled into the St. Moritz station. Temuri had heard that there was a Jewish hotel in town and thought that he could get his group something kosher to eat.

When they came to the hotel and told the owners, Mr. and Mrs. Bermann, their story, the Bermanns decided that these Jewish children must not be allowed to return to the Soviet Union disappointed and disheartened with *Yiddishkeit*. Mr. Bermann invited them all to stay for Shabbos.

Temuri demurred, explaining that they had no funds to pay anything approaching the cost of staying in the hotel. The Bermanns insisted that the children and their leaders be their guests — gratis.

On Friday morning the group sat huddled together self-consciously in a corner of the dining room, avoiding eye contact with the numerous guests who, not knowing their plight, viewed the youngsters as curiosities who were obviously out of place. As the day progressed, however, individual guests approached members of the group, greeted them and introduced themselves and became acquainted with some of the children and their backgrounds.

By Shabbos morning nearly everyone in the hotel was familiar with their situation. During *davening*, a *Rav* from Miami made a spontaneous appeal on behalf of the youngsters. Money was raised to enable them to purchase *tefillin*, *tzitzis*, *siddurim*, *chumashim* and other basic necessities of Jewish life.

By the time they met for *shalosh seudos* the youngsters were feeling at home and uninhibited. The boys sang the Israeli and traditional Jewish songs they had learned in the Georgian Jewish Youth Union back home in Tbilisi. People from other tables joined in their singing and soon their joyous celebration was being shared by all in the hotel.

Shortly afterwards someone asked me if I would be willing to address the entire group for a few minutes later that evening. At first I was hesitant, for I knew that none of them understood English. However, Temuri assured me that if I spoke slowly he would understand and would translate anything I said.

That night, long after Shabbos, the Russian youngsters, their leader and many of the hotel guests gathered in the lobby. I spoke for ten minutes, with Temuri translating after every few sentences. Then Temuri himself announced that he wished to speak.

Everyone wondered what he could possibly say to us. He had already thanked and expressed gratitude, both to the Bermanns for their hospitality and to the people who made pledges at the appeal. He had acknowledged the kindness of the many guests who had befriended the children. What more could he add now?

What he chose to say will forever be etched in the memories of the many who were fortunate enough to be there.

Temuri began by once again thanking everyone for all they had done on behalf of the boys and girls whom he would soon be escorting back to Russia. Then, to the surprise of all, he quoted a *Gemara* (*Taanis* 23a). He told the story of Choni HaMe'ageil, who fell asleep for seventy years. When Choni awoke he went into the *beis hamidrash* to see his friends, but no one recognized him. Even worse, no one even believed that he was Choni HaMe'ageil.

Choni became so frustrated and saddened that in exasperation he exclaimed, "אוֹ חַבְרוּתָא אוֹ מִיתוּתָא — Either friendship or death!" In his loneliness, Choni felt that if he had no friends and no one recognized him, he would rather not be alive in this world.

Then, his voice resonating powerfully, Temuri exclaimed, "For seventy years, my brothers and sisters in Russia have been asleep! For seventy years we had no connection with the outside world of Jews. We know so little, but we want to know more. We have such a limited background, but we want to attain knowledge. Please, please be our friends. Help us with learning, encourage us and inspire us. For if you and others like you don't encourage us with your friendship and genuine concern, then we are doomed to go back to Russia and die as plain simple Jews. אוֹ חַבְרוּתָא אוֹ מִיתוּתָא, Either friendship or death!"

All those present were electrified by his plea and moved by his sincerity. When he finished speaking, the lobby erupted in thunderous applause. Someone started a song about *achdus* (unity), and soon dancing was underway. The male guests of the hotel danced with the boys in the lobby, while off in another room, the women danced with the girls. People from Israel, Europe, America and Russia danced together with rapture and joy for more than an hour!

The songs with their words about Jerusalem, love of Torah and bonds among *Klal Yisrael* brought tears to the eyes of those of us who were simply at a loss for words. The rhythmic clapping, the cadence of foot stomping and ecstatic singing were transformed into vehicles which expressed heartfelt feelings of compassion and concern for the youngsters who would soon return to the cursed land of communism.

An older gentleman standing off to a side, observing the Jews from many countries joined together in unison on this *Motzaei Shabbos*, turned to me and said, "If only *Klal Yisrael* could constantly know such *achdus* (unity), *Mashiach* would come tomorrow."

According to the *Midrash Tanchuma* in *Nitzavim*, "אֵין יִשְׂרָאֵל נִגְאַלִין עַד שֶׁיִּהְיוּ כּוּלָן אֲגוּדָּה אַחַת," it seems that the gentleman was right.

May it indeed happen in our time.

~§ **Indexes**

Index of Personalities

Note: Included in this index are those historical personalities who played a role in the stories. Excluded are fictionalized names and narrators of the stories (unless they were personally involved in the story). The page numbers indicate the page on which the story begins, although the personality may not appear until later in the story. All titles had been omitted from this index to facilitate finding the names.

Index of Topics

Note: Included in this index are topics from all three Maggid books. **MS** indicates *The Maggid Speaks*, **AMT** indicates *Around the Maggid's Table*, **FM** indicates *In the Footsteps of the Maggid*.

Index of Sources

Scriptural and Talmudic index for all three Maggid books.
Note: **MS** indicates The Maggid Speaks, **AMT** indicates Around the Maggid's Table and **FM** indicates In the Footsteps of the Maggid.

This volume is part of
THE ARTSCROLL SERIES®
an ongoing project of
translations, commentaries and expositions
on Scripture, Mishnah, Talmud, Halachah,
liturgy, history and the classic Rabbinic writings;
and biographies, and thought.

For a brochure of current publications
visit your local Hebrew bookseller
or contact the publisher:

Mesorah Publications, ltd.

4401 Second Avenue
Brooklyn, New York 11232
(718) 921-9000